SOULS ON SAFARI

THE MIND IS A TROJAN HORSE

USE IT TO SMUGGLE BEINGS OF LIGHT

INTO THE CITADEL OF YOUR SOUL

SO THAT THEY MAY THROW OPEN

THE GATES OF YOUR HEART

TO THE SOURCE OF ALL LIGHT

Seán ÓLaoire, Ph.D.

Souls on Safari

Published by Wheatmark™
610 East Delano Street, Suite 104, Tucson, Arizona 85705 U.S.A.
www.wheatmark.com

International Standard Book Number: 1-58736-611-8
Library of Congress Control Number: 2006920867

TABLE OF CONTENTS

FOREWORD

"Let no one make the mistake of separating out the quest from everyday life. It is life itself!"

Paul Brunton

SOCRATES WISELY SAID: "The unexamined life is not worth living." If the spiritual quest is anything it is the examining of one's life, its meaning and direction. It is also written that, "You shall know the truth and the truth shall make you free." If we understand these two pearls of wisdom we can't go wrong by examining our lives, finding the truth within and living accordingly. We can become free to be who we are meant to be. Freedom awaits all who seek the spiritual path to enlightenment which leads to love and compassion for all sentient beings. Once we discover that the divine dwells within us and surrender to it, we fulfill the highest purpose of our life on Earth.

For some this book may be the first step on their spiritual journey. The spiritual journey is the most important adventure in our human experience. Though the real search is within not without, there are times when it is helpful to have a guide or mentor to lead us in our spiritual evolution. A phrase or two, coming from an inspired person, may set a subconscious process working in the mind and lead to a new truth or a new paradigm. An inspired guide can assist us in gaining a better understanding of what it is that gives our life meaning and direction and leads us away from the surface of the ego to the deep center of the soul.

5

Father Seán ÓLaoire is an inspired guide for many on the path to spiritual enlightenment. His homilies articulate what we are often unable to articulate for ourselves and introduce us to new paradigms of thinking. The old paradigms want us to give our heart to what our head tells us is not true. Father Sean's metaphorical rather than literal translations give us a deeper and more beautifully profound understanding of scripture than most of us have experienced in the past. His lectures and homilies involve a historical, metaphorical and sacramental way of seeing the scriptural traditions that can be transformational. It is important to expose ourselves to this new emerging paradigm of critical thinking and when we do this we expand our horizons and free ourselves from getting stuck in old paradigms.

It has been my sweet pleasure to transcribe and edit these great homilies. I have done so to bring Father Seán's inspiring message to a wider circle of those on the spiritual path. It is also my desire to have the inspiring spoken words of these homilies in written form as a more constant source for review, study and personal edification.

Included with these homilies is Father Seán's lecture on abortion, "Ideas on the Abortion Debate," and a transcript of a "made for broadcast" interview with Seán by Pat Burns filmed at the studios of "Still N' Motion," in San Jose, California. I am truly grateful to Pat for his time and energy in filming and taping this interview for me to transcribe and for creating the book cover.

I would also like to thank the "Companions on the Journey" especially Ron Alves and Michael Choy for providing the tapes of these homilies for me to transcribe and to my husband of 54 years, Robert, for his support and encouragement in this endeavor.

Mary Burns

INTRODUCTION

H OW HARD DO you think it is to hypnotize someone? Some will say, "Quite easy," others will protest, "I can't be hypnotized!" The truth is that all of us spend large chunks of our day being hypnotized. How would you know if someone were hypnotized? The trick is to watch their eyes. When we are focused on the external world and "watching" our environment, we blink quite frequently (usually every four or five seconds) because the eye needs to be constantly refreshed and lubricated. But when you are in a hypnotized state, even when your eyes are open, you are not processing the external world but rather are fixed on an inner landscape and, so, your eyes have less need to lubricate. Hence, you may go for 50 or 60 seconds without blinking.

So, watch people who are staring, with a glazed look, they are under hypnosis. Mostly, this is self-induced, though TV or radio can have the same effect. Nothing creates this effect, however, as effortlessly as stories—the ones we tell ourselves in the privacy of our own memories or imaginings, or the ones we hear from others.

The great storyteller realizes this, and is under a vow to tell only those stories that help dissolve the illusions of separation and forge the connections that allow us to remember our true nature, which is the source-nature of all other beings also. It is God. The "teacher" who encourages us to identify, xenophobically, with the differences among us is unworthy of the title "storyteller," and is merely a propagandist and proselytizer. And they are in plentiful supply in politics, in religion, in industry and in the mass media.

The true storyteller touches the soul and so ignites life and light and love in the listener. And the hallmarks of the true storyteller are four: he will, firstly, recognize the audience and its experience and issues; secondly, he will be interesting and engaging; thirdly, he will use this connection to help them remember their real nature; and, fourthly, he will empower them.

At the end of a really profound story, the audience will be left in awe NOT at the storyteller but at their own divinity AND the divinity of all others.

And that is the only purpose of this book of story-homilies.

Namasté,

Seán ÓLaoire–Tír na nÓg, December 7, 2005

ACKNOWLEDGEMENTS

THE SEQUEL IS rarely as good as the original. Godfather XIX probably won't be a huge box-office hit. "Souls on Safari" is the sequel to "Spirits in Spacesuits." If it's an improvement, the credit, resoundingly, goes to Mary Burns, who was less gentle with me and pruned with more abandon than she did in the first book! She has surgically removed many of the clumsy expressions of the spoken homilies, making both the ideas and the sentence-structure flow less turbulently. Her husband, Bob, diplomatic ex-fire-chief that he is, contrived to make all of this redacting pleasant—even for me.

Their son, Pat, who is the creator and director of *Still N' Motion*, once again brought his unique skill-set to designing the cover, shooting the photos and conducting the interview contained in the book. He is a professional but, more importantly, he has a great sense of humor.

As is the custom within our little Spiritual community, the *Companions on the Journey*, Michael Choy, who handled all the recordings for the homilies contained in the first book, trained his successor, Ron Alves, a nocturnal creature like myself, who has dubbed his heroic efforts, *Middle of the Night Productions*. My gratitude goes to Ron and especially to his wife, Jane, who must endure these anti-diurnal activities of his.

And, finally, a word of thanks to all my *Companions on the Journey* for the spiritual energy they create each week that allows these stories to be told.

May God continue to hold you all tenderly in the hollow of Her hand.

Seán ÓLaoire—Tír na nÓg, December 7, 2005

INTERVIEW WITH SEÁN ÓLAOIRE

T HE FOLLOWING "MADE for broadcast" interview was conducted by Patrick Burns at the studios of "Still N' Motion" in San Jose, California and transcribed for this publication.

Q. Tell us about the title of your first book, "Spirits in Spacesuits."

I have been convinced for a long time that part of our problem is that we misidentify. What I mean is that we think we are our bodies. During the 60's, we began to get in contact with our emotions as if our emotions were the ultimate truth. The scientific community tells us we are our thoughts and our minds. There is an old Hindu mantra that says, "I have a body but I am not my body. I have emotions but I am not my emotions. I have an intellect but I am not my intellect," and I add to that, I have a personality but I am not even my personality. Then I came up with the statement, I am a spirit in a spacesuit because I am convinced that our essence is non-material. It is God stuff and we are on safari on planet Earth. Each of us has a mission and in order to equip ourselves for that mission we take on spacesuits. We're on a planet that needs a particular kind of incarnated spacesuit. So we build these spacesuits for ourselves and the spacesuits have physicality, they have emotionality, they have intellectuality and as the spacesuit interfaces with the environment the soul creates the personality. So the essence of who I am is that I am a spirit, but in order to be on my mission, I need the equipment and the equipment is a spacesuit. So "Spirits in Spacesuits" pulls together the three pieces that define me: the essence, the mission and the incarnation.

Q. What do you mean by the subtitle, "A Manual for Everyday Mystics?"

I am convinced that religion has tried to lick people into shape and the essence of religion has been that you have to believe a whole bunch of stuff and you have to act in a certain fashion. The great spiritual teachers never ask us to believe anything. It is not about what I believe it is about a realization, it is about understanding who I really am. All the great teachers ask that question again and again. There is a great story in each of the Gospels of Matthew, Mark and Luke about Jesus traveling on the road to a little village called Caesarea Philippi. Jesus is walking in deep thought ahead of his disciples when he stops, turns around and waiting for his disciples to catch up says to them, "You have been with me now for a few years and you listen to people talk about me. Who do people say I am?" And they said, "Some people think you are John the Baptist come back to life. Some people think you are Elijah come back to life. Some people think you are one of the Old Testament prophets come back to life." Jesus said, "Okay, that is what the people say. They don't know me. What about you? Who do you think I am?" Then Peter said, "You are the Christ figure." And Jesus said, "Yeah that's it."

But I believe that Jesus had been asking himself another question before he asked the apostles. And the question he asked himself was, "Who do I think that I am?" That is the core question for everyone. We are constantly misidentifying. We misidentify with our bodies, with our names; we think we are our names. If you ask me, who I am, typically I give you a name, tell you the job I do, or that I am such and such a person's son. If you really set me down and say, "We have an hour to spend together and I would like to know who you are," I'm liable to string together a lot of memories and act as if I am the accumulation of those memories. The truth is that we are not any of those things. Every single one of us is God stuff; a soul on safari on planet Earth and we are all mystics at our core.

We have been taught that religion is about ethics, belief systems, rituals and liturgy. While all of these things might be important for

11

us if we are trying to live together in harmony, they don't go to the core of the thing. The core of the thing is that I have to come to the realization that I am a little piece of God on mission on planet Earth and that is the mystic in every one of us. You don't have to live on a mountain top to be a mystic. You have to be a mystic in your everyday work whether you are a postal worker, a psychologist, school janitor or a bus conductor, it doesn't matter. When I talk about "A Manual for Everyday Mystics" I try to explain how ordinary people like ourselves can go beyond mere religion and touch the core of what we really are. I think life on this little planet is about creating a species that will ultimately become aware of its own divinity and having realized that, begin to act toward all sentient beings in the realization that all sentient beings are articulations and manifestations of the divine. I hope that species is going to be homo sapiens. It may not be. We may destroy the entire experiment, but I am convinced at some stage, either through us or through a subsequent species, some species is going to develop on this planet that will recognize its own divinity and act from that place. For me that is what the Christ figures and the Buddha figures and all great avatars are about. They weren't just meant to be extraordinary individuals who were admired, put on pedestals, worshipped and have religions built around them. They are the prototype of where the human race is meant to be headed. We live on a planet that is 4.5 billion years old and life emerged about 3.8 billion years ago. Then this life went through extraordinary shifts so that a species evolved that developed self-reflective capabilities.

There are two more stages after that. Firstly, there is the stage that recognizes that we are souls and secondly, recognizes that we are the Spirit of God. That is where evolution is headed and that is what Christ and the Buddha represent for me. They are prototypes indicating that that is our future and that is where we are meant to be headed. We made the mistake of worshiping those people, creating religions around them, putting them on pedestals and then ignoring their teaching. So for me it is the discovery that there is a mystic within every single one of us because every single one of us is called to Christ consciousness or to Buddhahood.

Q. Does religion help us to deal with our everyday difficulties?

I think religion has been important in so far as it is the single greatest holder of tradition. But the difficulty with tradition is that it tends to stultify. If I use the metaphor of a tree: a tree has roots sunk deeply into the soil, it gets nutrients from the soil, but if all it has is roots, there is no tree. It has to develop a trunk, it has to develop branches and leaves and it also feeds itself through photosynthesis. The leaves drink in sunshine and convert that into energy which feeds the roots. The roots represent the tradition and the branches and the leaves represent what we are evolving towards and we have to interact and interface with each other. So when I'm cut off from my roots, there is no evolution possible. But if all I have is roots and I cut off the trunk, there is no possibility of further development because the roots need photosynthesis as much as the leaves need the root system.

There is always an extraordinary tension between the prophet and the king and you find this throughout all world religions. If there were only prophets there would be anarchy. If there were only kings there would be stagnation. The interaction between these two is the creative tension that allows the evolution to proceed. Religion has its function but religion should be an evolving phenomenon that takes cognizance of the evolution of the human species just as a family does. You are not going to treat a two-year old baby and a sixteen-year old teenager in the same fashion. You have to cut the teenager a lot more leeway. When your teenager becomes a 26-year old man and is married with kids of his own, you're going to treat your son at that stage very differently from how you treat your grandchild. A lot of religions find that a very difficult process. They find it very difficult to let kids cut the umbilical cords, develop and evolve. Religions tend to want to hold people in the status quo. Prophetic characters inevitably evolve who are inviting the religious system to make the next quantum leap. So there is a function for religion, but it has to be an evolving function.

Q: What types of conflicts do you see with today's religion?

We started as a species maybe 1.3 million years ago with a few people on planet Earth, not understanding anything about nature, having no scientific knowledge and life was extraordinarily unpredictable and could not be controlled. So we built images of God and we built gods in our image and likeness. While I do believe that we are built in God's image and likeness, religion tends to create God in its image and likeness and so the first religions were efforts to try to live with a totally unpredictable and a totally uncontrollable God; chaotic religions with various kinds of sacrifice to pacify a distant, demanding deity.

Then at some stage, a model of religion began to evolve where people realized that they needed some kind of law and order because without it there was ultimate chaos. This brought about the great law givers like Moses or the Code of Hammurabi in the Middle East. It was the realization that people needed ethical systems, norms, laws and regulations in order to survive. They started making gods who were lawgivers and law keepers and then they had a different relationship with God. God was no longer unpredictable. He was still uncontrollable, but not unpredictable and so they learned what the rules were and if one knew what the rules were and kept the rules, then things were fine. And that is where ethics came into being. Ethics are important, but that is a very elementary stage of the process. Some religions are still stuck in the punitive model of God who just gives laws and if one doesn't keep the laws one gets punished. Jesus realized that what is more important than law is love and when a community begins to act in love they transcend law. Not that law becomes unimportant, transcendence is epigenetic which means that every subsequent stage incorporates and builds upon, but goes beyond all of the previous stages so you don't reject what has gone before any more than the leaves reject the roots; you carry it with you, but you go beyond it. Jesus pointed out that the communities that work best aren't just the law-abiding communities but the loving communities and you find that in great bible stories.

There is a great story in Luke's gospel of the sinful woman coming into a banquet where Jesus was being cross-examined by a group of Pharisees and she let down her hair, cried on Jesus' feet, wiped his feet with her hair and poured costly ointment on his feet. This was unthinkable in Jewish custom. The Pharisees watching said, "Ah, it is obvious now that this guy is no prophet. If he were a prophet he would know that he is being touched by a sinner and therefore he is being rendered unclean." And Jesus said to them, "I have a question for you. A certain man had two debtors. One of them owed him a lot of money and the other owed him a little bit of money, but neither of them could repay him. Since they couldn't repay him he forgave both of them. Which of them do you think will love him the more?" So Simon, his host, said, "Obviously the person to whom more was forgiven." "You are right. You see this woman? I came into your house and you didn't even offer me water for my feet although I've been on a dusty safari. You didn't kiss me or embrace me and you didn't put oil on my forehead as a sign of respect. This woman has been washing my feet with her tears, she anointed my feet with costly ointment and she has been kissing my feet. I tell you her sins, and she has committed many, are forgiven because she has loved much, but the person who has loved little, little is forgiven." Jesus was pointing out that there is a huge difference between being a law keeper and a lover. The law keeper is always trying to be safe and go down the middle of the road neither too hot nor too cold. The lover is someone who is living with passion and when he makes mistakes they are passionate mistakes but when he is loving and when he is in love with God he is passionately involved with the process. That is where Jesus is taking it and there are religions that are trying to operate on principles of love, there are religions that are operating on principles of law and there are religions still operating on principles of unpredictability. Religion is moving through those phases.

15

I think there is a place even beyond love and it is the realization that every single one of us is God stuff. It is not that we love each other out of some sense of compassion for the human condition, but that we realize that this experiment literally is God experiencing Herself. For me, God exists, God knows She exists, but in order for God to experience Herself, She has to create and so She has created this extraordinary game that Hinduism calls Lila. Lila is a play of God and we are part of that play and the object of the play is to recognize and uncover the fact that we are God. So all great religious teachers, all great spiritual teachers and all great mystics, in my opinion, are not teachers in the sense that they are giving us information that we didn't already have; they are amnesia erasers. They are wiping away the veil that separates us from who we really are and remembering what we have come to do. I see religion moving in that direction but there are various religions and various groups within particular religions that are stuck at elementary stages.

Fundamentalist movements, whether it's within Judaism, Islam or Christianity, tend to be stuck in the legal part of it. For instance, there are laws you have to keep, laws that say you have to believe in the Lord Jesus or whatever the shtick is and only then can you be saved.

Q. Why do religions do that?

I think, and this is not to be in any way elitist, that there are different kinds of souls on the planet. There are very young souls on the planet in the sense that young souls are not very well evolved and there are very ancient souls on the planet who have been around many, many times. Even though I am a Catholic priest I believe in reincarnation. I believe we come onto this little planet many, many times. I think some souls evolve quickly and some very slowly and that there are souls whose experience of life and experience of self is that of fear and when you operate out of fear the response to life is always anger. All anger is fear based. There are people who have faced their fears and gone beyond their fears and gone through love

16

and compassion into Self recognition and these are the people who are inviting the whole system forward and the other people are like little kids on a diving board who are afraid to jump, but don't realize that what they are jumping into is a pool of cosmic compassion. All they see is a scary height, they are afraid and they cling desperately to what they know. Somehow the job at this stage is to wake up to the realization that if we cling to the fear, anger will be the result and annihilation will be the outcome.

Q. What is your definition of love?

I think love is alignment with the trinity and that sounds really esoteric, but it is not. The Christian, Hindu and Buddhist notion of trinity are not esoteric theological principles. Trinity is an extraordinary practical pragmatic psychological insight. To put it boldly, God the Father within the Christian model represents "Isness" or being. Christ represents God's total self-knowledge. The Spirit represents the love that God has for whom she knows Herself to be; it is being Self, knowing Self and loving Self. In the devolution from God to incarnation you go from being, to knowing, to loving. And in the journey back to God we go in the opposite direction. We go from loving, to knowing, to being. Now a lot of people will claim that you can't love someone until you know them. I would make the opposite claim. I would say you can't know someone until you love them. You have to love someone before you can know someone. It's not that you have to know someone first and love someone later. You have to love someone first and it is only by loving someone that you can truly know someone. It is only when you have truly known someone that you will both be free to be who you truly are. Yes, that is the God stuff. Love is the first stage of the journey back into our divinity because by loving we understand what the reality is and in understanding what the reality is we can be who we really are meant to be. Love for me is the beginning of the process back into divinity.

Q. Why do we experience so much prejudice in the world?

I think this planet that we live on is an extraordinary little planet. But it is only one system of millions of millions of planets throughout the known universe that has created intelligent life forms. There is something about this planet where we get to experience limitation and limitation brings prejudice and prejudice gives the opportunity of breaking through prejudice. So, for example, if you take a little child who has had chicken pox and a little child who hasn't yet had chicken pox; they are both chicken pox free. One has kicked it and the other still hasn't contracted it. They look the same but they are very different because the one who hasn't had chicken pox yet is always libel to get it so he is never safe. The other child will most likely not get it again. I think the whole point of experiencing prejudice is that when you encounter prejudice and go beyond it, you make a quantum leap in loving. If you haven't yet encountered prejudice you may be without prejudice, but you are prejudice prone and you will learn it from your culture at some stage. Before we come onto this planet as spirit beings we have no gender, we don't have ethnicity, we don't have socioeconomic status, we don't have I.Q. levels and we don't have religious affiliations. We don't have any of those confining and limiting boundaries. When we come onto this planet we have to make decisions. We have to decide if we are going to be born male or female, white or black, rich or poor, have a genius I.Q. or retarded. All of these limitations immediately create prejudices for us. But this is in order to break through the prejudices and learn to really love. For instance, a little infant and an enlightened Buddha are the same in that they are both prejudice free; they are without prejudice. But the little infant is going to learn prejudice and will have to contend with it. The Buddha being has encountered prejudices and gone beyond them so they are both prejudice free. One is pre-prejudicial and the other is post-prejudicial. We confuse them; we think that they are the same, but they are not because the Buddha has broken through it and the infant has still to meet it.

Encountering prejudice and going beyond it gives us the opportunity of growing into who we are rather than starting from a place of already accomplishing it. It's like the difference between a game of golf where you have been assured that every shot you hit will result in a hole-in-one no matter what you do. Even if you hit it backwards it will roll into the hole. There is not a whole lot of fun in playing that kind of golf. When you have to learn to master the craft and you get a hole-in-one or you go around in 76, that is an achievement. So it's coming in, taking on the limitations, learning the prejudices that are part of the limitations and then breaking through the prejudices. That's what enlightenment consists of; it's the break-through that creates enlightenment.

Q. If we are experienced, why do we have to go through this?

We have to go through this because even spirits need to evolve. There are young souls and old souls. It is the accumulated experiences of incarnation on many different kinds of planets or life forms that allow souls to develop and grow. Perhaps there are baby gods who don't know they are divine entities and have to grow into their divinity and it's by experiencing different situations that makes it happen. There are people on the planet right now who are really advanced souls and there are a lot of us who are somewhere in between and there is a whole bunch who are very, very young at the game. We are all creating the drama which is affording every one of us at every stage of the spectrum the opportunity of improving our game a little bit.

Q. Some religions see this as a place of test. Do you see it as a place of test?

I see it as a place of test not in the sense that there is a kind of reward or punishment or there is a God saying, "Okay, you have to run the mile in 3 minutes 44 seconds in order to qualify." It's not about that. I think we set ourselves a life of circumstances so that we become the kind of beings we want to become. But there is no God assigning rewards or punishments to the process and there is no God creating obstacles to trip us up. I am convinced that every single one of us, before we come in, create what I call a preconception contract with a group of souls to create a world drama which affords every single soul three possibilities: the possibility for self-development, the possibility to help others develop and the possibility of raising the entire consciousness of the planet. It's a three-part function. We pre-plan our drama. We come in with a cohort group of souls and we're going to safari with them through our entire lifetime. They will come into our lives no matter what we have to do to meet them. I don't believe in coincidence and I don't believe in luck. I believe that we bring into our lives the people with whom we have pre-contracted and it's to set up a drama in which every player is the star. There are no super stars in this drama; everyone is on stage 24 hours a day. Everyone is the center of his/her own drama and we assist one another so that every single one of us has the ideal optimized opportunity to do what we have come to do and what we have come to learn.

Q. What message would you like to get across to your readers?

What I've been trying to do in this book is to try to mine or harvest the great scriptural traditions of the world for their mystical core so that we can go beyond the metaphorical language in which they are being articulated or the kind of cultural environment out of which they grew or particularly the literalist fundamentalists interpretations of what they mean. When you go to the core of the Buddhist, Hindu, Hebrew, Christian or the Taoist scriptures, you meet the very same mystical essence. For me, the task and the passion has been to try to mine these systems and try to find out what is the mystical core of all these religions. When you get down to that place there are no theological, liturgical or ethical differences. You are at bedrock of the water table from which all the rivers of the world are sourced.

Q. How has being a Catholic priest affected you message?

I know that I'm a Catholic priest this time around. This is my mission; Catholicism is my birth family. I am not subservient to the Catholic Church as an institution and I'm not interested in it at all as an institution. I know that I've been Hindu and I've been Jewish in past lives. My purpose this time is to start with the home base of Catholicism and from that place invite Catholics to experience, experiment and survey the great mystical core of all the other traditions. My training as a priest in theology and scripture, my living as a priest in Africa for a long time and living here in the United States as a priest for a long time has given me the opportunity to take aboard what is really beautiful about Catholicism. There is a deep mystical core to Catholicism. There is an extraordinary environment that Catholic liturgy creates around the Eucharist which leads to a kind of numinous state; a place where I literally can sense and feel the divine. I think Catholicism has an extraordinary ability to create great symbolism. I don't agree with a lot of Catholic dogma and dogma for me is not that important. Great teachers never ask us to believe anything. They ask us to act with love and not to believe in a whole bunch of dogma. Dogma is totally superfluous to the process.

Q. What is the best thing about your community, the Companions on the Journey?

The Companions on the Journey is a group that was founded in 1997. It is a group of mainly liberal Catholics who have been disillusioned with main-stream organized bureaucratic Catholicism who are trying to create community for themselves where they have charge of their own liturgy, their own theological thinking and their own community organization. While what we have been doing is basically Catholic Eucharist, our theology is very eclectic. The community members come from Catholic, Protestant, Hindu, Buddhist, Muslim and Jewish backgrounds so there is great diversity. I would say that 80 percent of them are probably Catholic, but there are 20 percent who are from other systems. We have a great cross-section of theologies. Our method of self-government is more a Quaker model. It's a consensus model so there is no one in charge of anything, which means everything bumbles along very slowly and everyone's view is equally important. There is no hierarchy, bureaucracy and no one in charge.

I am the spiritual director for the group, but I have no organizational mandate whatsoever. I'm not in charge of the group in any sense of the word and I don't tell anyone what to do. It's a consensus driven model. In actual fact, I'm an independent contractor who this group has asked to preside over the liturgies, Eucharist and expose them to good theological thinking. That is my function.

Q. Why don't you say mass in a Catholic Church?

I am persona non grata in the Diocese in which we are situated. I don't belong to the Diocese so it's not a big deal for me. I worked in association with the diocese for about eight years after I came here from Africa. In 1995, the diocese told me that it no longer wanted me because my theology was too strange for them. My theology is not strictly Catholic and they told me that I would no longer be welcome to use any Catholic facilities for any liturgical functions. The Companions rent a Seventh Day Adventist Church for Sunday services and an Episcopal Church for Thursday and Friday morning services. It means that we are a pilgrim church and we don't have any real estate or any of the headaches that go with real estate. There is also the metaphor of being a pilgrim people who don't own the space, but are trying to create God's energy in a few different locations.

Q. Can you enlarge upon what you mean when you say: Life is not what happens between birth and death. Life is what happens between incarnation and enlightenment.

I believe there is only one life and it exists in a pre-incarnated form and in an incarnated form and in a post-incarnated form. The one life that moves through, for instance, this person you are interviewing today who lived before he had this spacesuit and will live after he has had this spacesuit is the same life that you have. So there is literally only one life. It is the God experiment. Whatever is happening, whether it's happening on planet Earth or happening on planet Vulcan, there is only one life. In the case of a single soul, that one life exists in three kinds of cyclic stages, in a pre-incarnation stage, an incarnation stage, and in a post-carnation stage. I want people to begin to think that life is not just birth to death. That doesn't represent life it represents just a stage in the mission, a stage in the safari. Life has existed long before I was born and will continue long after I shuffle off this mortal coil. Real life is the passion for mission. That mission started the moment I said yes to conception and that mission only ends when I reach enlightenment. In fact, I think it may not end even then. In Buddhism, there is what is called the Bodhisattva. The Bodhisattva is an enlightened being who has worked off his/her own personal karma and doesn't need to come back at all for continued evolution, but who chooses to come back until every sentient being is saved. While mission may begin at conception and end at enlightenment, in actual fact, it goes beyond enlightenment. It goes on until every being has reached enlightenment. It's not just between individual conception and individual enlightenment, it's between individual conception and enlightenment for everyone. No one finishes this race until everyone finishes this race.

I remember hearing a story a few years ago about the Special Olympics. One event for kids was the 100-yard dash although dash was a kind of euphemism for what happened. There were 20 or 30 kids from 15- to 30-years of age most of them with Down Syndrome all competing in the 100-yard dash. When the gun went off they all stumbled forward to run up the course. One little fellow fell and started crying and the whole group turned around and looked back at their fallen fellow and they stopped the race and they all went back and picked up this little boy, linked arms, walked up the entire track and went over the finish line together. The entire stadium stood up and gave them a standing ovation. I think that is what life is about. Life is about all sentient beings crossing the finish line together. I don't believe in individual salvation. No one gets to heaven until everyone gets to heaven. The old Christian notion that part of the joy of heaven will be to have ring-side seats looking down at the agonies of the damned is the worst contortion of the teaching of Jesus.

Q. If we have multiple lives, why can't we see our past lives?

There are many, many ways of seeing a past life. How much of your first six months on planet Earth do you remember right now? You probably can't remember any of it. Some of the most important things that ever happen to you happen in that first six-month's period. The fact that we don't have conscious access to experiences doesn't mean that these experiences haven't formed who we are. Even if I were to say to you, what were you doing on the first of July, 1979, you probably couldn't tell me. We don't have conscious access to most of our life experiences. But all of these experiences form us. They are the reason we are who we are. Every experience we've ever had has been part of the formation of the personality that we now have. All the information from past lives, in fact, has formed us and is part of the reason we are who we are. So in that sense we have unconscious access to it constantly. For example, subsequent generations of computers are hardwired with what previous generations of computers needed by way of software. Subsequent generations built upon new knowledge and incorporated that into the hard wiring of the new systems. I think in subsequent lifetimes we have hardwired into us all the knowledge of the previous times. The fact that we don't have conscious access to much of this information doesn't mean that this information isn't profoundly affecting who we are and how we are responding.

Q. Is humanity getting better?

I believe so. The measure of it is the extent of the crisis we face as I look at human history. In some sense, the only difference between the violence we are experiencing now and the cave man experience is that it is much more difficult to do international damage with a cudgel than it is with an intercontinental ballistic missile. But the anger, the selfishness and the fear is the same. At one level we are being driven by the same kind of fear and anger except that now it's being wedded to a much more lethal technology. At the same time the level of consciousness that is growing on this planet is extraordinary.

When you look at human rights, women's rights, even recognition of animal rights, all these realizations are very recent in history. Humans are maybe 1.3 million years old as an experiment on a planet that is 4.5 billion years old and a universe that is 13 billion years old. But even within the human experiment, it's only for the last 2500 years that the great avatars have been coming among us. The Buddha figures, the Lao Tzu figures, Socrates figures, the Jesus figures have only recently begun to come among us. We are very young at this experiment, but even in that period of time we have made extraordinary progress.

The fact that we are now facing an extraordinary crisis reminds me as I look at evolutionary history that there has never been a significant shift in functionality that is not precipitated by some kind of global crisis. This happens in evolutionary biology all the time. I see it as a psychologist when I'm working with couples or individuals; no one makes a significant shift in his/her level of functioning unless it's occasioned by some kind of personal crisis. We are facing this crisis simply because as a planet not only the human species but also the sheath of consciousness surrounding the planet itself is being called to the next evolutionary shift from mind to soul. We've gone from just being physical stuff that we study through physics to being a life form studied by biology to being intelligent beings studied by psychology and the next part of the shift is being souls that are studied by theology and finally spirits that are studied by mysticism. So we are on the brink of the next two phases as a planet and that is why the crisis is happening. Otherwise we wouldn't be making the shift.

Q. How do you think your message will help the people of the world?

A teacher's function is not to tell people what they don't know. It is to awaken them so they remember what they know in the core of themselves. My hope is that if enough people are articulating the truths that they know at the core of themselves and are networking with other people, eventually a critical mass will be reached. You don't need a majority in order to make a huge shift in thinking. A significant minority is enough, often less than 10 percent. If there are enough teachers on the planet helping to wake people up to the realization of what they know deep within themselves and those teachers are networking with other groups there will be an extraordinary shift in consciousness and I'm adding my two cents to that process.

Q. What is happening in America that is not happening in Africa?

I think America has an extraordinary opportunity. One of the things I felt strongly after the 9/11 incident was that America, given its extraordinary resources, not just its physical resources or wealth, but its brain power gave us the opportunity to spearhead human evolution. The pity has been that those in political authority chose to go back to a level-two religion and even a level-one religion of unpredictable, uncontrollable, distant, demanding deities that visit their anger upon the people. We're being offered an extraordinary opportunity to think differently and to lead the thinking. What I would have loved to have seen in the wake of 9/11 was to have declared a five-year moratorium on retaliation and bring together the great spiritual, political, military, ecology, psychology, medical and agricultural people to a five-year meeting to brain storm how we can do life on planet Earth differently instead of just going back to level-one religion or level-two religion which is an eye for an eye and a tooth for a tooth. The reason I'm excited to be living in this country at this time is that we do have the resources, we do have the freedoms and we do have the intellectual power to be able to create a paradigm which will allow the human species to break through into Christ consciousness. It's a real exciting time to be alive and it's a very exciting place to be alive. I couldn't be doing this work in Africa; I couldn't be doing it in the third world.

In East Africa, I wouldn't have the resources, the technology or the audience that is capable of making differences in the world. When I was in a village in Africa, I was dealing with the local community helping to provide water and food and change the local environment, hopefully for the better, but it would never make a huge impression on what's happening on a global scene. Here I can be a factor in that.

Q. Where do you see the best chance for change?

As we go off on an aberrant direction, even the ones among us who are asleep begin to realize that things are getting so bad so quickly that instead of leaving it up to the leaders to make decisions for us we need to rouse ourselves and organize ourselves. So this very aberrant swing is a wake up call for me. Part of me thinks it's like brinkmanship happening. I felt before we went into Iraq that if the peace movement succeeded too quickly it would prove its own undoing because we would all just go back to sleep. The war happened and devastation happened and many lives have been lost. The ideal would have been some kind of brinkmanship where it would get serious enough for enough people to wake up so that they would remain awake forever, but that it wouldn't have to translate into the death of a lot of innocent people. We've transgressed that boundary. My hope is that because things are getting so bad that more and more people are going to wake up and they will wake up sufficiently to stay awake and not just wake up until the crisis is over and then go back to business as usual.

Q. Are you familiar with the modern religions that tend to be more scientific and shun the concept of God?

I think these people misunderstand what science is about and a lot of scientists misunderstand what science is about. There is a notion now called "Scientism" which is an aberrant form of science. In the same sense that you have fundamentalist religion, you've also got fundamentalist scientism, which isn't good science at all. Science should be open to investigating the data and on the basis of the data recognize patterns, set up hypotheses to explain the patterns, set up experiments to test the hypotheses and then build models that work. Scientism doesn't do that. For instance, Scientism believes that only the material world is real and if something isn't material, and if it can't be empirically validated by our instrumentation or by the five senses, it doesn't exist. Scientism is totally closed to investigating a whole realm of human experience; that is fundamentalist science. It's really bad science and just like the fundamentalists religion it is the refusal to accept the findings of real science. In the past, the fight has been between fundamentalist religion and scientism. A wedding needs to happen between mystical religion and good science and when you bring those two together, extraordinary things can happen. For my doctoral dissertation I did an experimental study with 496 people on the effects of intercessory prayer at a distance on self-esteem, anxiety and depression levels in the population. This is an area where I tried to bring together the best of real science, random, controlled, double blinded experiments with an esoteric phenomenon like intercessory prayer. You can do that when you bring good science together with mystical thinking; then you have an extraordinary synthesis. When you bring fundamentalist religion together with scientism then you get just an extraordinary fight with each group accusing the other of being blind.

Q. What is prayer?

For one thing, there are lots of different kinds of prayer. Most people only think of intercessory prayer; that's only one kind of prayer. There's prayer of praise, prayer of thanksgiving, prayer of adoration, prayer through meditation, but most people think about prayer of petition so let me concentrate my response on that. Prayer of petition is where you want a specific outcome and you pray to some God to affect that outcome. When I was doing this prayer study I investigated a few different notions on prayer. There are some people who think that prayer of petition or intercessory prayer is merely chatting about the inevitable. Even if God exists, since God is omniscient, presumably God has factored all pieces into the equations including the prayer that is to come ten years down the line. There is not going to be any change because God has factored all the pieces and he has come up with the equations. Prayer of petition is just wasting your time or chatting about the inevitable, for God is going to do what God is going to do. Now I don't think that's true and I don't believe that.

There is an idea that prayer of petition is what I call the satellite-dish model. Suppose I want to pray for my brother Séamus living in Ireland, but because of the curvature of the Earth I can't pray for him directly, so I have to bounce my prayer off God like a satellite-dish in the sky and God directs my prayer down to Séamus. God is some kind of intermediary bouncing my requests onto their targets. Now I don't believe that is true either, but a lot of people operate with that model. There is a model that I call the Abrahamic model. It's the model that you can argue with God. There's a great story of Abraham arguing over the fate of Sodom and Gomorrah saying to God, "If there are 50 good people in these cities are you still going to destroy them?" And God says, "Well, if there are 50, I'll save them." "What if there are only 45?" "Okay." "Suppose there are only 40?" "You got a deal." "Suppose there are only 30, 20?" And he goes right down to 10. So are there some things you can argue about with God and you can bend God's arm and get what you want? I don't think that is how prayer works.

There is a notion I call the Mosaic model. There's a story of Moses in the desert where the Israelites are having a battle with the Amalekites and Moses goes up on the hilltop and he's got his hands raised and he's appealing to God to help his side and as long as he can keep his hands in the air, the Israelites are winning. But his arms get tired and they begin to droop and then the Amalekites begin to win so two guys come one on the left side and one on the right side and they prop up Moses' hands and then the Israelites win.

There are some people who think there is some kind of trick to prayer. If you can figure out what the trick is you get what you want; it may be a pilgrimage to Mecca or it's the Nine First Fridays or going to Lourdes or whatever. I don't believe there's a trick to it at all.

I think of prayer like a sprinkler system in a lawn and you have all these underground pipes connected to one faucet. There is a source; God's love for us. By this love, the water flows through the entire system and sprinkles the lawn that is human life. But there are nexus points where the pipes join and when they get clogged up, an area of the lawn gets no water. The sprinkler in that area isn't going to work because it's all clogged up. What clogs it up is prejudice, a lack of forgiveness, and bad theology. The object of prayer is to free up the blockages within the pipe system so that the water within the pipe, which is within the system already, is free to water the entire lawn. Prayer is not where we are bending God's arm. I don't think God is involved in prayer at all. I don't think prayer is about asking God to make any change in the outcome. I think prayer is about human beings freeing the blockages in the water system so that people can benefit from our compassion. I don't think prayer involves God at all. Prayer is about our consciousness and our mindfulness which allow the blockages within the system to be dissolved so the water can flow freely to its targets; I call it laserized intentionality. It is not asking God to intervene at all.

I don't believe that prayer involves God at all. We are not appealing for a transcendent entity to intervene in human affairs and change an outcome. But since we are God, we are, in fact, praying to God; we're trying to access our own inner divinity. Except that for most of us it is really difficult to believe and do that so we create symbols outside of ourselves in order to try to focus what's within, but most of us project this image outside in order to focus and then we think the action is out there. It's as if you are watching a movie screen and you think that John Wayne is actually riding across the stage from left to right and you take out your gun and start shooting at him when in fact, the action is happening in the projection box. But it is very hard to see a movie if you're looking at celluloid frames. That is a very boring way to watch a movie. By projecting onto a screen we get the illusion of change and of time and of speed and of size. It allows us to see very clearly what is happening on the celluloid frames. But if we think it is actually happening on the screen we are deluding ourselves. When we pray to God, it's to help us focus on an image of something that's within ourselves. But if we think it is outside and we are praying to an entity that is going to intervene from the outside, we get it wrong. Prayer is an aid to self realization, it's an aid to becoming fully aware, it's an aid to laserizing my internationality, but it's being driven from the God within me and my target is the God within you or the God within whomsoever I'm praying for.

Q. What is sin?

I do not believe that sin is the transgression of precept. I do not believe that sin is breaking law. It is only tangentially related to that. Essentially sin is the conscious, deliberate decision not to grow. If I'm faced with an opportunity in which I can act out of my divinity and I can radiate love and compassion in a situation and I choose instead to identify with my ego or my persona and I choose not to grow; that is what sin is. It frequently involves breaking a precept or transgressing some kind of law, but that is tangential to the process. That is only the effect or the symptom or the epi-phenomenon. It is not the core of the essence at all.

Q. Do some people get stifled by sin?

I think many people are over-awed by law and by convention, by culture and by upbringing and they are not thinking for themselves; they are not contacting their own soul wisdom. There is a place beyond mind-set and that is soul-set. There is wisdom far deeper than our thoughts and that is our spiritual knowing, but most of us have been taught to distrust that. We have been taught to follow dogmas, listen to teachings, believe in a whole bunch of stuff and totally disregard intuition and native wisdom.

I watch little children from the time they are born as they absorb their phenomenological world. They drink in all of their extraordinarily awesome experiences and they ask great questions. At age five and six, we send them off to school, we ignore their wisdom and we fill them with data and information. Data and information

31

just allow us to manipulate the external world, but they don't bring us into alignment with our truth. That is what wisdom does. That's what soul does and kids instinctively know that until the education system makes them distrust that. Then religion picks up on education and continues it into our adulthood. Religion continues to tell us to distrust our intuition or wisdom or soul-sense and to listen instead to revealed dogma and the church belief system and a whole bunch of ethical norms.

Q. Why are we so accepting of propaganda?

In the United States our propaganda is much more subtle. Having lived in Ireland for the first 26 years of my life and in East Africa for the next 14 years and now here in the states for about 17 years I see that this culture has an extraordinary ability for self deception. Because life in America is so good and we have so many freedoms, we believe our own lies much more readily. We take aboard these lies because they are far more subtle and therefore the damage is much more devious because we can't recognize them and therefore it's hard for us to do something about them.

Q. The Bay Area is a very materialistic area. How does this affect our spirituality?

I think it is a very materialistic part of the world, but at the same time I don't know of any other segments of the population who are more aware of, interested in and involved in rights and equalizing opportunities for the world's population. In many places in the world, people are so involved in the daily grind and survival issues that they don't have the resources or the time to spend on thinking of a bigger picture. There is a sub-group within this culture well enough off to have the leisure time, training, expertise and the resources to begin making change. I know some extraordinary people in this area. In spite of the fact that they are often well to do they are using their material wealth as a resource to try to make changes globally. And that is part of the excitement. There are a lot of people, of course, who are just trying to get richer and richer on the backs of many people getting poorer and poorer.

Q. What is your ultimate goal for your books?

I would love to think that I could be part of a networking group that is waking up people to the realization that this is a game and we are playing the wrong game. Some of us think the game is prestige, some of us think the game is politics, and some of us think the game is wealth but none of these things is the game. The game is to seek and remember. The game is to seek and wipe out the amnesia for whom we really are and the game is to seek and cause to evolve on planet Earth a species capable of recognizing its own divinity. I would love to be part of that movement to wake up enough people so that this movement results in a consciousness shift for the whole planet and that would then affect everything we do from our politics to our agriculture.

Q. Do you believe in evil?

There is a shadow part to every single one of us. In speaking of the shadow, Carl Jung said, "the shadow is 80 percent gold." Unlike Freud who believed that the unconscious was a repository for the suppressed trauma of our lives, I believe that Freud had only part of the truth. There's going to be 20 percent of this shadow that is filled with the darkness or the trauma of my experience in life. The other 80 percent is unrealized potential. If I'd been born in a different family maybe I would have been encouraged to be a musician, which I'm not. If I'd been born in a different family maybe I'd be encouraged to be an ice skater, which I'm not. The family I was born into was interested in academics so I majored in that. So there are all these parts of us that never get developed because of the particular family we are born into or the culture we are part of.

What is evil? I think it's unrealized potential and the frustration that comes out of that and the failure to deal with our own egocentricity. If I don't deal with my own egocentricity, I'm going to have to project onto some other person or some other segment of community. I think we do this as individuals and we do this as communities and we do this as cultures and we even do it as a global community. There's a lot of constellated unacknowledged shadow material that the entire species has disassociated from and it's polluting the consciousness sheath around the entire planet.

I had a vision a few months ago in which I saw the universe as a pregnant woman. I was watching her silhouette and she was pregnant with planet Earth. I could see that the expectant mother sometimes looked vibrant and healthy and sometimes looked really wan and listless. I came to the realization that instead of there being a single umbilical cord connecting the planet to the universe there were six billion umbilical cords and there was liquid passing through these cords and I noticed that the quality of the liquid influenced the health of the mother. I came to the realization that every human being on the planet is connected to this consciousness sheath around the planet and is being sustained by it and is also feeding stuff back into it because the umbilical cord does two such functions: it feeds the baby because the mother sends nutrients in and the baby eliminates through the umbilical cord back into the mother and she gets rid of the waste matter on behalf of the child. If our thoughts or our words or our actions are violent then we are sending all of this toxic material back into the womb and back into the membrane that should be feeding us but we're polluting it and poisoning it and it is unable to sustain us anymore. I believe then, that evil is that unresolved stuff that influences selfish decisions that individuals make, communities make, nations make and the global community makes. When we become conscious of that then we need to do three things. We need to watch the quality of what we think. We need to watch the quality of what we say. We need to watch the quality of what we do. We need to make sure that we are not putting violence out there or judgment out there, we need to be putting compassion out there and then as this membrane receives more and more compassion from inside, it becomes more and more capable of nurturing us and then the evil dissipates. Until we realize this as individuals, communities

34

and nations we just keep projecting our stuff onto others and then punishing them

Q. What concerns you about our society?

I remember, in April 1978, in a deep meditation, having a vision in which Jesus was crucified, died, rose from the dead and then was recaptured and re-crucified and then a whole group came out the second Sunday to watch him rise from the dead as a spectacle, but it never happened and the whole crowd went away disappointed. In my vision, after Jesus rose the second time, he said to me, "Who do you think disappointed me the most?" I said, "I suppose it was Peter. Peter was allegedly the rock on which you were going to build your church and three times he denied that he knew who you were." Jesus said to me, "No it wasn't Peter. Peter did what he did because he was afraid and I can understand fear." So I said, "Well, if it wasn't Peter it was Judas. Judas was one of the 12 and he sold you for money." And Jesus said, "No, it wasn't Judas. Judas put a lot of cunning and a lot of craft and a lot of commitment into what he did. It wasn't he." So I said, "If it wasn't Peter and it wasn't Judas, then it must have been the High Priest. The High Priest was a scripture scholar and the leader of the spiritual movement, he should have recognized the messiah when he came; instead he crucified you." And Jesus said, "No it wasn't even he. He stuck to his guns. When I rose from the dead the first time, he crucified me again. No it wasn't he." And I said, "If it wasn't Peter and it wasn't Judas and it wasn't the High Priest, I give up. You tell me who it was." And he said to me, "It was the mob. The bored, listless mediocre mob; all they wanted to do was be entertained. It didn't matter that I was feeding them miraculously or that I was dying on the cross or that I was rising from the dead. They just wanted to be entertained. They couldn't care less about what I had to say. All they wanted was entertainment." What disappoints me most is that the vast bulk of us are just mediocre. We're neither hot nor cold, we're not doing a whole lot of damage and we're not doing a whole lot of good. We're just meandering through life in this soporific state of being half awake. It's not so much the leaders, the ones that are leading us to hell in a hand basket, at least they are bringing power and passion and a commitment to what they are doing. Most people are just drifting through life aimlessly.

Q. Is that a result of fear?

I think it's a result of a few different things. There used to be an old statement in Rome at the time of Jesus that the crowd would shout out, "Give us bread and circuses." As long as we have food in our bellies and entertainment, we couldn't care less what you guys do at the top. Leaders know that and they know that if you can give people bread and games you can do pretty much what you want. Leaders throughout history who have agendas whether they are political agendas or religious agendas have learned that if you can satisfy people's basic needs for entertainment and food you can do pretty much what you want with yourself and lead them any way you want. I think leadership all throughout human history has cynically manipulated us.

Q. Does God forgive sin?

Someone said to me one time, "Can God forgive everything?" I said, "No, God can't forgive anything." God is the only "person" in the universe, to use an anthropomorphic term, who can't forgive and doesn't forgive. Because in order to forgive, He first has to hold a grudge against me and then subsequently let go of it. And since God, as the ineffable ground of our being is totally incapable of holding a grudge, God is the only person who can't forgive. Forgiveness comes from inside each other.

It is very interesting to me that at the end of the Jewish year, before the book is closed, there is a ceremony called, Kol Nidre. Kol Nidre is people acknowledging their misalignment, but none of it is about offending God. There is not a single statement in that entire liturgy about offending God. It's all about offending each other because you can't offend God. You can offend someone else, but you can't offend the transcendent, ineffable ground of our being.

Forgiveness is never a question of asking God's pardon for having upset Her. Forgiveness is always coming to the realization that all sin is about a failure to grow and that failure to grow effects my relationships, affects my culture and affects my world. And therefore those of whom I need to ask forgiveness are my brothers and sisters. All forgiveness is about the acknowledgement of the misalignment I've created between my essence and myself and between myself and other selves; but I can't really be misaligned from the ultimate ground of my being.

Q. What Catholic teaching bothers you the most?

For me one of the saddest things about being a priest in the Catholic system is the exclusive rules about receiving the Eucharist. Eucharist was probably the most healing thing Jesus ever did in his life. It was much more healing than raising people from the dead, the cripples he cured or the blind to whom he gave sight. The Eucharist was the end of exclusivity. It was Jesus inviting everyone in from the highways and byways to this banquet of God's table; it was the end of exclusivity and elitism. To be told as a Catholic priest that I must exclude people from that banquet who are divorced and remarried, gay, or non Christian is totally abhorrent to me. The essence of the Eucharist is its inclusivity, which means that every single one of us is equally beloved of God and we are all called to this banquet table. Eucharist is a symbol of the love that God has for us and the fact that we are all equally beloved of God. One of the things that we do at our community on Sunday is we tell people, "Everyone here today is welcome to receive communion with us because every single one of us is equally beloved of God and this is symbolic of how God feeds us." So it is really upsetting to me to think that Jesus' single greatest teaching about inclusivity has become the criterion for exclusivity in Catholic teaching.

Q. Why does the Catholic Church stress obedience to its rules and use guilt to shame people who disobey those rules and leave the church?

The church is shooting itself in the foot because of what it is retaining. The church is retaining, as part of the fold, people who are obedient and it is losing from the fold people who are creative, the ones who can really bring the system forward into its mystical core. The ones who are just concentrating on the roots and maintaining the status quo are the ones who are being retained. That has happened throughout history. The church has lost its greatest creative thinkers and mystics.

Q. This interview will be published in your next book and for possible broadcasts. Will this be just more bread and circuses? How do you feel about that?

There's a great Sufi story about a man living somewhere on the borders of Afghanistan and every week he'd load up his donkeys and take them across the border. Every week the soldiers at the border would stop him because they were convinced he was smuggling stuff. They would search the bags around the donkeys and they'd look in the donkey's ears and open the donkey's mouths and this was done week after week after week and he would go back and forth with the donkeys and they never figured out what he was doing. And he <u>was</u> smuggling. He was smuggling donkeys! I think that that is what we are doing here. I'm trying to smuggle donkeys, trying to go into a place where people go to be entertained and I'm going to smuggle in a donkey. And the donkey is some kind of truth and some kind of being awake and if only one person in the audience finally gets it that this is about donkeys and that the donkey is what's hidden and one person wakes up, that's enough.

Q. How can we tell when we are passionate about a cause or if we are just being fanatical?

I think there are two huge differences between someone who is passionate about a cause and someone who is fanatical about a cause.

The first difference is a sense of humor. Fanatics have no sense of humor; they never laugh about their stuff. Someone who is passionate can. And the second big difference is a sense of time. I think if someone is passionate about God's work then it has to be God's timeline. If I am insisting on my timeline of the process then it's my stuff, my agenda and it's my ego; it's not God's time anymore. And so I need to allow it to happen at its own pace, do my damnedest, but then let it happen at its own pace and view both my efforts and the results with a sense of humor. We have to laugh at ourselves.

I remember when the Dalai Lama came to Saint Patrick's College in Menlo Park. There was a grand procession in the college auditorium led by the Archbishop of San Francisco to introduce the Dalai Lama. As the Dalai Lama came in he was beaming from ear to ear while the Archbishop, deadly serious, was walking in the procession with all solemnity. The impression the Archbishop gave was, "I am an important person." And the impression the Dalai Lama gave was "You are important people." The Dalai Lama was laughing and smiling in awe at his audience and the Archbishop was totally self-engrossed in his own importance. That sums it up for me. If I can't laugh at myself and be in awe of others rather than be in awe of myself and despise others, I've no idea what spirituality is about.

Q. Why did you name your second book, "Souls on Safari?"

When I try to explain the concept, Spirits in Spacesuits I find myself using a lot of different terms. I believe that our essence incarnates onto this planet and in order to do that we need some kind of equipment in which to live in this environment. We come here for a purpose; we are not coming here just to visit. Our incarnation has a purpose. In Kenya, the word safari doesn't mean an exotic journey to watch wild animals. A safari just means a journey. It could be a safari to the schoolhouse or a safari to Nairobi; it is just a journey.

What I wanted to say is that our purpose here is that we are on a journey. It is a journey of remembering. It's not so much that we are here to learn or discover. For me, we are here to remember to lift the cloud of amnesia that incarnation induces. It is a journey from God back to God and we go through the woods of various kinds of illusions. Most of us hold the illusion that we are separate from God, that God is angry with us and that we are sinners and need to be redeemed. I really don't like the Christian term redemption which comes from Latin and means to buy back. The notion of redemption connotes that somehow a deal was made between God and Satan and that, because of our sinful nature, Satan owned us and by Jesus dying, God bought us back from Satan by the sacrifice of his son. That imagery makes no sense at all.

Q. What are we trying to remember?

We are trying to remember that ultimately there is only God. God is playing an extraordinarily creative game of hide and seek with God. God is, God knows who She is and God loves who She finds Herself to be and in order to experience Herself, God creates. In the very same way, for instance with a couple in love, there is something about the nature of love that wants to create something apparently other than self in order to personify the love or incarnate that love. Why would a husband and wife who are blissfully in love have the desire to have a child? Parenthood is an incredible responsibility, but there is something about being in love that makes us desire to reproduce or create in some fashion. What is created, although it contains our DNA and is influenced environmentally by us, is totally unique as far as the soul is concerned.

God, in order to experience Herself, needs to create so everything that *is* is merely a creation of God. Hinduism says that, "Rocks are God sleeping, plants are God waking up, animals are God walking, human beings are God thinking," and I add to that the phrase, Christ-conscious human beings are God becoming aware of Herself. In this extraordinary burst of creativity on God's part, in order to experience different facets of Herself, She creates everything from just minerals all the way to human beings and beyond it. I don't believe that we are the highest life-form in the universe. Every articulation of God is a unique way in which God experiences herself.

For me, remembering is about understanding and a stripping off of the veil of illusion that I'm separate from God and need to be redeemed. Every single one of us is God. There is nothing but God. But there are articulations of God that are totally unaware of their Godliness and there are articulations of God that believe that they are sinners and there are articulations of God that are just happy to be flowers, bees or dinosaurs. There are also unique sub-groups that become aware that they are God, and that everything that seems to separate them is an illusion created by amnesia. These are Christ-conscious beings or enlightened ones with Buddha nature or avatars, etc. Remembering is about stripping away the illusions that we are separate from God.

Q. Give me an example of some of those illusions.

The most devastating illusion is that we are separate from God and that God is some kind of distant deity who needs to be feared, obeyed, honored, worshiped and that our behavior really upsets Her. That is the biggest illusion of all. Subsequent to that illusion is the illusion that we are separate from each other as individuals. We are no more separate from each other than the five digits of my hand. They are all articulations of the same hand and all have the same usefulness and as long as they cooperate and realize that they are all part of the same hand, they are in business. But if they begin to act as if they are separate entities and be in conflict with each other, then you have an autoimmune disease. The essence of autoimmune disease is that the system doesn't recognize itself and is at war with itself. In a sense, all conflict is an autoimmune disease. Whether it is an interpsychic conflict where I don't like myself or I have self-esteem issues or an interpersonal conflict in a relationship or intercommunity or international conflict, all this is ultimately an autoimmune disease or the system failing to recognize itself. When we don't recognize that we are God then we are bound to be separated from each other. We separate ourselves from nature and exploit it because we have no respect for it. When we break through the illusion, we know that nature too is an articulation of God just as we are except that nature is a non-self-reflective articulation of God and we are a reflective articulation of God and Avatars and enlightened beings are reflective of the fact that they are indeed God and everything else is God.

Q. Why do you refer to God as she?

For me, God is totally ineffable and inexpressible. Therefore, when we speak about God as the ultimate ground of our being, we use metaphors. Since the metaphor of God as father, lawgiver, king and despot has been used and abused over millennia, I want to mix different metaphors. We are basically trying to communicate that God is ultimate love. Mother love very often can be more real than father love. Most people insist on using the image of God as father, so to counterbalance that, I occasionally use female pronouns and talk about God as mother. All pronouns which attribute personhood to God are totally made up. God is not a person. It is anthropomorphic to think that God has human characteristics, but it is the best we can do. When we have an experience of the divine, all we can do is try to express it in the terms that we hold most dear. As human beings, we think that personhood is the single greatest attribute so we attribute that to God as well.

Q. Doesn't it also limit God by giving God a name?

Absolutely. A lot of early Christians, particularly the Greeks, spoke of what God is not. They refused to say what God is. They would say; x, God is not x; y, God is not y, and z, God is not z. It was a way of ruling out our mistaken notions of God. It crept into the west when Meister Eckhart, a 13th century Christian mystic, said, "I pray daily to God to rid me of God." In other words, whatever theologies I create or notions I have about God are wrong so I pray to rid myself of those notions. When I do this I can hold myself in the center of the absolute, pregnant void of the mystery. It is a void not of nothingness but of no-thing-ness. It's not as if nothing exists, it is no-thing-ness; there is no separation and everything is possible. It is the field of all possibility. When Jesus talked about the Kingdom of Heaven or about the father, he insisted on using a plethora of allegories in the hope that if he used enough of them we wouldn't take any of them literally. But, of course, we have done just that. Jesus would never say the Kingdom of Heaven *is*. He said the Kingdom of Heaven *is like*. This was to emphasize that it is an allegory and not an ontological description of what heaven is like. He was giving us a allegorical description of a state of consciousness. For instance, "the Kingdom of Heaven *is like* the farmer going out to sow seed;" or "the Kingdom of Heaven *is like* fishermen on the lake;" or "the Kingdom of Heaven *is like* a woman baking bread;" or "the Kingdom of Heaven *is like* a merchant in search of fine pearls." Jesus used allegories that made sense to his audience.

Even to ascribe being to God is meaningless since being is itself a human category. Once we have an experience of the ultimate ground of our being, then we mentally try to put it into some kind of terms so we can begin to wrestle with it.

The great mystical experience of God goes through four stages. The first stage is the actual experience itself which is totally ineffable and can't be articulated. The second stage is that we are left after the experience with some kind of symbolic residue. The third stage is that we then try to wrestle conceptually with the symbols. And fourthly, we create theological systems to make these concepts logical and consistent with each other. By the time we get to the theology, we're three stages from the actual experience and every intervening stage brings its own cultural prejudices and individual biases.

If two or three people have a deeply mystical experience, each person will have to interpret, or make sense of it according to each one's cosmology. If I am a fundamentalist, whether, Christian, Jewish or Islamic, I will see God in very black and white terms and impose my views on it. If I'm a scientist and I don't believe in God whatsoever, I will explain it away as a grand mal seizure or a random firing of neurons in my brain. If I'm a religious person I will try to make it conform to what I've been taught. If I'm a true mystic, I won't try to explain it at all; I've had the experience and the experience is enough in itself. I know that as soon as I begin to speak about it, I've lost it. In the Taoist tradition, Lao Tzu says, "Those who say don't know, and those who know don't say." The true mystic will not even attempt to articulate the experience. The theologians will articulate it in fine detail but they won't have had the experience. They describe what they have not experienced and the mystic is not describing what he has experienced.

Q. If we incarnate to this planet, from what place do we incarnate?

I think it is a journey through states of consciousness. I have a belief that life as we experience it is a dream that the ego is having and the ego is a dream that the soul is having. The soul is a dream that Spirit is having and the Spirit is a dream that God is having. These are nested dreams within dreams within dreams. The journey away from God takes one into more and more illusion or deeper nesting. The journey back to God is shuffling off these illusions.

When we think that we are awake, we are actually in our deepest sleep. What we call "waking consciousness" is actually our deepest sleep and most cloying illusion. That is when we are really caught in the illusion that we are separate from God, separate from nature and separate from each other. When we go to sleep at night and we dream, we shuffle off the physicality of that illusion. In our dream state, we are not aware at all of our physical bodies; we are operating at a psychological and spiritual level. We are creating mind states and emotional states, but we don't have to physicalize it any more. All of the energy that goes into our waking consciousness to create physical aspects to reality is now freed up to create emotional and intellectual aspects. This is why our dreams are much more intense than waking life because there is extra energy available for the mental and emotional processes.

As we go from dream sleep to non-dream sleep, then we get rid of the illusion that we are separate because the soul ceases to exist at that stage and there is just pure spirit. That is the nearest we get in a 24-hour cycle to home base. When Jesus said at one stage, "In my father's house, there are many mansions," he didn't mean that there was one place for the Jews, another for Christians and a third for Muslims in separate quarters in which they are quarantined from each other. It is not about that. We are able to create heavens that are nearer to the source depending on how successfully we have dismantled our illusions. So the different mansions have to do with the different states of consciousness that we safari through in our journey into the oneness with God.

After we die and get completely rid of this physical spacesuit, I think that we experience the level of heaven or hell that we are prepared and ready for. If I am a mean spirited, angry, prejudiced character and believe that life sucks and I can't trust anyone, then that is what I create on the other side and that is my hell. If I believe that the ideal life for me is that I would be with my grandparents who have died and all my buddies that I know here on earth, I can create a heaven that is populated by all these people. But if that's how narrow my thinking is, that is my experience of heaven until I get rid of that illusion and then I'm ready for the next level. The journey on the other side is also a safari where layer by layer we peel off the skin of the illusion of separation and we finally merge totally with the ultimate ground of our being and then the game is over.

Q. What happens then?

A new game starts and that's the end of game one.

Q. What's game two? We don't know yet?

I have no idea. Be as creative as you can be and multiply by ten and that's the beginning of game two.

Q. It's almost as though we create this physical existence. If that is true, where do we come from?

We came from God's attempt to experience Herself. That goes for everything. The entire phenomenal world comes from God's intention to experience Herself. Whether this is a physical, emotional, intellectual or spiritual dimension, all that is merely another aspect of God experiencing Herself; that is all that it is. Each of us is circumscribed by our culture, religious upbringing, personality and history because we incarnate onto planet Earth many times until we figure out how we can be spirits in spacesuits or souls on safari in such an environment and learn how to love. When we have mastered that, presumably there are other dimensions where we can incarnate to experience different conditions to test ourselves and see whether we can still learn to love.

I believe that planet Earth is one of the toughest places for us to be because of our propensity for prejudice, anger and greedy self interest that is just about balanced by our propensity for compassion, love and altruism. It's a very balanced struggle. I think that other places have it easier where the default position is towards love and compassion. While that may be a more pleasant environment in which to grow, we have a more accelerated rate of the growth.

Q. It seems that northern California, one of the fastest living places on the planet, makes it a real struggle to maintain a balance between physical existence and enlightenment.

I agree with you. At various stages in human history, there have been power spots, places where there have been great breakthroughs. Civilization happened on this planet basically around four great rivers over the last 12,000 years. It happened around the Yellow River in China, the Nile River in Africa, the Tigris-Euphrates in the Middle East, and the Indus in India. When you have a large confluence of people coming together, the accelerated growth creates a great spectrum of possibilities for good and evil.

The same thing can be said about the northern California bay area. There are 130 different languages spoken in Silicon Valley. People are here from all over the world bringing their traditions, intellectual know-how, adventurous spirits; it's a melting pot where you find violence on the one hand and deeply compassionate people on the other. This area is a real power spot right now.

Q. So when people come together there is great potential for growth and great potential for evil but if they never came together you wouldn't see that?

Yes, exactly. What tends to happen is that when you bring people together, the engagement of people with each other in different mind-sets and different cultures, creativity begins to flow. People come face to face and that brings out the fears in us and also the creativity. But wherever people are encouraged to think and cross cultures, there you will see an extraordinary growth of human ideas. We all have unique hits on how to do the human experiment. Every one of us has his/her own way of trying to wrestle with the ordinary questions of survival and the great existential questions of the whole purpose of life; even if we do it unconsciously through our actions or through philosophical rumination or through meditation. We are all doing it in our own fashion. When you bring people together with their unique ideas and have the courage and ability to listen to each other, then you get quantum leaps in growth. I think that is what is happening in the great metropolitan areas. You get an extraordinary increase in crime and an extraordinary increase in human creativity.

Q. Is violence increasing?

Two things come to me when I hear that question. The first one is that I think sometimes the political leadership wants to create fear because they can manipulate a population that is fearful and then offer more security in the guise of withdrawing civil rights. One of the ways of creating this fear is by convincing people that they can't trust anyone and artificially inflating the reports of violence in any area. Often what we hear is not a representative sample of what is actually happening. I think that is one way in which violence seems to be on the increase.

The other way is that today's improved technology matched with a pathological person allows the amount of damage to be greater. It is not that s/he is more violent; it's just that the technology is available to make bigger, more impressive violence.

Q. The United States is considered the third most violent country in the world. This is attributed to the fact that the people of the United States are free and have a choice to do the right thing or to do the wrong thing.

There is a great story of the fall in the Judeo/Christian scriptures where the first sin is eating the fruit of the tree of the knowledge of good and evil. That is the ultimate bifurcation point, because only then are we truly free. At that stage we can make moral choices. We can't make moral choices until the hard-wiring is in place and we can imagine walking in someone else's moccasins. There is a bifurcation point that happens when we learn to choose between the two and that leads to great possibilities for evil or for good. Up till then we are living an amoral life style; neither good nor bad, it's just almost instinctual and driven almost by a reflexive response to life.

Q. So one chooses to live as one chooses?

One does. Choice is basically about a decision for consciousness and awareness and that awareness starts with a self-realization. I need to realize that I am an articulation of God and therefore you too are an articulation of God and the God in me recognizes the God in you. That is the great Hindu greeting, Namasté; the God in me recognizes and honors the God in you. That then begins to move through all articulated nature. I have the same respect for people of other cultures, other religious belief systems, animals, plant life and for the planet. The choice for awareness is the realization and choice to be conscious of the God in all things. My definition of sin is that sin is not the transgression of law or the breaking of a precept or the trampling of a commandment; to me, sin is the conscious, deliberate decision not to grow. It is to stay in my own unawareness rather than to choose consciousness.

Q. What are we going to read in "Souls on Safari?"

The second book will be even better and I don't feel that I am the author of it at all. I think that the quality of the lectures and homilies in this second book will show an improvement. I believe that my job on Sunday mornings is to try to become some kind of channel or conduit for spiritual ideas to flow through so perhaps as I am aging and getting my ego a little bit more out of the way, that channeling is better able to come through. As I listen to some of the tapes of my homilies from the last year and a half, I'm sometimes amazed at the ideas that come through and it's not me creating them, it's more like I'm some kind of channel for them. So I'm enjoying the ones I've heard as well.

THE ULTIMATE WEAPONS OF
MASS DESTRUCTION

"Truth is not that which is demonstrable—it is that which is ineluctable."

St. Exupery

TIMING IS EVERYTHING. This time the timing couldn't have been timelier. It all happened at exactly the right time. It was excellent. On Sunday, October 31, 2004, two days before the presidential elections, the weapons of mass destruction were finally found. They are even more devastating than expected, even worse than our intelligence had feared. As you would imagine, the elements of which they are composed in themselves are totally benign, but the configuration in which they have been conjoined and the manner in which they have been applied allows them to be used with devastating consequences.

The weapons of mass destruction have been found and they are: the Scriptures. In human history, there has never been a weapon that has been discovered, exploited and applied with more devastating consequences than the scriptural traditions of planet Earth.

The great scriptural traditions: Judeo/Christian, the Upanishads, the Pitakas of Buddhism, the Koran, etc., have all been used and abused in various ways. Our scriptural traditions are really the record of human attempts to make sense of our experiences vis-à-vis the great existential issues of living and dying on planet Earth. They start out based on some kind of a belief in God. They were intended to be metaphorical, parabolic and allegorical explanations of how life is experienced. Properly understood, they are symbol, metaphor, story

50

and parable. Unfortunately, in the hands of fundamental literalists they quickly became weapons of mass destruction.

The first abuse of the scriptures was the notion of justifying genocide. This came early in the scriptures. There is an injunction in the Hebrew Scriptures that is called the Bann. The Bann was allegedly a command or mandate from God that when you capture your enemy's town it was incumbent upon you to kill all living things.

There is a story in the book of Joshua where the newly freed Israelites crossed the Jordan and upon arriving at Jericho surrounded the town and God's command was that every soldier was to march straight ahead and kill all living things; specifically every man, woman, child, ox, donkey and camel. There was to be no living thing left. This injunction appears in the bible frequently. There are records where God became really upset with particular Commanders in Chief who failed to enjoy and employ this injunction in its fullest ramifications. Occasionally a compassionate leader might spare the children only to incur the wrath of God who was indignant at the breaking of the injunction to kill all living things. So genocide was justified from the scriptures.

We use the scriptures to justify our total conquest of nature. Nature quickly became the enemy. For some kind of perverted reason, everything of the Earth was of Satan, while everything of the heavens was of God. There is a phrase in Genesis in which God allegedly gave Adam and Eve the right to spoil, exploit or be responsible for nature. Throughout history we have regarded nature as being merely a resource to meet human need. And the consequences have been devastating.

We have used the Judeo/Christian Scriptures to justify the subjugation of women on our planet. In both the Hebrew Scriptures and in the Christian tradition, women should keep their mouths shut in church and if they have questions they should ask their husbands privately when they go home rather than disturb the congregation by talking in church. There was also the notion of the subjugation of the feminine principle: the feminine face of God and the feminine aspect of nature.

There was the alleged biblical injunction to enslave the black community based on a story that we find in the book of Genesis. It came after the flood that allegedly destroyed all human beings and which only eight people survived: Noah, his wife, their three sons and their wives. As they subsequently began to repopulate the Earth, there is a story in which Noah is the first recorded drunk. Noah got drunk and was inside his tent lying naked and his son, Ham, came in and seeing his father's nakedness, started to giggle and went out and told his brothers what he had just seen. The two brothers were shocked and they took a blanket into the tent and covered him so as not to see their father's nakedness. When Noah woke up and heard the story, he pronounced the following curse. He said, "Cursed be Ham. From this day forward he shall be a slave to his brothers." In the Hebrew cosmology, Shem was the father of the Semite people, Japheth was the father of the Caucasian people and Ham was the father of the African people. This text has been used throughout history to justify the enslavement of the black community especially in the southern states of this country. It is mandated, not just allowed, that blacks be subservient to both Caucasians and Semites.

One of the most devastating abuses of all is the notion of the second coming of Jesus. There was the notion that Jesus who developed Christ consciousness throughout his life and who was the prototype of where the human race was meant to be headed was going to come back at some stage and beat up on those who didn't believe in Christianity. This notion is called "The Rapture." The Rapture is the notion that the born-again will be swept up to the heavens. The only people left on planet Earth will be the unsaved, who will inherit the planet for a period of time until Jesus comes back with his legions and then there will be a titanic Armageddon and all the unsaved will be wiped out.

Saint Paul is responsible for some of this. In his first letter to the Thessalonians he wrote, "I don't want you to misunderstand me because those who have fallen asleep in Jesus will not be anywhere less fortunate than those of us who are still alive when he comes. Rather, this is what will happen. God will send his angel with a trumpet and will awaken those who have died in Jesus and they will be the first to rise. Then the rest of us who are still alive will rise up and we will meet them in the clouds." The Thessalonians took him literally and they stopped working because if Jesus is coming back imminently what is the point of working? Paul then had to rush off a second letter to the Thessalonians, "I didn't mean it literally. We have no idea when he is coming back and therefore here is my new rule: those who don't work shouldn't eat." Paul tried to back off from what he said in his first letter. Unfortunately it continued to be taken literally. Those are some of the ways that the scriptures have been used to abuse others.

It is almost as if we are being offered a treat of, "all you can eat for ten dollars." We will combine some of these excesses, abuses and misunderstandings of the bible and we'll package them for you and for ten dollars we will give you a version of the bible, a paraphrase, built specifically on these five misunderstandings and particularly three of them. One of the three notions is the notion of Armageddon. This is the notion that there is going to be a bloody battle to end all bloody battles led on the one side by Jesus and on the other side by Satan. In past generations, people were happy just to opt out of society when they thought that day was about to come. Throughout history there have been accounts of people who have left their towns and villages and gone to the mountain top thinking that Jesus was coming back to do his shtick and time after time they proved to be false. There is a newer version of that because now there are millions of people who are not content to opt out and let Jesus come back when he is ready; they are actually trying to precipitate his coming back. They are trying to foist on planet Earth the circumstances they believe will occasion his imminent return. They are hell-bent on creating Armageddon in our time. There are millions of right wing fundamentalist Christians who are hell-bent on forcing Jesus' hand by trying to create the political, sociological and geographical conditions that they believe are indicated in the bible as the prerequisites for the second coming. They are literally putting billions of dollars into this project. Then they co-opt the other two pieces.

The first of these two pieces is the notion that nature is intrinsically evil, so why should we protect it? Why should we have any concern for it? And the second of these says: if this is the last generation to inhabit planet Earth, what is the point in protecting the environment? Why shouldn't we be drilling in the Arctic? Why shouldn't we be devastating the wilderness? There will be no one left to inherit it. For a short period of time, the only ones left will be the sinners while we the enlightened, enraptured people will congregate in the clouds with Jesus to marshal our forces to return. If the only ones left behind are the sinners, why should we leave them anything? Why should we leave them forests, clean air or clean water? Why not use it all up now? I'm not exaggerating; there are literally millions of people putting billions of dollars into this project. The belief is that Jesus is imminently about to return and they are trying to force the circumstances. If Jesus didn't have the perspicacity to rise from the dead three days after he was buried, he would be turning in his tomb to think that these people believe that they represent Christ consciousness or that they represent Jesus. It is a super abuse of the Scriptures to lump three of these together and try to precipitate the end time, devastate nature in the process and cause everyone to be lost except those who believe in Jesus as their personal savior.

Theocracy is the notion that you can run the affairs of the human community according to divinely revealed principles. The law of the land and the law of your scriptural traditions are synonymous, i.e., you believe that the scriptural tradition to which you subscribe is the basis for all of the legislation that needs to be enacted in the community. It is the belief that all politics, warfare and business must be conducted according to the precepts and the revelations of your particular scriptural tradition.

Theocracy comes in two guises. There have been many examples throughout human history. Early Judaism was a theocracy. Islam, for the main part, is still a theocracy. Most of the countries in the Arab world are theocracies attempting to foist the Koran as the law of the land. As long as the papal armies had control of Europe they foisted Catholic belief system as the law of the continent. Humanity has done it throughout history. There are two versions of theocracy. There is one form that is driven by religious fanaticism. Religious fanatics are quite happy to co-opt the politicians, military and big business in their endeavor to impose their own narrow, sectarian agenda on a community. That is one form of theocracy.

There is another form that has begun to emerge in the last 50 years. This is a theocracy that is driven initially by the politicians, big business and by people who neither have an interest in God nor even a belief in God, but have an over-arching interest and belief in the power of religion as a tool to whip the masses into the service of their own very secular agenda. In America, we have been blessed with a blend of these two. For the last several years we have managed to blend these two forms of theocracy into our system. It has created some very strange bed fellows. It has produced an extraordinary conjoining of fundamentalists, bible thumping Christian groups with Roman Catholic bishops. Fundamentalist Christians see Satan under every liberating liberal idea. They have joined with some Roman Catholic bishops acting as if they are the mouthpiece of Jesus purporting to speak for God and admonishing servile congregations by telling them that a vote for democracy disqualifies them from participation in Eucharist.

The strange bedfellows in the Midwest part of our country are really loyal, patriotic, ordinary families willing to send their sons and daughters to a foreign war to fight terrorists who have been bred in record numbers in the laboratory of the current régimes' paranoia. The Alice in Wonderland part of all this is that now the good guys have become the bad guys and the bad guys have become the good guys. Those who want to stop this slaughter of children and take our soldiers back and prevent them from going in the first place are un-patriotic. The men who sit in their offices sending others to war while none of their own children ever get involved in the conflict and become cannon fodder; these are the good guys by some extraordinary quirk and twist. The people who want to take back $500 billion that has been used in this war and put it into education, medical insurance and social security, are un-American. Those who prepare to waste the resources of this country by fattening themselves; somehow these get to be the good guys by some twist of fate. Those people who are trying to create a situation in which there are fewer and fewer young people ending up in our jails, are the bad guys. The two greatest growth industries at the moment are our prison system and our war machine. Most of our money is going into these systems. The phrase, "No Child Left Behind," sounds absolutely true because if this thinking continues for another four years there will not be any child left behind. Every child will either become a felon or cannon fodder. They will all be used up while the big wigs sit back and watch. Is this what it means to be patriotic? Is this what it means to be American? Is this what it means to be a follower of Jesus?

While I believe in the separation of church and state, there is a huge confusion going on. You cannot separate spirituality and politics. Indeed, we have to separate church and state, but not spirituality and politics. Any spirituality that has a hands-off approach to politics is merely irrelevant esoterica. On the other hand, any religious system that seeks to use the White House, Congress or Supreme Court to promote its very narrow sectarian dogma and enshrine it in the laws of our land, is very un-Godly.

There is a dance to be danced. In this respect, I find the liberals as guilty as the conservatives. Liberals who want to take spirituality totally out of the national political debate are eviscerating the dialogue just as the conservatives who want to impose and use religion to foist a very narrow sectarian belief system on all of us. To be truly spiritual people, we have to be involved in politics. And to be truly spiritual people we have to separate church and state. There is no discrepancy between these two points.

It is one thing to inveigh against and confront the excesses of our times; it is another thing to create a vision. I don't want to just point out what is going terribly wrong; I want to look at what is going right in our world today.

There was a meeting some weeks ago of a group called the Bioneers. They are a group of people from all over the world who have been meeting for about seventeen years. Their shtick is that they look to nature for solutions to human problems. They are looking at how creatively nature deals with an issue when it is presented to see if we as human beings can learn the same thing in our political systems, education models, agricultural policies and everywhere humans are doing life. One of the talks was given by Paul Hawkins. As he gave his presentation, in the background there was a screen which continuously displayed a list of organizations throughout planet Earth that are trying to do life differently on the planet right now. The list contained groups involved in politics, medicine, agriculture, law and every possible human way of relating. This list scrolled continuously for the entire hour that Paul Hawkins spoke. He said, "If I were to allow this list to continue scrolling all day Friday, Saturday, Sunday and Monday it would still not be finished. That is how many organizations on planet Earth, at the moment, are trying to make a difference; trying to do things differently." But you won't hear any of that on the mass media. If you are watching main-stream television, or reading main-stream newspapers, you get the odd mention of the odd one of these. Planet Earth is on fire. It is not on fire with fear or zenophobia, it is on fire with extraordinary Christ conscious human beings many of whom have never heard of Jesus, but none the less have put on Buddhahood or Christ consciousness while trying to make a difference on our planet.

It is not a question of just opposing what is going on; it is a question of embracing a new vision. There are millions and millions of awakened people on our planet making a difference in everything we do as human beings. There is a vision and it is the only vision that there has ever been. It is the ineffable Spirit of God bubbling through creation, manifesting itself in more and more extraordinary configurations and it will not be stopped. It cannot be stopped. It is a bubbling forth, an evolution that is taking us as individuals from egocentric concerns to global consciousness. It is the bubbling of the Spirit that is taking us from ethnocentric military, economic and political policy to beginning to think with cosmic consciousness as the community of sentient beings inhabiting planet Earth. It is the kind of vision that will create charismatic leaders who will lead more by their example than by legislative injunction. It will create people who leave behind the distant demanding deities who will recover, remember and discover the God at the core of every single one of us and of every other living being. This vision is unfolding and it will not be stopped. But a journey of a thousand miles has to start with a single step and a vision of a 1000 years hence has to start with a single vote. I appeal to you when you go to your poling places, let love and compassion be the things that direct your choices and not fear and not xenophobia.

SUPER SOUL SUNDAY

"There is no rung of being on which we cannot find the holiness of God everywhere and at all times."

Martin Buber

OR THE LAST 11 years I've been spending three days a week at my place in the woods near Healdsburg. This is where I sometimes do my meditating and occasionally I do some writing, but mostly I just watch to see what nature is doing. A few months ago I was sitting by the creek and I saw a leaf fall and get tangled in a spider's web. After a few moments, the spider came out to investigate thinking perhaps that dinner had arrived. Seeing the leaf caught in her web, she circumambulated the leaf to see where it was attached and assess the damage.

She carefully nipped one of the strands holding the leaf and the leaf tumbled down and got snagged on another stand of the web. I watched her look at the leaf and then go around again and snip another strand, but the wind blew it back and it caught yet another strand of web. She continued snipping the strands, but still the leaf would not drop out of her web. At one point, she looked closely at the leaf and after a while she figured out that there was no solution but to cut up her whole web. I went back to my reading for a few hours and when I looked up there she was on a different branch spinning a new web.

In the world of the microcosmic, a single falling leaf is an act of God. I began thinking, as I watched other leaves fall down, next spring will the same leaves come back out, then begin to fall again?

Will they be different leaves, new leaves, or will they be just reincarnations of the old leaves? Am I going to watch the same leaf but just in a different season? Does a leaf have a soul? I thought about a hierarchy of souls or gradation of souls.

Do you think that cells have souls? Does every manifest thing have a soul? Do souls go all the way from cells-souls right up to the galaxy-souls? Are you looking at simple souls or single souls when you look at a single cell? Are you looking at a very complicated soul when you look at a galaxy? Are there lesser souls than single cells down to the atomic level? Are there souls greater than the galaxies?

There are different levels of souls. The simple soul is the essence of a single celled organism. The next level is when a community of cells get together and create an organ like a heart or lung. I call those super souls. At some stage organs get together and create an organism or a person and I call those mega souls. Then a whole bunch of beings get together on a planet and the soul of the planet is what I call the ultra soul. Then this planet is just one of billions and billions in the cosmos and I call the essence of that a cosmic soul.

If the super soul is the essence of an organ, what is the human body symbolically and mystically about? The eye is a super soul dedicated to seeing what really is. It is not just about seeing things in the physical cosmos, it is a super soul dedicated to seeing to the core and the essence of all that really is. The ear is a super soul dedicated to hearing the harmony of the spirit. It is hearing the hymn of the universe. It is hearing the song of God, the Bhagavad-Gita. The function of the ear is that it is a super soul designed to hear the Bhagavad-Gita.

The function of the nose is the personal contact with the fragrance of the journey into enlightenment. Touch is the super soul dedicated to the manifestation of the boundaries around the ego so that we can transcend them and recognize the God image in everyone else. Skin is a super soul that is dedicated to having the inside of God bump up against the outside of God. The function of taste is that super soul that gives me the real flavor of what God is so that I am seduced into going all the way. The heart functions as the super soul dedicated to manifesting love in our time and in our world.

The lungs are super souls dedicated to the dying and rising of all the spacesuits in which God experiences Herself in an incarnation format. The liver is a super soul that is dedicated to discerning the distinction between the value and toxicity of an experience. The stomach is that super soul that is dedicated to the extraction of life's blessings from every human experience. The kidneys are twin super souls dedicated to the shedding of the addiction to any experience once it has delivered up its message. We don't need to hang on to them any more. The legs are the super souls dedicated to taking us on the journey into enlightenment that ends exactly where it started except with the realization that the journey has been a journey back into the core of ourselves and the core of each other. We should remember that these spacesuits, or bodies we inhabit that enable us to have the experience of reincarnation, are extraordinary clusters of lesser entities. They are a cluster of super souls that create the mega souls of the incarnation of a single human being in our world, which is an ultra-soul composed of all the mega souls adding up to the cosmic soul that is the essence of the entire universe where we now find ourselves.

Physical light is the presence of Spirit or God in the manifest realm. It is extremely powerful. The human body is full of light. There are about 100 trillion cells in the human body and 100 trillion atoms in every cell and each atom contains a single proton of light. It's not technologically possible, but if it were possible, the light in a single human body could light up a baseball stadium at one million watts for three and one-half hours. It would take seven people to create enough light for the World Series! The cosmos, in which we reside, contains one million particles of light for every particle of matter. It is basically a cosmos of light. Matter is a minor contaminant in this cosmos. Moreover, light is the source and the origin of all life and energy on this little planet. There is no energy source or life form on this planet that does not ultimately owe its existence and its continued survival to sunlight. Even at a physical level light and sunlight are extraordinary.

When you go to the metaphysical level it is even more extraordinary. At the metaphysical level, light is the manifestation of Spirit in the immaterial, nonmaterial, mystical or the esoteric realm. Light is the word that has been used to symbolize enlightenment, awareness, discernment, consciousness, intuition and insight. All these words can be used as metaphors for light. The one word, light, can represent all these great breakthroughs in human spirituality. Isaiah used light to symbolize ultimate liberty.

When people live in fear, they are slaves. The history of Israel has shown this metaphorically again and again. During the first phase of evolution, we lived in fear of greater forces, greater tribes or greater communities than ourselves. We became enslaved by them. The history of the planet has been one conquest after another. Israel experienced a prolonged period of slavery from 1700 B.C. to 1250 B.C.

About 1250 B.C., Moses liberated the people and they escaped from Egypt and went out into the desert. This is the second phase or the anger phase. When fear finally gives birth to anger then action happens, rebellion occurs and liberation may transpire. They are liberated, but they are only politically free and only militarily free, and they do not believe in themselves yet. They were forced to wander for 40 years in the desert. In actual fact, within six weeks of leaving the land of Egypt, they arrived at their old home, but they still didn't believe in themselves. They sent in spies to reconnoiter and they came back and said, "We have no chance. The people in this country are giants. They will swallow us up." So they went back into the desert and they wandered for 40 years because although they were free politically, they were not free mentally, spiritually and emotionally. They were still in bondage. That is what happens with anger. Anger never frees anyone. It can make one politically free, but it never makes one spiritually free.

There is a third phase in the process. This is the phase of belief in oneself. It is only when you believe in yourself that there is true freedom. After 40 years of wandering in the desert, they believed enough in themselves to actually enter the Promised Land.

We see the very same thing happen 700 years later during their return from exile in Babylon. In Babylon they were enslaved for 70 years. They were physically, politically and mentally enslaved and then in the year 529 B.C. when the Persian Empire overthrew the Babylonians, the remnant of Judaism was set free to return to their land. They were free politically again, but they didn't believe in themselves. They went back to the land of Israel to a devastated countryside, a city in ruins and a temple that was no more. Isaiah tried to encourage them into phase three which was a belief in themselves so they could rebuild their city. They finally accomplished it.

The problem is—what happens in Phase four? The end of phase three offers a bifurcation point. What typically happens is that once we have escaped slavery and broken through the mental slavery and once we have reached both inner and outer freedom and have a belief in ourselves, what do we believe about others? We can become arrogant and we can impose our way just as their way was imposed upon us. Many servile people who have finally grown into a belief system of themselves, become aggressors. This is the history of Israel and of the United States and the history of every other country. Every country has experienced colonialism of some form and having shuffled off the yoke of colonialism has invaded and taken land that was not previously theirs. The bifurcation point allows us to go, now that we believe in ourselves, into a disbelief in the rights of other people or allows us to truly believe in the rights of others as much as we believe in our own rights.

The bifurcation point of Israel was an invitation into mysticism like the Kabala or an invitation into the domination of the land in 1210 B.C., which they did, or domination of the Samaritans which they did in the year 529 B.C. The domination that happens again and again in our world when people who ultimately have escaped inner and outer slavery finally believe so strongly in themselves that they are offered the opportunity to believe equally in others. When we reach stage four and when we opt to believe in the rights of others as much as we believe in our own rights, only then, is true spirituality possible.

Anything that masqueraded as spirituality in the first three phases is merely a religion of slavery. It is either the religion of the slaves or it is the religion of the slave makers. But it is a religion of slavery. The hallmarks are always the same. It is the notion of being the "chosen people" or that salvation exists only through the Catholic Church or that we are the elect or that salvation is for some special group of people. In practice it always leads to inquisitions, crusades, and proselytizing. Whenever you see a notion of special-ness, chosen-ness and salvation-only-for-us-ness, or wherever you see the practice of inquisition or the enforcement of viewpoints on others, wherever you see these you are in the presence of religion that is based on phases one, two or three and it is not about true spirituality.

True spirituality is the ultimate liberation because it recognizes the God not just in me or my child; it recognizes the God in all of the tribes and in all other sentient life forms. We live in an extraordinarily exciting time. We live at a time in world history when the world is desperately trying to birth this true spirituality. We live in a period in American history when we are trying desperately to birth this true spirituality. But we live in a world and in America at a time when the old religions of slavery are exercising an extraordinary strangle hold on the throat of this development. The positions of power have been seized by fundamentalist thinkers. They seem to be in control, but the spiritual evolution will not be stopped. True spirituality will continue to unfold until finally leaders will emerge who recognize deep in their souls that rights and responsibilities are the same for everyone. At that stage we will be truly free. At that phase, we will have gone from super souls to mega souls to ultra souls to cosmic souls. At that phase, we will truly understand what life is about. The light of Christ is not the light of the interrogator's lamp shining in the face of the accused to try to extract some confession. That is not the light of Christ. The light of Christ is a gentle, radiance of Spirit

64

emanating so powerfully that it ultimately dissolves the illusion that we are separate from God and separate from each other. The light of Christ is that light that will bring the final missing piece to the jigsaw puzzle of human evolution. It will be the realization of who we truly are. It will dissolve the amnesia for the memory of where we come from, who we are, what our mission is and what our destiny is.

THE MIRACLE IS THAT WE DON'T
SEE THE MIRACLE

"The spirit shall look out through matter's gaze and matter shall reveal the spirit's face."

Sri Aurobindo

THERE IS A language which I call Mythish. Mythish is even older that Irish, more beautiful than English and more mellifluous than Spanish. There are very few people that speak Mythish well and there are two kinds of people who totally misunderstand Mythish. One group thinks that Myth is bunk and they refuse to pay any attention to it. They think that it is just stupid stories made up by unsophisticated people to explain stuff that science still hasn't caught up with. There is another group and they do even more damage to it. These are the fundamental literalists who think that they speak Mythish but in actuality they don't understand the first thing about it. They reduce myth, which is an extraordinary metaphorical articulation of truth that is so profound and so deep that there is no way to express it theologically, philosophically or scientifically and they reduce it to its literal fundamentalist underpinnings. They think that that is the meaning of it.

There is the beautiful story of the three wise men coming from the East to visit the baby Jesus and bring him gifts of gold, frankincense and myrrh. The first group thinks that Mythish is ridiculous and says it never happened. The second group thinks it absolutely happened and that Jesus was given a gift of gold, frankincense and myrrh and he kept all these things. And this group also believes that

Herod, a paranoid schizophrenic in constant fear of being over-thrown, would allow three men from the East to come looking for a king who would supplant him. That he would give this group two years to find the baby Jesus, who was born only six miles down the road, and wait for them to come back is ridiculous. This group thinks that that literally happened and has not understood what this Myth is about. It doesn't understand the difference between wisdom and knowledge or the difference between truth and mere facts. There is a very big difference.

Facts are really a mapping between the terrain and the representation of the terrain; between the map and the territory. A factoid is a fact that doesn't change the world in any way.

Truth is very different. Truth has nothing to do with facts. Truth is that which transforms and ultimate truth is that which transforms radically. Until we get the difference between facts and truth we won't understand Mythish. We don't understand the meaning of the story of the three wise men. Until we can distinguish between wisdom and knowledge, we can't get the meaning of this story. Knowledge is merely the ability to manipulate the external environment. It is very important to us. It allows us to survive in the world. It allows us to invent stuff, make our houses warm, cars run, etc; that is knowledge.

Wisdom is very different. Wisdom is that which brings us into alignment with truth. Wisdom is that which grounds us in our connection to God. Who are the wise people? What does it mean to be a wise man or wise woman? The wise person is a person who recognizes the difference between truth and mere facts, between wisdom and mere knowledge. The wise person is a person who is grounded in truth and the truly wise person is a person who can recognize Christ consciousness.

Christ consciousness does not just come to us in the Christian story or in Jesus the carpenter from Nazareth some 2000 years ago. Christ consciousness came to us before Jesus and many times since Jesus. The truly wise person is the person who has the eyes to see that Christ consciousness can be found in any tradition in all parts of our globe. This Christ consciousness always comes with gifts: the wise man or woman do indeed bring gifts of gold, frankincense and myrrh, but they are symbolic gifts. Gold represents royalty. It does not represent that we live in a political society with the king at the top and the rest of us at the bottom. It means that we are all royalty and everyone on planet Earth is entitled to security, shelter and respect. It means that we recognize the royalty of all living beings by according them the kind of dignity and justice that is their birthright. That is the gold that the wise person brings to the infant i.e., nascent Christ consciousness.

The frankincense was a gift brought to honor the divinity of Jesus. Jesus was God and so are we. There is nothing except God. There is only God. According to a beautiful Sanskrit poem, "Minerals are God sleeping, plants are God waking, animals are God walking and humans are God thinking." There is only God. The frankincense represents that. It does not mean that three people came across the world to meet a little baby and an angel in Bethlehem 2000 years ago because they recognized that he and only he was an incarnation of Divinity. It wasn't about that at all. It was recognition of the divinity in every one of us.

Myrrh is a traditional Christian symbol representing death. Do you think that the wise men recognized that this little child was going to be killed? I don't believe that at all. Myrrh is not recognition of death, but the recognition that only life is real. It is an embalming for life. It is the recognition that there is only one life; that this life dips into incarnation and out of incarnation on a cyclical basis and that there is only the one life threading all of that together. There is life as a little baby and there is life in elder-hood in the very same way as a tree has within it all the possibility of spring, summer, autumn and winter.

Saint Francis of Assisi stood beside a dormant fruit tree in the middle of the frostbitten winter and said to it, "Speak to me of God," and the tree burst into bloom. It was not a miracle. It was Francis' ability to see within the dead tree the four seasons. All of the possibility of spring resided within the dormant tree in winter.

Within one lifetime, reside all the possibilities of our extraordinary incarnation on planet Earth and the disincarnating and the reincarnating that comes afterward. It represents the fact that there is only one life joining all of us together. Every one of us is an articulation of this single life. There is only one life breathing itself through us. There is only one God articulating Herself in us again and again. This was the gift of the myrrh that the wise men brought to the infant Jesus.

Wisdom happens in three stages. It happens locally, globally and cosmically. This is represented in Mythish by the story that the first ones to come to adore the infant Jesus were local shepherds from the fields looking after their flock. The second group to come was an international group; the three wise men from the East and the third group were the angels; the cosmic travelers. It represents the fact that when Christ consciousness lights up, everyone is impacted by it. First came the local, then the global and then the cosmic community. Every time someone awakes to Christ consciousness it is a local event, a global event and a cosmic event.

The wise person always navigates by soul wisdom. What drives the safari of the wise one is always the soul. What drives the safari of the worldly wise is always the head and emotions in combination. One of the greatest fallacies and illusions under which we humans live is that we are rational animals. We claim humans are rational animals. We are not rational at all. We are emotional beings who have learned how to think; there is a big difference. Some of us are so good at very quickly adducing reasons to support our emotional responses to life that we think that we are responding rationally to life. Almost none of us responds rationally to life. We respond at a visceral gut level and some of us are so good at immediately adducing evidence to support our emotional response that we think we are behaving rationally, but we are not. Only the truly wise person is navigating according to the soul, the rest of us are navigating mainly according to our emotional responses to life. Very quickly we begin to move into fear. We are born with only two emotions. We are born with the ability to feel fear and the ability to feel love. Both of these bifurcate and create combinations and permutations which lead to all the other virtues and vices. When fear is turned inward, it becomes depression. When fear is turned outwards, it becomes anger. When love is turned inward, it becomes self-esteem. When love is turned outward it becomes compassion. One of the permutations is greed. It's always fear based; a running away from the fear that resides at the center i.e., fear of death, fear of being conquered and the fear of not being loved. It can lead to extraordinary power. There are no more powerful orators on the planet than persons living by greed and adducing reason to support their bid for power. These powerful individuals seem to control much of our world. The military, politics, and unfortunately, our churches are in their hands. These are the people who drive the system. They have left off wisdom and have opted for fear.

The Greek word, epiphany, means that a god has incarnated among human beings. Has this happened just once? According to the Christian myth, for those who do not speak Mythish, it happened only once 2000 years ago to a carpenter's son, born in Bethlehem who was named Jesus. The truth is that when you begin to speak Mythish well, you realize that as you move into all the great myths of the world, you find the same motifs again, and again. You find it in Irish, African, Greek and Scandinavian mythology. The notion that the gods appear among us comes up in all the world religions. It continues to happen through all the eras of human history. As Jesus said, "Split a log, and I am there, turn a stone and I am there. There is no place where I am not."

Epiphany happens everywhere. God among us happens again and again. In fact, to say it happens is the wrong term. To happen, gives the impression that there is somehow a void and then it happens and then there is a void again. The only reality is epiphany. The only reality is that God is. It is our awakening to that reality that looks like an epiphany. The truth is that God is and only God is.

70

We tend to think that the important figures in history are the great political, military, economic or great slave masters. When the history is written, these people will be mere footnotes in the prologue. The 21st century does not belong to them. The history of the 21st century belongs to the mystics. It belongs to the people who understand Christ consciousness. It is happening now. It did not happen with just the infant Jesus 2000 years ago.

There is a great Jewish tradition that in any period of human history there are only 36 holy ones (Zaddikim) on the planet. I think that they miscalculated or maybe that was true in former times or maybe we needed 36 holy ones to hold the position temporarily. There are a lot more than that on the planet Earth at the moment. There is a filigree necklace of human beings joining hands across the globe of human consciousness and creating a template that is leading us to the next quantum leap in our evolution as a species. We can be part of that necklace or we can just wait for it to happen. Jesus is such a person in that diadem as are the Buddha, Mother Theresa, Thich Nhat Hanh and the Dalai Lama. The question is; are any more of us going to wake up and join hands and learn to form this necklace? Where are we looking for leadership? Are we expecting some cataclysmic event to project us into the next stage of our evolution? My belief system is: you don't need to look that far. If you really look into the eyes of a baby, watch a butterfly in flight or if you have ever really seen a sunrise or sunset, then you have already seen God. You have already had your epiphany. We do not have to wait for some cataclysmic event to change world history.

My prayer for you is that you stay ready to receive your epiphany.

WHAT HAVE YOU GOT IN YOUR MOUTH?
THE TONGUE AS METAPHOR

"It is difficult to find happiness in oneself, but it is impossible to find it anywhere else."

Schopenhauer

D O YOU HAVE any idea how sophisticated and versatile the instrument is that you carry around in your mouth? The tongue is an extraordinarily sophisticated and versatile piece of equipment. The tongue is loaded with taste buds. This is God's gift to us. In fact, if you are Italian you are basically taste buds on legs. If you are Irish, you are the victim of a very cruel evolutionary mishap. You don't need taste buds if you are Irish. Given the quality of Irish food, taste buds are never employed. The Irish have found a new use for taste buds. We love the taste of words.

We need the tongue to speak. The tongue is capable of making the most extraordinary contortions. It is capable of extraordinary numbers of positions within the mouth without which language would be totally impossible.

In Kenya, there are some interesting uses for the tongue. If a little child gets something in his eye, the mother of the child will use the tip of her tongue to take a foreign object out of her child's eye.

We need our tongues in order to suck. It helps us create a vacuum or semi vacuum in our mouth without which we would not be able to suck. We used our tongues in Kenya to suck out snake poison.

The Turkana people in Kenya use their tongues to point. A Turkana man carries his entire possessions in his two hands. In his left hand he carries a three-legged stool, which he uses as a pillow when sleeping and to sit upon when he is at council meetings. In his other hand, he carries a spear. If you ask a Turkana man directions, he points the direction with his tongue.

We use the word, tongue, metaphorically in many ways. We speak about tongue as a language: biting your tongue, holding your tongue and tongue twisters are just a few ways we use the word tongue. We use tongue very specifically to talk about the word of God.

Words have extraordinary power. Simple words can absolutely change your life. When the first time someone spoke the magic words to you, "I love you," what happened to your heart? Or if you are at your doctor's office and the doctor says to you, "You have cancer," how does that change your life? When you are waiting for the election results and someone says the words, "the winner is," that can change the entire country or globe for the next four years.

It is said that "Sticks and stones may break my bones but words will never hurt me." It is foolish to think that words can't hurt us. Words have an extraordinary ability to change our paradigm, our thinking and our feelings. Words are the first stage of the incarnation of ideas into action. They are the connectors between the transcendent and the immanent. They are the connectors between the immaterial and the material. They are the connectors between God as father and God as mother. All the great teachers not only use words, they talk about the power of words and the importance of words.

The Buddha, 550 years before Jesus said, "Words are the most accurate diagnostic tools ever invented and they are great for psychotherapeutic interventions." (My terminology, his idea.) In other words, if you really want to understand who you are, listen to what you say. Words are great self-diagnostic tools. If you want to know what kind of person you are, listen to the conversations you have. Are you speaking words of compassion, empathy, love and encouragement? Are you speaking words of cynicism, bitterness and anger? Then that is who you are. Listen to what you speak and then you know who you are. If you want to change who you are, change what you say. If you find yourself speaking cynically, start speaking encouragingly and lovingly. If you hear yourself speaking very critically, speak words of love and encouragement to people and then that is who you become. Words have an extraordinary ability to diagnose our condition and to intervene taking us in the direction we want to go.

This notion of the word of God goes through seven great stages. The first stage is that God is the totally ineffable, unknowable ground of our being. The second stage is that people have mystical experiences of this ineffable, unknowable ground of our being. Stage three is they have to try to unpack them. Whatever mystical experience you have you have to unpack it using your own personality with all its gifts, talents, strengths and biases. You have to unpack it in the cultural paradigm in which you were raised.

Stage four is the oral presentation. All the great scriptures of the world were originally oral traditions. They were handed down as stories for hundreds of years before they came to stage five which is when they were written down for the first time. In the case of Islam, they were written on pieces of parchment, leaves and bones. Whenever Mohammed spoke it was recorded on whatever kind of material was at hand.

Stage six is that it got translated. As this revelation became more popular and better known, it got translated into different languages. There are basically three ways of translating scripture. The first one is a literal translation. You may think that the literal translation is the best. In a literal translation, you translate a noun with a noun, an adjective with an adjective and a verb with a verb. But it doesn't work because languages show life with symbol and metaphor and when you begin to translate something literally, you totally lose its meaning.

For example, when I was living in Kenya, I had a visit from an American priest. He came to bring financial aid and to help us run a hospital for disabled children. I took him with me to local villages to say mass. I invited him to speak and I translated for him. I remember at one stage he used the phrase, "You push my buttons." How do you translate the notion of that to people who don't know what a button is? So the first way, translating literally, is meaningless.

The second way of translation is to try to encapsulate the meaning and translate according to the meaning, but then you run into trouble and you have to be inventive. When Jesus spoke about the wheat and the cockle, he knew that his audience was made up of agricultural people and would understand the imagery he was using. Wheat and cockle are alike in the early stages of their germination, but cockle is a weed that imitates wheat. Jesus tells a story about a farmer that sowed wheat in his field. But when he was asleep, an enemy came and sowed cockle among the wheat, which would destroy the wheat. After a few weeks, some of his workers began to see that something was wrong with the wheat. "Someone has sown cockle in your wheat. What shall we do? Shall we pull them up?" The farmer said, "No, if you pull up the cockle you will tear up the wheat with the cockle. Let them grow together and then when we harvest them, we will separate the wheat from the cockle and we will keep the wheat and we will burn the cockle."

When I was in Kenya, I had a hard time teaching this story because the Kenyan people do not have wheat in their diet. I had to make up words to get this story across. In order to get this message across, I had to invent new words. That also is what happens when you start translating the word of God into other languages. Often there are no categories in the host language for the ideas in the language for which you are translating.

Finally there is stage seven: the whole interpretive process that goes on in the minds of the listeners. The listeners bring their own talent, gifts and pathology to the listening. They bring their cultural biases and insights to the listening as well, so it is going through a much different iteration. For some people, it comes out in a very loving understanding of our interactions with God and with each other, but for other people, it comes out very punitively and often it's abused. We certainly have abused the Judeo/Christian scriptures.

Because of this seven stage process and because the interpretation has to come through our own particular biases and our own cultural prejudices, we constantly abuse them. We have abused the Judeo/ Christian scriptures in order to dominate women, nature and the black people in this country and other places.

Islam has an interesting idea. There is the story of Mohammed when he had his first encounter with the angel Gabriel. The angel Gabriel caught him in a bear hug and said to him, "Recite, recite." Mohammed was not a learned man; he could neither read nor write. He said to the angel Gabriel, "I can't!" The angel caught him again in a hug and said, "Recite, Recite!" Mohammed said, "I can't!" The third time the angel hugged him and commanded him to recite Mohammed began to recite.

Islam claims that the word of God is only an oral tradition and that when you write it down it gets interpreted. It needs to be heard in an oral format in Arabic otherwise you will misunderstand it. Islam claims that any effort to translate the Koran is, in fact, an interpretation of the Koran. You cannot translate it because it needs to be heard in Arabic. It is the sound of the language itself that is a part of the revelation. There is a notion that the Koran is the earthly book form of the sacred book in heaven called the Kitab. The Koran is to the Kitab as Jesus is to God. We believe that Jesus is the incarnation of God and Islam believes that the Koran is the book form of this divine revelation. Unfortunately the monotheistic religions, in particular, ran with their own particular revelations. Having gone through this seven-stage process, they claim that they and they alone have the ultimate truth. Judaism claims that the Jews are the chosen people, the Hebrew language is sacred and that revelation ended about 400 years before the birth of Jesus.

Christianity will come along later and say, "Rubbish." There is a new "chosen people" and it is us Christians. There is a new sacred language and it is Greek so the New Testament will be written in Greek. Revelation ended with the death of the last of the apostles.

Six hundred years later, Islam will say, "Not true." There is a new "chosen people," they are the Muslims and a new sacred language, Arabic, and a new revelation that ends with the death of the prophet Mohammed.

In my opinion, God continues to speak in many different languages. Every folklore, proverb or mythology of the world is God continuing to reveal herself to us. The word of God continues to happen as we listen.

In the year 721 B.C., ten of the tribes of Israel were taken by the great Assyrian Empire and they are never heard of again. There is a great mythology about where they went and what happened to them and where they might be today, but in truth, they are gone.

About 130 years later, the great Babylonian Empire which had suppressed the Assyrian Empire, took over the two remaining tribes of Israel and took them into captivity in Babylon. They remained there for about 70 years. In the year 529 B.C., the Persians overthrew the Babylonians. The Persians liberated the Jews to go back to the land of Israel, but only 24,000 chose to do so. Those that went back found that Jerusalem had been destroyed and the temple was gone. They were very dispirited, but they made a half-hearted effort to cultivate the land. Reports went back to Babylon that the Jews were not doing well. A Babylonian priest, Ezra, and Nehemiah, a royal cupbearer, were sent back by the Persian Emperor to try to encourage the people. The priest, Ezra, recovered the sacred scriptures and read them to the people. He told them: "You are a liberated people; this is the good news, now let's dream a new vision." Ezra was quoting Isaiah. Later Jesus takes up those three themes in his message of good news, liberation and a new vision.

We normally think of Jesus as a priest. In one story, Jesus is a lector. He is asked to read from the scriptures. He read, "He has sent me to preach good news to the poor, to proclaim liberty to captives, to restore sight to the blind, to release the prisoners and to declare a year of favor from the Lord." This was proclaiming Jesus' mission.

After reading this, Jesus gave this short homily: "Today this scripture is being fulfilled in your hearing."

What was that about? Was Jesus saying: "The entire history of humanity has been leading to this moment? Here I am, Jesus, the incarnation of the second person of the blessed trinity, I have arrived." Is that what he was saying? I don't believe that at all. What he was saying was that anyone who really understands and hears the word of God should be able to say; today this scripture is being fulfilled even as you listen. This is our vocation. Anyone who wants to put on Christ consciousness or adopt Buddha nature should be able to make that same claim. If we really understand who we are and we really understand why we are here, every one of us should be able to make that statement. There is good news being preached to you, you are being liberated and a new vision is being offered to you.

When you walk among a group of people, your presence should be good news, if you understand Jesus. When you walk among a group of people it should be a liberating experience for everyone, if you understand Jesus. When you walk among a group of people you should be offering them a whole new vision of the world if you understand the message of Jesus.

An American idol said one time: "Make my day, go ahead, make my day." This is not the boastful taunt of a gun-toting cowboy. This is a jaded world looking for a new vision, liberation and for "new" good news. He is asking desperately, go ahead make my day. Do we have the courage to let that be our mantra that can truly "make the day" of the world in which we live? Our very presence can be good news, liberating for everyone and offering a new vision for the future!

WHO DO YOU LOVE THE MOST?
THE NEED TO FEEL SPECIAL

"To tie oneself to a special group and to its ideas is to form another attachment for the ego."

Paul Brunton

I WAS LUCKY ENOUGH to have five siblings, four of whom are still alive, and I have 19 nieces and nephews all of whom are still alive, thank God. I also have six grand nieces and nephews all of whom are alive and kicking. Two of my nieces are "Irish twins." For two months out of the year they are the same age because they are born ten months apart. When I came home to Ireland while I was living in Africa it was always the same story with my nieces and nephews. Each wanted to be treated special as though I could choose one over the other. I couldn't because they were all special to me.

Who gets to be God's chosen people? We think that maybe because we come from the Judeo/Christian system that that phrase only applies to the Jews because they were God's chosen people, but that title fell to the Jews by default.

The beginning of the world happened in the year 4004 B.C. if you are a fundamentalist. An Irish bishop, Bishop Usher, looking at the biblical evidence estimated that the world was created in the year 4004 B.C. Another scholar, looking at the evidence also from the Book of Genesis deduced that it actually happened at 9 a.m. on a Tuesday, October 23. So if you were a fundamentalist, the world was created at 9 a.m. on a Tuesday in the year 4004 B.C. On that glorious occasion, God created Adam and Eve and the first agreement was made with them. They were in some sense especially chosen among all the animals. This is the first notion of a chosen people. As yet there was no other people and definitely no Jewish nation at this stage. Adam and Eve were just two people who hadn't as yet worn fig leaves. Then because of a sin that they committed they got kicked out of the garden. God got really upset and he kicked them out and he closed the gate and no one could get into the garden of paradise until the Messiah comes to re-open the gate.

God quickly figured out that it wasn't such a good creation. He kind of screwed up. His first draft didn't turn out too well. He decided to wipe the whole thing out about the year 3000 B.C. This can be dated accurately from the genealogy contained in the Book of Genesis. Only eight people survived; Noah and his wife and their three sons and their wives. God made a new agreement. In Genesis we find out what this agreement was. According to this agreement, God made a new covenant, not between himself and Noah, not even between himself and all human beings, but between himself and all living beings. Six times God said: "I make my covenant between myself and all sentient beings." As yet, there was no Jewish nation. Even though there are human beings, the covenant God was making is not with human beings. It was between God and all living things.

This is the beginning of a cosmology of genetics. According to the Jewish tradition then, all the peoples of the world were descended from these three sons. Because of the inadequacy of the scientific data at the time, they wrongly presumed that there were only three races. There was the African race that was descended from Ham. There were the Semite people who were descended from Shem. And there were the Caucasian people who were descended from Japheth. In the Hebrew cosmology, all the races of the world came from these three sons of Noah. They hadn't heard about the Indians or the Asians; these two races were left out of this cosmology completely. This was the beginning of some kind of notion of choseness. As yet, there still is no Jewish nation.

Fast forward to the year 1850 B.C., and you have Abraham, who lived in his father's house while his father made statues of gods for all of the temples in the area. One day Abraham heard a voice and the voice said, "Abraham, I want you to leave your father's house." Abraham said, "Me, I'm not old enough." God said, "No, you are big enough and you are ready to go. You have to leave your father's house and go to a place I will show you and I will make you the father of a great nation."

Abraham left home with his wife and his cousin, Lot, and they went into the land of Israel. God made a third covenant with him. "I will choose you and I will make you the father of a great nation. You will be my people and I will be your God." There was no monotheism at that stage; there were lots of gods. God said to Abraham, "I want to be your God. Your father has his own gods, but I want to be your God." That was the agreement; it was not monotheistic.

When it came to the time that Abraham's son, Isaac, was about to get married, he sent back to the old country for a girl because he did not want his son to marry a local girl. When his grandson was about to get married, Abraham again sent back to the old country for a girl to be the wife of his grandson. Then at some stage, they all emigrated to Egypt and were then enslaved for 450 years. God had forgotten his people, but one day God came upon Moses while Moses was tending the flock of his father-in-law who was a priest of another religion. Suddenly Moses saw a burning bush and heard a voice that seemed to come from the burning bush say, "Put off your shoes. The land on which you stand is holy ground. I am God and I want you to go back into the land of Egypt and set my people free. I am the God of Abraham, Isaac and Jacob." Even at this stage there was still no monotheism in Judaism. Monotheism was the idea of a Pharaoh in Egypt. The Pharaoh, Akhenaton, lived about 150 years before Moses and claimed that there was only one God. This idea proved so popular that the priests killed him and the idea of monotheism got quickly quashed.

Moses led the people out of exile into the desert until they reached the Promised Land. He gave them a new covenant; the Ten Commandments. The first commandment is always misquoted and always misunderstood. We think that God said, "I am the Lord your God, you shall not have false gods before me." That is not what God said. What he said was, "I am the Lord, your God. You shall not have strange gods before me." Strange as in foreign or other gods, in other words, you are not allowed to have those other gods in front of me. I want to be the top god. They can have their god, but you have to be my people and I will be your God. The Ten Commandments are not monotheistic. The very first commandment is not an injunction to monotheism, it is not "the" God saying there is only one God and you're not allowed to believe in other gods. He was not saying that. He was saying, I am your God and I don't want you putting other gods in front of me. I want to be number one on your chart. That is all he was saying. Monotheism had still not arrived in Judaism.

By 800 B.C., 400 years after Moses, there was a great prophet, Elijah. He was really upset that the people who had now reached the Promised Land, had conquered it and had settled it and had now become agriculturalists; the ex-slaves who had been nomadic pastoralists for 40 years were now a settled agricultural community. They were getting fed up because they didn't need a war god anymore. They had conquered the land. What they needed was an agricultural god. They began looking around to change their investments. They wanted to take out a second mortgage, amalgamate all their finances and put all their money where it really counted i.e., into a god who knew about agriculture. They were no longer interested in a war god.

They began to follow a god called Baal. Baal is a word for "master." Elijah got upset that they were leaving Yahweh in order to follow Baal. Elijah arranged a large contest on Mount Carmel in order to distinguish which of these gods was more powerful; Yahweh or Baal. Of course, Yahweh won the contest. The people went back again to follow Yahweh who had demonstrated that he could send rain and was beginning to understand agriculture. The people felt that if he could send rain maybe he did know something about agriculture so they followed him and no longer followed the other god. But Judaism was still not monotheistic. They had just opted again to follow Yahweh, but there were many other gods available.

The story continues until 500 B.C., when Judaism finally did opt for monotheism. The evolution had gone from a tribal deity to a top god to an only god. So by default the claim they made that, "We are God's chosen people," made them the chosen people of the only God. The original claim was that they were the chosen people of a particular God, one of the many. Then all the other gods proved to be false so there was then only one God and by happenstance he was the God that chose them. So they believe that they were the chosen people.

This is not peculiar to Judaism. It happened in many different areas. Within 200 years of the birth and death of Jesus, Catholicism wrested the title from Judaism claiming that Judaism had dropped the ball and God had changed his mind and Catholics were God's chosen people. Six hundred years later Islam said that both Judaism and Catholicism had dropped the ball and God was really fed up with both of them and God had made another choice and chose the Arab world of Islam.

The Masai of Africa were totally convinced that they were the chosen people. The Masai believed that all the cattle on planet Earth belonged to them. They were enjoined by God to repatriate all the cattle on the planet. Cattle raiding for the Masai, is not just a kind of recreational activity, it is the divine injunction: "Go get your cattle back. I gave them to you why did you let other people steal them from you?"

The great religion of Japan, Shintoism, has the belief system that God chose the Japanese nation as his particular patrimony. Of course, if you are lucky enough to be Irish, you know that all the other stories are made up and that there is only one chosen people; the Irish! There are Irish and those who want to be Irish. All Irish blessings end with the phrase, May you have the health of the salmon, may you always have liquid in your mouth and may you die in Ireland because that is God's chosen place and if you die in Ireland, you go straight to heaven. The Irish knew that they were God's chosen people. All this is based on the need to be special.

What is this terrible need, psychologically speaking, to be special? I believe that the birth of the ego is an extraordinarily painful process and so in order to birth an ego, the psyche has to be seduced with some kind of perks. The perks are that you will feel special and unique and that you will be different from everyone else.

Two problems emerge as the child's ego develops and two great mistakes can happen. In psychology we call them borderline personality disorder and narcissistic personality disorder. A borderline personality disorder is an ego that is so fragile that it doesn't adequately develop and particularly it doesn't have boundaries. The world spills in and the fragile boundaries melt under the onslaught of other people's agendas and invasiveness. The ego never really fully develops. Such people are very fragile throughout their lives and tend to be suicidal; they tend to attract extraordinary amounts of drama and abuse into their lives and are very difficult people to be around.

The other disorder, narcissistic personality disorder of a newly emerging ego is much more serious. This is where boundaries also aren't developing and the ego spills out into the world. There are no boundaries so the world melts under the onslaught of self importance, i.e., I just spill out into the world and everything is my oyster. These people become the Donald Trumps of the world; they are very difficult people to be around. Not only for their immediate family, those with whom they are in intimate relationships, but they make an impression on the world. They make the world a dangerous place to inhabit. You find a disproportionate number of these people in politics, in the top echelons of government, church activity and among industrialists, executives in Hollywood and every place where people are promoting themselves and their own agenda to the absolute detriment of an entire society or even the global community. This is narcissism gone awry. Why do we have these extraordinary needs? The reason is that the ego needs to be seduced into birthing itself.

Without an ego we wouldn't be able to function. The ego needs to have adequate boundaries to protect itself against the world and even more important, to protect the world against it.

The problem would be fine if the ego could limit its narcissistic activities to just the immediate web of interpersonal relationships. However, it spills out into families and nations. When the narcissistic ego spills out into the family system, then you get the notion of "old families" or royalty or political dynasties. As if any family is older than any other or more royal than another, every single family goes back to the beginning. Every one of us goes back to a little tribe of Africans who lived about 200 thousand years on the plains of Kenya. So we are either African or descendants of Africans. The notion of royal family is based on two myths: the myth of the first born and the myth that the lineage can only pass through the male. In actual fact, every child is equally a descendant of the parents whether s/he is first born or 15th born. To attempt to trace our royal image by excluding women and excluding everyone who is not a first born is totally ridiculous. We have built this notion of old families, royal families or political dynasties. That is what ego looks like when it spills out into the family system.

If it stopped there, it wouldn't be so bad, however, it spills out into national identity and into religion. What spills out from these systems is that some nations are particularly beloved of God or that some religion is especially chosen of God. Then, at that stage, we have a real problem. There is a stage beyond that wherein the ego expands to the level of the entire species. We believe that as a species we are truly the center of the universe. For the last 400 years, this heresy has been under scientific onslaught. Bit by bit it has been chipped away for those who have been paying attention. But for those of us who are still asleep, we are ignorant of the data. It started with the Copernican revolution. Copernicus demonstrated that the Earth is not the center of the solar system. This was so upsetting that he was found guilty of heresy and liable to hell fire. Our little planet is not the center of the solar system.

Fast forward to Charles Darwin who demonstrated that the human species is not the center of biological life on planet Earth; we are merely one step in the evolution from the primates to our own time. This was really upsetting to the church. In our own time, Carl Jung showed that the ego is not the center of the psyche; it is merely the center of the conscious psyche. There is another center to the entire psyche that he called the Self with a capital S and which spiritual people call the soul. The ego wants to be the center of attention, but is not even the center of the psyche; it is merely the center of waking consciousness. The ego is the center of the tip of the iceberg. That and that alone is what it is.

In the 1950s, Frank Drake, a famous astronomer delivered the second most important formula of the 20th century. He estimated the number of civilizations in the Milky Way Galaxy which are capable of communicating with other civilizations outside our solar system. It is a probability equation. The best estimate of that equation is somewhere in the region of one to two million. There are approximately one or two million such civilizations just in the Milky Way Galaxy. If that is the case, then by the law of averages, at least half of them are more advanced than we are. We can't be the center anymore.

Quantum mechanics tells us that this universe of ours has 10 to the power of 27 brand new universes called into being every second per cubic centimeter of 11 dimensional mathematical spaces. That is a lot of universes. We are losing our place constantly at the center of everything. We are clinging desperately to the need for religious or national narcissistic personhood. It has gone like this: Mesopotamia (Iraq and Iran), to Egypt, to Greeks, to Romans, to Spaniards, to Portuguese, to British, to Americans and it is now on its way to China. What has been the trajectory of religious narcissism? Political narcissism has gone from the religions of Mesopotamia, to Egypt, to Judaism, to Christianity and to Islam to pan-fundamentalism. What happens when these two schemes get together? When narcissistic religious thinking gets together with narcissistic nationalism then you get theocracy and it is a very dangerous state? Then the separation of church and state is in grave danger of dissolving. At this moment, politicians and fundamentalist Christians and top level industrialists are clambering into bed in an orgy of copulation in order to beget the second coming of Jesus. What will be the cost of the second coming of Jesus when you get copulation between industrialists, politicians and fundamentalists? The costs are global conflagration and the destruction of the ecology of planet Earth. The reward for that is global domination and global grip on the economy by the winner. So if they win, we will be faced with a world in which the survivors will only be born-again Christians that will inherit a world denuded of trees, Jews, Arabs, Catholics, gay people and liberated females. The survivors will inherit a world denuded of diversity, creativity and life.

When you fall asleep, the ego which is merely the CEO of waking consciousness has to give way to the soul which is the CEO of dream consciousness. As surely as that process happens to every one of us on a nightly basis so surely will it happen to the human species as well. The national ego and the global ego of the human species will inevitably give birth to a soul of the human race and the soul of planet Earth.

Recently, in the last 2500 years, spirit has been implanting little probes of Christ consciousness in the human experiment. Beginning merely 2500 years ago with Lao Tzu and Confucius in China with Zoaraster in Persia, with the Buddha in India, with Jeremiah and Jesus in the land of Israel, Spirit has slowly been implanting little templates of Christ consciousness on the task of human evolution. The template has been laid down well and truly by these intrepid explorers. Now the energy of Spirit is irresistibly pouring itself through into the story of human evolution. Therefore, I appeal to everyone to stop listening to the prophets of doom whose theory is based on fundamentalist fear and are articulating their belief system with a superficial misunderstanding of human history and are using as their resources mere religion while eschewing the mysticism of spirituality. Do yourselves a big service and do the world a big service, stop looking at the nightly news. Go visit your grandchildren. Look into the eyes of a new born grandchild and you will see everything you need to know about tomorrow.

Prejudice—"They're All the Same"

"There is little hope for us until we become tough-minded enough to break loose from the shackles of prejudice, half-truths, and downright ignorance."

Martin Luther King, Jr.

I'M A SUCKER for going to movies that upset me. And even if I know that they are going to upset me, I still go to them. I recently saw "Mississippi Burning." It was a brilliant story of three civil rights workers from the East Coast who went to Mississippi during the 60s in order to register the black community to participate in democracy for the first time. These three young men were murdered and there was an enquiry to find out what happened. Of all the scenes in that movie that most upset me was the interview with a young white mother at the end of the movie. She looked to be a teenager and she spoke in the interview while nursing her baby. She was asked, "What do you think about this affair." She said, "Well, you know, you got to keep them blacks down cause if we aren't on top of them, they'll be burning our churches, raping our women and killing our kids." She was describing exactly what she believed would happen if the black community were in the ascendancy and she described, in fact, what had been happening for hundreds of years and what was currently being perpetrated on the black community. In other words, in order to protect the white community, here's what we need to do to the black community. What upset me the most was that she was nursing her baby as she mouthed this level of prejudice. Her little baby was drinking in that kind of prejudice with his mother's milk. It upset me that the next generation was being nursed with the milk of prejudice by their mothers.

Prejudice is always a fear based xenophobic generalization extrapolated from a single experience to an entire community. If I have some kind of an experience with a single member of a particular group, then I generalize that experience and make the entire group the same. Often this incident is a non-representative sample of my experiences with this particular group, but for some reason, I generalize this one and make it true for the entire group. What is even more upsetting is that often this one experience is not even my own experience. It is an experience that some ancestor of mine had and passed on down the line of relatives who finally passed it on to me. Very often I haven't had any experience with the group that I'm discriminating against. I merely trade on borrowed experience from the past that was non-representative and could be generalized to an entire group of people.

A truly enlightened community should be a community where there is a one to one mapping between the resources and skills on the one hand and the needs on the other hand. A truly enlightened group operates on those kinds of principles. We need to look at the resources and the skill sets of the community members and match them one to one with the needs of the members of the group.

Unfortunately, the vast bulk of human communities operate on a totally different principle. The vast bulk of human communities throughout our entire history have been predicated on a model of the stratification of prejudice and privilege. There is almost no community on planet Earth that has not been based, predicated and organized around the hierarchical stratification of privileges and prejudices.

When you look at prejudices, they often fall into two categories operating simultaneously. There are prejudices for and prejudices against: the prejudices for result in the notion of a chosen group, an elite or an "in" group. If we are part of this group then we are prejudiced in its favor. The prejudice against is where we discriminate against another class and we give them names accordingly. Very often these names start off fairly innocuously. They are merely descriptive of whom these people are, but very soon they become pejoratives. For instance, the title barbarian is a Greek word. The Greeks divided the world into Greeks and non-Greeks. The word for non-Greeks was barbarian. This just meant non-Greek, but very quickly it became a pejorative. Within Judaism, the Jew and the gentile (Goyim) was a way of breaking the world into people who are us and people who are not us. Very soon the word Goyim became a pejorative. Within Catholicism, we talk about the Christians and the pagans. The word pagan was just a Roman word for people who were not Roman. Very quickly within Christianity it became a pejorative word indicating those who were not saved. Islam does the same thing; the believers and the infidels. Every group has the "in" group and the "out" group. There are some organizations that are built around the notion of prejudice for and the out group is only there by default. They are harmless groups. If you are part of the golfing community you are prejudiced about golf and golfers. You are not prejudiced against anyone; you are just prejudiced on behalf of golfers. You don't organize campaigns against basketball or baseball players, you just play golf and you believe that golfers are the most important people in the world.

Then there are those who organize specifically for prejudice against. Their reason for being is that they organize around a prejudice against another group. These are the dangerous people. They get their own sense of identity not by positively reflecting on what they have in common, but by creating an enemy They find out who they are by being different from the outcast class. Very often it goes through a staged model. This process happens where we first begin to project, then we separate from, then we isolate the group, then we vilify the group and then ultimately, if we have the authority and the power, we persecute that group. That is how discrimination against or prejudice against operates. Every one of these stages drives us further and further from the truth that there is only one of us and every one of us is built in the image and likeness of God. The image of God within every one of us is both light and dark. What tends to happen is that we claim the light for the "in" group and we project the dark for the "out" group and then trouble starts.

If you want to watch a movie, there are two ways to watch it. You can sit down and watch John Wayne come into town and there is a big gun fight and at the end of the movie he rides off into the sunset. It will take one and a half hours to watch that process. Or you can look at the celluloid roll of film frame by frame, but that does not have the same effect as watching the projected images. We buy into four illusions in order to watch a movie properly. We have to buy into the illusion of size because we are seeing a ten foot John Wayne when in fact even John Wayne wasn't more that six feet tall. We have to buy into the illusion of motion, i.e., John Wayne rides across from the left side to the right side of the screen on a white horse. It is an illusion. We buy into the illusion of change that things are different at various stages and we buy into the illusion that time passes. All of this information is already on the celluloid roll of film. The notion of projection gives us an ability to see in much more detail and much more clearly what is on the roll of film. We have developed that ability as human beings. We have developed the mechanism that Carl Jung called projection whereby in order to understand what is inside ourselves we project it outwards. But it is a two part process. We are meant to project it outwards in order to see it more clearly so we can introject it and take it back in, but we seldom do that.

Growing up in Ireland I went to our local Lido Theater which was a big barn with wooden benches. On Saturday mornings we would see Roy Rogers or Tarzan. The price of admission was two milk bottles. Before we would go into the movies we would pack our pockets with stones and we would sit watching the movie and as soon as the bad guy came on the screen there would be a hail of stones. The movie would shut down, the house lights would go on and the usher would come in and escort two or three kids out of the theater. We would all be good for ten minutes. When the movie restarted, we would wait again for the bad guys and throw our remaining stones at the screen. Then on would come the lights again and two or three more kids would be thrown out. That is a case of projection when we don't understand what it is about. We were totally convinced that we could assist the good guys by pelting the bad guys.

If that sounds hilarious to you; it is. If that sounds like what is happening in our world; it is. This is what happens with prejudice. Instead of projecting in order to see clearly what lies in the human heart so we can work upon it we project it onto another group or individual and we throw stones at them thinking that it is out there. All violence in our world is the result of projected unclaimed shadow material. When we do this as individuals it leads to interpersonal conflict. When we do it as communities, it leads to racial profiling. When we do it as nations, it leads to warfare. When we do it as a species, it leads to ecological disasters. The very mechanism of prejudice is this notion of projection. A notion that should really assist us in our spiritual development but because we do it so unconsciously we get the first part right and then we forget to do the second part. We forget to introject what we have seen written in large movement to make it very obvious to us what lies in the human heart and we think instead that we are watching it out there and we fill our pockets with stones and we cast the first, second, third and the fifteenth stone at the enemy.

No matter how often we incarnate and no matter how evolved we are when we come back, every one of us still has to start as a little baby. A very enlightened being will accelerate through this process of being a baby, but we each have to go through it. We can't skip stages. Therefore, even if Jesus comes back on this planet, (I do believe that he has been here many times) he has to start as a little infant and work his way up. As soon as you are born into a family you are going to be surrounded with prejudices. You will take them in with your mother's milk. Jesus had prejudices of his own that he had to work through in his own process to get to where he needed to be.

There were four main prejudices in Judaism at the time of Jesus. The really blessed ones were Jewish, male, healthy and wealthy. If you were really beloved of God you had all these four characteristics. If you were merely Jewish, healthy and wealthy but you were not male, you were lesser or, God forbid, if you were not Jewish or only a woman and you were a barbarian, sick and poor, God really had it in for you. These were the prejudices at the time of Jesus and he had to contend with them.

By the time he got into his public ministry, he had managed to shuffle off two of these prejudices. He knew that health and wealth had nothing to do with God's blessing and neither had sickness and poverty anything to do with God's curse. Jesus said, "I have come to attend to those who are ill. It is harder for a rich person to get to heaven than for a camel to go through the eye of a needle." For a period of time, though, he got stuck with the other two prejudices. He was prejudiced against women and non-Jews. The Father, as he does for all of us, or the Spirit, as she does for all of us, built into the life of Jesus opportunities for him to meet face to face with his prejudices so he could break through them as in the encounters with two foreign women and a Roman centurion. They would help him break through his prejudices against the goyim and mere women.

One day, as Jesus was preaching, a centurion said, "My son is very sick. Could you please come and lay your hands on him?" Although this centurion was a Roman he had been very good to the Jews and had helped build the synagogue and the people wanted Jesus to attend to the Roman's son. Jesus set out to go to the man's house but the Centurion said, "He can't come into my house. I'm a gentile, if he comes into my house, he will be ritually defiled. Tell him he doesn't need to come. I know he has the power. Just tell him to say the words and my son will be healed." This was related to Jesus while he was en route. Jesus was astounded. He said, "I tell you that I have never found such faith in any place in Israel. Go tell him that his son is cured." Jesus had never met faith or the respect that this centurion had accorded him in his life. This was a huge learning experience for Jesus.

There is another story in Matthew's gospel where Jesus is on vacation. He had taken his twelve disciples and gone out of the land of Israel and in a strange little town a woman recognized him. She ran up to Jesus saying, "Jesus, Jesus, please come into my house. My little daughter is seriously ill." Jesus ignored her and kept walking. But she kept screaming, "Please, please come to my house." The people in the village wondered what the men had done to make a local woman scream at them. Peter got embarrassed and said, "Do something, for God's sake. Everyone is watching us." The woman came face to face with Jesus and said, "Please, my little daughter is dying." Jesus said to her rudely, "I was sent only to the lost sheep of the house of Israel." The woman grabbed his feet pleading, "Please, please, my little child is dying." Jesus said again, "It is not okay to take the food from the children and throw it to the dogs." This woman's love for her child was more important than the insult she has just received and she said, "That may be true, but all I want is the little pieces of food that fall off the table onto the floor." The Spirit hit Jesus between the eyes. He got it and his ministry changed significantly. It was a foreign woman and a foreign soldier that brought Jesus to his senses around his prejudices against foreigners and women.

Jesus had a second encounter with a foreign woman. Let me give the historical background so the story makes more sense. In the year 930 B.C., the Kingdom of Israel was split in two. On the death of Solomon, there was a civil war in the country that divided the country in two: a northern kingdom that retained the name of Israel and consisted of ten tribes and the southern two tribes based in Jerusalem. In the year 721 B.C., the great Assyrian Empire came and demolished the northern ten tribes and took them into exile and they are never heard of again. They are the lost tribes of Israel. The Assyrian Kingdom dominated the Middle East for another 130 years.

In the meantime, in the northern kingdom, the Assyrians, took away the local population, left a few stragglers, and gave the land to some of their own soldiers. These soldiers intermarried with the local population. In the year 598 B.C., the Babylonian Empire came and invaded the southern kingdom of Judah and deported the last two remaining tribes and they were in exile for 70 years. Then in the year 529 B.C., the Persians overthrew the Babylonians and they released the Jews to go back to the land of Israel. In the meantime, as the two southern tribes were taken into exile, a few stragglers were left there and the land was given to the Babylonian soldiers. The half-breeds that emerged between the Assyrians, Israelites and the Babylonians became the Samaritans. When the little Jewish remnant went back to the land of Israel the city was demolished, there was no temple and the land had been totally desecrated. They attempted to rebuild their temple. The Samaritans came and offered to help and the Jews said, "No, you are unclean and we want nothing to do with you." Thereafter there was this tremendous antipathy between the two communities. For the next 600 years right down to the time of Jesus this continued. In 1900, there were only 150 Samaritans left in the world all living in the land of Israel. Today there are about 600. They are the most inbred population on planet Earth. Strangely, they are no more genetically handicapped than any other people.

Jesus had to pass through Samaria on his way from Galilee to Judea. The Samaritans would not let anyone stay over night in their town and wouldn't feed them or give them any kind of hospitality. That is why Jesus was outside the town at the well, hot and thirsty when the woman approached. At that time, Jesus showed himself to have two extraordinary prejudices. He said to the woman, "You people worship what you don't understand. At least we worship what we know because salvation is of the Jews." To say this to an entire people as if the ground of our being, the God of all creation spins this little globe in this huge galaxy of the Milky Way and picks out one little group of people, the Jews, is an extraordinary prejudice. Moreover, not only was he prejudiced he was extremely rude. He commanded the woman, "Give me water." He forgot to say please. He used no title for her until well into the dialogue at which stage he called her woman. He harangued her about her marital status which was none of his business. He said to her, "Woman where is your husband?" She answered, "I am not married." Jesus said, "You've had five husbands and the man you are with now is not your husband." This was none of his business. In spite of all this the woman conducted herself with extraordinary dignity. She kept calling him Sir in spite of the insults that he heaped upon her. She said to him, "You want me to get you water. You don't have a bucket how are you going to get water?" Even when she continued to talk with him she still addressed him as Sir.

Jesus continued to ignore her personhood and refused to call her anything except woman. Finally he got it. When you look at the subsequent life of Jesus between the Samaritan woman and the Roman centurion, Jesus did finally get it. He finally let go of his last two prejudices against women and gentiles. Thereafter there were women among the disciples of Jesus which was very unusual. There was no Rabbi at the time of Jesus who would have women disciples. He lay to rest his prejudice against women and his prejudice against gentiles. If you really want to give up something for Lent and if you really want to understand what Lent is about and what resurrection means for this Lent, give up a prejudice.

God's Contract with Humans

*"He who asserts his own ego in conflict with others will thereby provide
them to assert theirs."*

Paul Brunton

WHEN I WAS a child in Ireland in the late 40s, packages came
for us from America. They arrived at unpredictable intervals and their unpredictability was part of the excitement
because if they had come at regular intervals, we would have known
when to expect them, but we never did. Sometimes there would be a
year between packages and sometimes eighteen months or even two
years. When they did come the excitement was almost unbearable.
My grandmother who I called Big Mammy had distant relatives living in Boston. Every so often they would package up some clothes
and send them to us. There wasn't ever a whole lot in the package
for the men and boys because boys don't care much for clothes. Girls
are much more creative. Girls will use several different outfits in the
course of a single day. Most of what came was for the girls. The boys
would still gather around because the packages were from America
with exotic stamps and lots of brown paper that we could use to
make footballs for playing soccer. That was the advantage for the
boys.

I remember one particular year a package came and it consisted
of only one single item; a big fur coat. My grandmother went ecstatic.
She was a small woman fairly rotund and when she put the coat on
it reached to her ankles and she looked like a cross between a grizzly
Bear and Nikita Khrushchev. She absolutely loved this coat. I re-

member one time she went to the movies at the Ritz Movie Theater in Cork City about a year after she got this coat. While watching the movie, she huddled up in her lovely bear skin. When she came out of the movie at about 10:15 at night, it was really cold. She pulled the coat around herself and it was so cold that she pulled tightly on the coat to warm herself. Now the more tightly she pulled the colder she got and finally she gave the coat a big tug and the two halves of the coat came around and met in the front. Someone in the theater in a fit of jealously or whatever had taken a razor and sliced the coat down the back seam. So that when she pulled on the coat the two halves came away. We have a saying in Ireland, "It's an ill wind that doesn't blow some good to somebody." It wound up becoming two blankets; one on her bed and one on my bed. She never patched her fur coat. It never again became a coat. It existed from then on as two blankets.

Jesus talked about the same notion; the idea of patching something up. The notion of a covenant that is very dear to the Judeo/ Christian spirituality is based on the notion of some kind of business agreement of two parties: on the one hand, God and on the other hand, people of various stripes. It consists of duties, obligations and rights. Each party has duties that it must perform and has rights to which it is entitled. There is a long history of the evolution of this notion within Judaism. For instance, starting with the first covenant, probably between God on one side and Adam and Eve on the other side, the agreement was as follows. Adam and Eve could live in the garden of paradise and their duty and obligation was to not eat the fruit of two trees in the garden. Everything else they had access to, but they couldn't eat the fruit of these two trees. That was the first covenant or contract between God and human beings. It didn't last very long.

Shortly after this was the second covenant. This was the covenant between God and Noah and the seven other people that had been spared from the flood: Noah and his wife, their three sons and their three wives. This is a new covenant. According to this covenant, God gave Noah the entire earth to dominate and exploit and he allowed him for the first time ever to become an omnivore. Up to then they were vegetarians now they became omnivores and carnivores. God gave Noah total right to dominate the planet. That was the second agreement.

Twelve hundred years later there was an agreement made with Abraham. This was a covenant between God and a select few. It wasn't between God and all living beings anymore, as the covenant with Noah had been, it was a covenant with God and a select few. According to this covenant, God was going to bless the progeny of Abraham and eventually give them a land all of their own.

After about 600 years, God rescinded that covenant and made another covenant with Moses. In this covenant, God gave Moses a constitution, he gave him a law, 613 precepts and he promised him that he would inherit a special land of his own.

About 200 years after Moses, God made a different covenant with King David in which he promised David that his dynasty would survive forever and that a son of his would continually sit on the throne of the land of Israel.

About 400 years after that another covenant was made to two extraordinary prophets, Jeremiah who lived about 600 years before Jesus and Ezekiel about 550 years before Jesus. Now for the first time ever the covenant was not an exterior thing. It was not about land, progeny or dynasty. It was about an affair of the heart. They both talked about a covenant not written in stone or not about laws, but written in the human heart. About 600 years later, Jesus would speak to that in depth. Jesus talked about "A kingdom within you and among you," covenant.

That is a brief history of the notion of covenant. My belief system is that the notion of covenant is always based on insecurity, fear and the need to be special. What it does is that it leads to the shifting of alliances among people of various kinds and it always results in some kind of fundamentalist thinking no matter where you find it. The essence of fundamentalism is just two elements, i.e., firstly, you take a very complex, profound system and you reduce it down to its bones so that ordinary people can understand it and secondly, you identify and demonize the enemy in order to incite the masses. Whether it's religious wars, business competition or ethnic strife this is inevitably what happens. It starts with the notion of chosen-ness and it always results in the notion of some kind of covenant. And what it leads to then is stereotypes where all we see is gender, ethnicity, denomination affiliation or socioeconomic status. We categorize people and we come up with the "out" group and the "in" group; that is what happens with covenant.

Personally, I do not believe for a moment that God ever made a covenant with the human species. How could we make a business agreement with the ineffable ground of our being? How do you make a contract with a totally, invisible, sacred, ineffable entity? How, if God has no name, can God validly sign a contract? If God has no face, how can God produce an I.D. in order to sign a contract? The notion of God making a contract with anyone is totally ridiculous. There is a contract, but here are the parties: the God-in-me and the God-in-you; what the Hindus call, Namasté, i.e., the God in me recognizes and honors the God in you. All contracts are valid only because of their attempts to express the divinity we all share. They are not between a special group of people and the ineffable ground of our being; they are preconception agreements we make before we come here so that when we get here we can recognize the divinity in every person, culture, nation, denomination, religion, gender and socioeconomic status. We can see through these artificial barriers and we can see the God within and that is the only valid covenant, i.e., the covenant I make between me and my Self because my Self means your Self and it means all Selves. Hinduism will say, "Thou art that." Everything you have read about the transcendent divinity is you at your core.

When you can get beyond the accidents of birth, ethnicity, IQ level, gender, socioeconomic status, racial characteristics, denominational affiliation and national identity and see to the core, the covenant you are making is really a covenant between you and your Self. It is the covenant of the God within you recognizing the God within everyone else. That is the only meaning of covenant it seems to me.

When I look at the history of the notion of marriage on planet Earth, I see that marriage has gone through different iterations. Probably the first understanding of marriage was when people finally made the connection between coition and conception or the fact that when a man lies with a woman a baby is conceived and is born; they didn't make that connection for a long time. When they first made this connection then it became very important to have some kind of contractual agreement between the woman who was carrying the baby and the man who thought that the baby was his. Marriage, in its first effort, was to try to create some kind of protection or bill of rights for the male and female and for their children.

The first understanding of marriage had to do with the paternity of children, their protection and their evolution. Later on, marriage began to be used as a way of cementing relationships between families, communities and sometimes between entire nations, for instance, when the King of Spain's daughter married the King of England's son in order to try to forge some kind of alliance between those nations. Marriage became a contractual agreement where you could cement together disparate elements of the population or you could create some kind of harmony and peace. That was the second iteration of the meaning of marriage. At some stage, the notion that marriage was about companionship i.e., people seeking companionship and dedicating themselves to each other so as to provide a kind of friendship throughout a life time. That was the third iteration of the notion of marriage.

Later in Europe the notion of romantic love came into being. This was the notion that you followed your heart and married the person with whom you fell in love. It was no longer a contractual agreement any more in order to have children or to cement community relationships. And it was not just about companionship in your old age; it was this biochemical attraction of falling in love with someone. Subsequently people like Carl Jung talked about it as the sacred mystery or the sacred conjoining. It was the notion that marriage is a symbolic quest where a female who is incomplete because her male side is not fully developed will marry a man whose female side is incomplete so that by modeling to each other the contra gender elements of what it means to be a total human being they can each become total human beings. So we marry it in order to develop it not in order just to live with it. Marriage is not meant to be an agreement whereby males and females continue to be males and females but rather a complementarity that allows both parties to develop the total psyche of what it means to be built in the image and likeness of God.

At some stage the Israelite prophets began to build this imagery into their understanding of covenant. Although the notion of covenant was very ancient in Israel, only with Hosea for the first time ever do we find this covenant with God having some kind of marital elements in it. Hosea will talk about this covenant between God and Israel as a marriage contract between a husband and wife. He will be one of the first people to take a personal experience and build it into a global cosmology. He took his own personal experience of his own marriage and he built from it a cosmology of the relationship between his entire culture and God. The history of his experience was that he married a woman who proved unfaithful, left him, abandoned him, became a prostitute and God said, "I want you to take her back because this will be the image of what my relationship with Israel is like. I married Israel and Israel abandoned me and became a prostitute, but I will take Israel back." Hosea took his wife back and they had two children together and then she abandoned him again. God invited him again to take back his wife. Hosea used his own personal experience of marriage as a metaphor for the relationship between God and Israel. In my opinion, it wasn't a particularly helpful image because when we look at the relationship between God and Israel, God allegedly married Israel in the desert and there was a honeymoon period. The Israelites looked back and they said, "Yes, when we lived in the desert, God gave us manna from heaven and there were all these great signs and we defeated all our enemies." But when you actually look at what that honeymoon period consisted of they were <u>lost</u> for 40 years; that was a lot of fun! They were constantly complaining that they didn't have enough food, not enough water and they revolted so badly against Moses that he sent a plague of serpents to bite them and kill them; some honeymoon. When you look back it always appears much nicer from a distance.

When I look at this marriage of Israel to God, I find on the one hand extraordinary infidelity on the part of the "wife" and I find domestic violence on the part of the "husband." He beat her again and again. Time after time she is exiled. Time after time invading armies come in and wipe her out. God would be guilty of domestic violence and his wife would be guilty of infidelity.

I'm going to use that now as an image of a conflict between God and us at a time perhaps in our own culture when, unfortunately, 50 percent of our own marriages are ending in divorce. It doesn't look to me like it is a very adequate metaphor for the relationship between us and God. God, in my opinion, had a very unhappy and a very unsuccessful marriage.

Look at what Jesus did to this in his own time. He totally exploded this thinking. He brought a whole new kind of thought to the process of our relationship with God. He totally interiorzed it and he would say, "I and the Father are one." Then he went on to say, "The same things I do you will do and even greater," because Jesus was inviting us not into some kind of external contract with a distant demanding deity but into the recognition of the God who lives among us and within us. It is a totally different paradigm and the world wasn't ready for it yet and the world crucified him and the church that he bequeathed this extraordinary insight to wasn't ready for it and it too eviscerated the teaching.

It is the same kind of paradigm shift that is going to be necessary for our times and our thinking. That is the way it has to go. Look at how the scientific model works; this is precisely what it does. Your typical scientist will look at a lot of totally meaningless data, and then begin to identify some kind of pattern that may explain the data. Stage two is the identification of some kind of pattern. Stage three is a hypothesis to explain the pattern. Stage four is to set up some kind of experiment to test the hypothesis. Stage five is to replicate it in some laboratory to see if the results are consistent. Stage six is that you now have a new principle. Stage seven is that you have a whole new model that now science can continue to work with. Later on however, anomalous data begin to come in and then the scientific model has to be tweaked a little bit and is bulging at the seams to contain the new data. At some stage, unfortunately, so much anomalous data begin to come in that the old model is totally inadequate. It happened in the 20th century. It happened in 1915 with Relativity Theory. It happened in 1920 with the Quantum Mechanical revolution where the old Newtonian model was totally inadequate and we had to build a brand new model that could contain all of the Newtonian data and all of the quantum mechanical and relativity data. We tried patching the old paradigm like putting my grandmother's coat back together again. It never works because more and more anomalous data begin to come in as we experience God more and more deeply until finally the old paradigms are passé. We can't patchwork them anymore. We can't pour the new wine of fresh insight into the old skins of ancient thinking. It can't happen. Although the process is epigenetic, we build on it, but in its old form it is no longer an adequate model for our thinking.

In the times in which we live, there is going to be no solution to human problems as long as our paradigm is based on the notion of contracts between the transcendent divinity and special groups on planet Earth. Whether they have to do with our gender, ethnic or racial divisions, the notion of nation as the ultimate or the notion of socioeconomic status conferring some kind of divine benediction, is flawed. As long as we continue to build our thinking on these totally outmoded ideas, there will be no solution to human problems. We are called to a bold new way of thinking and a totally different way of transcending ethnicity, race and socioeconomic status, the gender divide, the notion of nation as ultimate and the notion of churches as the revealed word of God. We need to go far beyond those.

I would like to pose again the notion that what we badly need in our time is at least a five-year moratorium on the production of all weapons both conventional weapons and weapons of mass destruction all over the world. Not just in designated locations, but all over the world across the board, a total moratorium of the production of things that kill human beings. I will propose that in its stead there be a five-year conference funded by the military budgets of the nations of planet Earth that will bring together great agriculturists, doctors, educators, psychologists, spiritual people and environmentalists to brainstorm as a global community for five years as to what kind of lifestyle for the entire species will bring peace and harmony to our planet. Their findings should be enforceable, not through violence, but because they will be so appealing and so much of God that they will be adopted easily. We should then try this new lifestyle for a hundred year period. We've tried war for 5,000 years and it hasn't worked. Let's try peace for 100 years and see what happens.

The end of the world is very near. I believe it very strongly, but the end of the world is not what is going to happen in the nuclear holocaust. The end of the world is going to happen in a blinding flash of global enlightenment. The end of the world is coming; the world as we know it is passé. There is a whole new world being born. Today would be a very good day to die.

Temptation—The Clarion Call
to Christ-Consciousness

"Whenever the world falls into decay and the human ascent towards divinity is seriously endangered, God descends to Earth to release the jammed wheels of history."

Huston Smith

ART OF MY work as a clinical psychologist is to work with people who are recovering from addictions of various kinds. One thing that I have seen over the years, especially in working with people who are recovering from alcoholism, is that in the early years of recovery they have horrific nightmares: a nightmare that consists of the horrible feeling that they have fallen off the wagon. They have scenarios in which they believe they are drinking again. These nightmares are so powerful that they wake up in the morning and often for the first waking hour of consciousness they are convinced they have fallen off the wagon. Part of the reason they have these nightmares is because alcohol suppresses the REM sleep i.e., dream sleep. An alcoholic's dream-life is really deadened. After alcoholics give up alcohol, they have what is called a REM rebound with lots and lots of dreams. This is particularly found in the first two or three years of recovery.

This morning in my meditation I had a vision of Jesus having a vision of the same thing happening to him except that for Jesus, it wasn't a nightmare about falling back into alcoholism it was the fear that he had given in to the three temptations. Satan's imagery was so intense that I could picture in my mind the pictures in Jesus'

107

mind implanted by Satan as part of the temptation. It was the horrible realization on the part of Jesus, "My God, I've given in to all three temptations." It was the temptation to turn all the stones of the desert into bread. It would have meant that he would, by way of economic hegemony, agree to take over the economy of planet Earth. And then he had the horrible realization, "My God, I blew the second temptation." I bowed down and I worshiped a false God which gave me total control over planet Earth. I have total command of the military and political process. Then the third temptation was to stand on the parapet of the temple in Jerusalem and throw himself down and start a brand new world religion and take control of the religious process of planet Earth with all that that would lead to. As I watched him writhing in agony, this was so real that Jesus was completely convinced he had actually blown every single one of the three temptations. And as he watched the conclusions and the aftermath of having said yes, yes, yes instead of no, no, no: a vision of the world unfolded in which there were 40 percent of the world's population starving for want of food, and there were 112 armed conflicts raging simultaneously in which religion had been turned into a weapon by one group or another to encourage the massacre. Jesus watched this entire thing unfold and realized the awful truth that it was his failure in all three temptations that resulted in the extraordinary apocalyptic vision he was having. Over all of it was the sneering face of Satan saying, "What are you worried about, you said yes, it's your fault you sold me your soul?" Jesus then writhes in agony because he believed he had in deed sold his soul to Satan.

This was an extraordinary temptation of Jesus and the vision in his mind of believing that he had succumbed to the temptations with horrible consequences. He had said yes, yes, yes instead of no, no, no. This is not just a temptation for the Christs of the world. This is not just a temptation for the leaders of the world whether they are religious people, politicians, military or economists. This is not a temptation just about those people. This is not just a temptation facing nations. It is not just a temptation facing particular communities.

It is not just a temptation facing us globally. It is the individual temptation of a life on the line by all six billion of us. This is a temptation for every single one of us because Satan is real, not perhaps as some kind of demonic entity somewhere in the cosmos, but residing in the individual human heart, the collective human heart, the national human heart of every nation and in the global human heart of homo sapiens. Satan is very real.

There is the temptation in all of us to constantly say yes to that which leads to violence. The good news is that there are angels ministering to Jesus. There are angels within us and among us. I am totally convinced and I see more and more in my meditations that there are angelic presences very close to us. There are beings from other dimensions that are very close and are watching very carefully to what is happening to the experiment of planet Earth. Except that they are not allowed to intervene. They are only allowed to come in if they are channeled by people who are open to them. They can only be a meaningful part of this experiment if there are souls willing to become conduits in order to embrace their presence among us. More and more they are here, they are watching, hoping, willing and they are ready, but it is going to take more and more channels and more and more conduits to bring them into the craziness of our times.

Then there are the beasts in Jesus' temptation story. The beasts in our midst seem to me to represent the magnificent menu of vices on the plentiful platter of evil. They are inside every single one of us. They are in us as communities, nations and globally. There are these extraordinary choices of beastly vices available to us if we choose to say yes, yes, yes instead of no, no, no. Then there is the whole notion of the temptation itself. Is temptation a bad thing? On the contrary, temptation is a really good thing. Temptation is the only way we will possibly wake up. In the absence of temptation, there is only soporific sleep. In the absence of temptation, enlightenment is not a possibility. In the absence of temptation, we just go about our merry way in mediocrity. Temptation is perhaps the greatest gift of God to us. So Satan has two places, there is the sneering face of Satan that sticks us in the muck of our decisions and there is the face of Satan that allows us the possibility of becoming wide awake and saying no to vice and yes to love.

I look at the history of world religions and see this notion of "drawing apart." We find it in every single tradition. It is not just in the Christian tradition. We find it in all traditions. In earlier times, particularly, when there were very few of us walking on the planet and the population of the planet was in the millions rather than in the billions. It was quite easy, even expected, and quite normal for individuals or groups to draw apart on a regular basis and go off into the desert for solitude. It didn't have to be the desert it could be the forest, the mountains or the ocean side; any place where they could get away to create space in their lives. As long as they were able to do that as individuals and communities they could bring back some semblance of peace and sanity into their civilization and into their togetherness. As the numbers increased and they got more and more urbanized it became very difficult for people to make that safari into the wilderness. Then the churches began to dogmatically legislate "time apart." They said, "You have to abstain from meat on Fridays or you have to fast during Lent." This was an effort to try to bring the wilderness into civilization in a good sense, but it was dogmatically legislated with law and it didn't work because you can't reduce love to law. You can't force people to be enlightened by making up stuff to believe in or to engage in meaningless practices. It hasn't worked as Catholics and we abandoned it thirty years ago, but we have replaced it with nothing in the meantime. Tuesday and Sunday are indistinguishable from each other in most of the Christian world. There is no difference between our activities on Sunday and our activities on a Tuesday. There is no difference between Christmas day and tax day for most of us. It is business as usual. There is no drawing apart anymore. We have lost the ability to go off into the wilderness on a regular basis and refresh our souls and that other system of legislatively bringing the wilderness into our lives isn't working. Where are we going to go from here?

I believe that there are three stages to the process of emerging from this darkness. The first one is; we have to create space in our lives in order to dream our dreams. Every one of us has to manage to do it individually. For some of us it is possible to go off into the forest on a regular basis. For other people it is not possible. There are mothers and fathers among us who have work to do and somehow they have to create a wilderness of their own in the midst of their environment, but it has to be created. There is no way you can dream your dreams if you do not create the space for the dream to unfold. That is the first stage; you have to create space and wilderness in your weekly life.

Secondly, once you have created the wilderness and once the dreams have begun to come, you have to have the courage to pursue your dreams. There is nothing worse than a person with an unfulfilled dream. There is nothing as eviscerating of human evolution as someone who has created a space and allowed a dream to emerge and then not have the courage to follow where that dream may lead.

The third part of that process is that I have to have the sensitivity and the compassion and the love not to trample on your dreams in the pursuit of my own dreams. Any dream lived on the back of other people's dreams is a nightmare rather than a dream. The processes are: create my space to dream my dream, follow courageously where my dream leads and sensitively and compassionately ensure that my dream does not create a nightmare for you.

There are two ideas I want to propose about what revitalizing Lent might mean for us. One of them is preparation for death and the other is preparation for resurrection. When I talk about preparation for death I don't mean that you think morbidly about your demise and the time when you will shuffle off this mortal coil; I am not thinking about that at all. I'm thinking about the daily death of ego, of breaking the illusion that this is the only reality. I'm thinking of killing the ego before it kills us. We have to prepare for the death of the ego and we have to prepare for the death of illusion and we have to prepare to kill the myth of separate identity. Then we have to prepare for the resurrection. The resurrection to the remembering of who we really are and what we have come to do.

I sometimes go down to the local park and there will be little children all dressed up in their magnificent uniforms playing soccer. I look at the children on the field and there are some who seem absolutely bored with the game. They do summersaults and cartwheels all over the field and they have no idea where the ball is at any stage. Then there is another group that seems absolutely frightened of having to play the game; they don't want the ball to come near them. Then there is a third group that has no idea how the game works but is totally enthusiastically involved in chasing the ball all over the field.. Then there are always one or two children who want to be stars and when they get the ball, they try to control the ball by themselves for the rest of the game. They want to be the center of attention. Then there are a few who get it that this is a team sport and that there is a reason why there are 10 other guys on the team and they play as a group.

I see that happening so often in life. We have the same approach to life; we come onto this planet and there is a whole bunch of us who are bored by the whole experiment. Then there is a bunch of us who are absolutely scared that life will actually ask us to do something. We think that perhaps life will present us with the ball and everyone will be expecting something from us and we live life avoiding the ball at all costs. Then there is a bunch of us constantly chasing around looking to where the ball is and wanting to be right there where the action is, but we have no idea what we are going to do should we get the ball. Then there are those among us who want to be the stars. We want to be the person that everyone is watching. We want to hold the ball for the entirety of life and want to be the focal point of everyone else and that is how we live our lives. Then there are a few enlightened beings who realize that we came here as a team; all six billion of us. We are meant to play this game together as a team. There is a purpose, a plan and a mission to it and every single person is important to that plan. So I won't hog the ball for myself. I see that that is a way of revitalizing us. I see that as a way of bringing back that vision and preparing for that kind of resurrection.

Jesus had his wilderness experience for fourty days. I see a lot of people in the course of counseling and giving spiritual direction attempting a wilderness experience. I watch what happens at the end of their wilderness experience when they come back into the "real" world. I see so many different responses. Having had the time to look deeply into their own souls and therefore by looking into their own souls seeing the soul of the planet they come back and there is a plethora of responses. There are people who are absolutely scared because of what they have seen. They have looked within themselves and they have looked into the soul of the world and they come back filled with fear. There are people who come back and they are totally depressed by the experience; it proved to be an over-powering experience. There are people who come back and they are filled with anger at the injustices of what they saw as they looked into their souls and to the soul of the planet. There are people who come back and they are paralyzed by mediocrity and inactivity. They put their heads down and they hope they won't be noticed. These are some of the responses of people coming back from the desert.

If we come back from the desert and all we come back with is anger or fear or inactivity or mediocrity we have no right to call ourselves followers of Jesus. If we do not come back with the urge to preach good, new thinking, if we do not come back with the urge to heal, if we do not come back with the urge to liberate and we do not come back with the urge to open the eyes of the blind we have wasted the desert experience and we have no right to call ourselves followers of Jesus or to claim Christ consciousness.

Look at the very first temptation where Satan says to Jesus, "Turn these stones into bread." Obviously, the real import of this temptation is not that Satan was saying to Jesus, "You've been fasting for 40 days you must be really hungry, why don't you turn these three stones into three loaves of bread and eat today?" He was obviously saying to Jesus why don't you, through magic, feed everyone on planet Earth?

I look at our attempts to feed or not to feed the planet right now. I look at genetically engineering our food. Is this what it means to turn the stones of our deserts into food for people on the planet? Is it by poisoning our resources? Is it by killing the poly culture of agriculture or killing the little farmers in India who have spent 5,000 years breeding different kinds of seeds and making it a crime for them to use their own seeds? We have somehow managed to hold all the food on planet Earth in five great international moguls; the "mogulization" of the food supply of planet Earth. Is that what it means to turn the stones of our desert into food? Or is it to liberate people to grow food according to their own tradition so that people have both a livelihood and a food source that is not dictated by great groups living elsewhere? Is that what it means? I think about the economic models that we have managed to create lead to a reality in which 40 percent of planet Earth is on the brink of starvation throughout the year. I look at some great saints who have been among us in recent years. I look at Cardinal Dom Helder Camara, Archbishop of San Paulo for many years, who very famously said on one occasion, "When I give food to the poor, they call me a saint. When I ask why is it that the poor don't have food? They call me a Communist." Why is it okay to give handouts to some people but when you ask questions why is it that most people don't have enough to eat suddenly from being a saint you become a Communist? Some people regarded Jesus as a great guru or even a god and then there were those who accused Jesus of being a drunkard, a glutton, a friend of tax collectors, a sinner and a law breaker. How could people look at the same Jesus as he engaged in the same kind of activities and preached the same mission have such different hits on who Jesus was?

I think about Noah and I think about the covenant that God made with him in Genesis, Chapter Nine. There are 14 references to the covenant, nine of them have to do with the planet and all living things and five of them have to do with human beings. In some parts of it God said to Noah, "I make this covenant between me and you." That is said four times. On one occasion in this passage he said, "I make this covenant between me and your descendents." Five times this covenant is between people and God, but six times in this passage he said, "I make this covenant between me and all living things." On three occasions in this passage he said, "I make this covenant between myself and the entire Earth." Nine references out of fourteen are to nature and five references out of fourteen are to humans. So this is a covenant between God, humans and nature. Here is the bummer. It may well be that the covenant part to nature is going to outlive the covenant part to humans. There is a real possibility that the covenanted part to humans is going to dissolve and be no more because there won't be any more humans left with whom to have a covenant. But nature will survive. It is guaranteed that nature will survive. There is a possibility that there will come a time in the not too distant future when some exotic new creature perhaps a bird pecking at a dung hill that has been newly unearthed by a mud slide will find a little red code book on how to push the nuclear button. It will peck at the pages and the pages will fly off and disintegrate and this exotic little creature will continue pecking at the dung hill of human history.

My final vision during my morning meditation was this: I had a vision of six billion souls standing shame-facedly in front of God, the ineffable ground of our being and saying, "Experiment homo-sapiens ended in our watch." And God said, "Let's see, homo sapiens why does that name ring a bell? Oh, yes, I remember. That was cosmos Number 2354." "Yes, that was it." "And there was a Milky Way and there, now let me get this right, oh yes, it was planet Earth. I remember that. Oh, yes, homo sapiens. Wait a minute. Wasn't that the place I sent Gautama Siddhartha and the Buddha? Wasn't that the place I sent Jesus the son of Joseph who became the Christ? I think that was the place I sent Mahatma Gandhi. And wasn't that the place I sent Francis of Assisi and Mother Teresa? I don't get it. Which part of 'Love thy neighbor' was so difficult to understand?"

True Patriotism and Sacrificing the First Born

"Our primary vocation is global and universal and should never be subjugated to the norms and laws of any one political or religious system."
                                                             Diarmuid O'Murchu

I T WAS ONE of the funniest books I ever read. It was called, "The Comic History of Ireland." I read it about 30 years ago. It was material culled from the examination papers of Irish students. In those days, Irish students had to do two very important examinations, one called the intermediate-certificate midway through high school and the leaving certificate at the end of high school which was to prepare you for college or for life. Of course, it did neither, but that was the theory.

If you were an Irish student of history whatever paper you were assigned and whoever the main character was, it was mandatory that you begin your essay with, "so and so was the greatest Irishman that ever lived." The feeling was that you would thus establish rapport with the examiner so that if he believed the same thing, he would mark you gently. The authors of the book culled from those examination papers the reports of the students and their understanding of Irish history.

There were two phrases that kept repeating like a mantra throughout the entire book: "He was the greatest Irishman that ever lived." The second mantra that kept repeating itself was: "They became more Irish than the Irish themselves." If you know any Irish history this happens again and again. When the Danes began to inter-marry with the Irish, they became more Irish than the Irish themselves. Then the Normans came and they became more Irish than the Irish themselves. When the English came in the 1600's, having pinched what was left after the Danes and the Normans were finished and inter-married with the Irish, they became more Irish than the Irish themselves.

In Ireland, as I was growing up, I tried to figure out how I could be more Irish than the Irish or how I could be a real Irish person. There seemed to be five categories that we employed as kids that would ensure our Irishness. The first one had to do with physical appearance. If your hair was blond or red then you were definitely more Irish than someone whose hair was brown or black. If your skin was pale or freckled you obviously were more Irish than someone who had a dark complexion. If your eyes were blue then you were more Irish than someone with green eyes who was more Irish than someone with brown eyes who was more Irish than someone with black eyes. The first category had to do with physical appearance to prove your Irishness or the extent of your Irishness.

The second had to do with location. If you were a city dweller, you were not quite as Irish as the fellow who came from the countryside. If you came from the countryside, you were not quite as Irish as someone who lived in the really remote part of the country; he would be more Irish than you.

The third had to do with religion. You were really more Irish if you were Catholic than if you were, God help you, non-Catholic. If you believed in the Pope and fairies then you were really Catholic; more than a Catholic who didn't believe in the Pope or in fairies.

The fourth category had to do with being a English speaker. You obviously were not as Irish as someone who was fluent in Gaelic. But even if you were fluent in Gaelic you were not quite as Irish as someone who was a native born speaker of Gaelic. Not someone who learned Gaelic while in school, but was born into a family whose mother tongue was Gaelic; then you were even more Irish than the other guy.

Then the fifth category had to do with entertainment. So when you were dancing, if you were waltzing, you were not quite as Irish as someone who was step-dancing. If you were singing rock and roll it did not make you as Irish as if you sang what we call old style singing. If you were engaged in games; if you played hurling or handball you were much more Irish than someone who played cricket, golf, soccer or rugby because these were English games.

Using the same kinds of criteria or the same kinds of parameters how do you define who is more American than someone else. Would the same parameters apply? Take physicality; for instance, are Americans who emigrated from Europe more American than people who emigrated from Asia and Africa? Is hair color, skin color or eye color important in deciding who is more American? Is location important? If you come from one of the 13 original states of the union on the East coast are you more American than those born in the Midwest or those born in California? Does that make them more American? And what about birth, does the place where you were born, does that determine how American you are? If you are born in this country, are you more American than someone who is naturalized? If you are born here but your parents were born in the old country are you as American as someone whose parents were born here? And how about the guy whose grandparents are all born in America, does that make him more American than you? Or what if one side of your ancestors came off the Mayflower but your daddy was an Italian emigrant? What do you do then? Can you compromise your American-ness? What makes you more American than anyone else? Is it physical appearance or religion? If you are Christian in this country does that make you more American than someone who is non-Christian? If you are a Protestant Christian does that make you more American than someone who is a Catholic Christian? Are you more American if you play baseball rather than cricket because baseball is American and cricket is English? Are you more American if you play basketball rather than soccer, football or rugby? What creates American-ness? Who is more American than anyone else? Does it have anything to do with any of these categories?

Why are we all living in America right now? There are some of us who managed to live in America by arranging forbearers who got to be born here and there are some of us who became American by choice and we had to make our own way to this country. Which of us is more American? What are we here to do? Does our American-ness have to do with any of these factors? My belief system is, of course, being truly American has nothing to do with skin or hair color, where I happen to be born, my religious affiliation, the language I speak or the games I play; none of this has anything to do with being American.

We are living in America because every one of us has made a preconception contract to be part of an extraordinary population at an extraordinary time in the history of an extraordinary nation. We have come, it seems to me, for four purposes. We have come because every single one of us is committed to spiritual evolution. We have come because we are committed to helping each other in his/her spiritual evolution. We have come here in order to spiritualize an entire cultural nation and we have come in order to spearhead the evolution of the entire human species. That is much more important than where we happen to have been born, how long our genealogy extends in this country, what color we are, what religion we espouse or what games we play.

What about true patriotism, who or what is the true patriot? Is it true patriotism to say "My country right or wrong?" If my country happens to be America or Ireland or Egypt or any place else does that make me more patriotic? Am I more patriotic to the extent that I blindly follow the current crop of leaders? Does that make me more of a patriot? Does blind fidelity to the mandates of whoever happens to be in positions of power make me a more patriotic American? For instance, does blind obedience to Papal Infallibility make me a better Catholic? Am I a better Catholic for thinking for myself and for following Jesus and spiritual, mystical teachings rather than just dogmatic edicts? What makes me a true patriot of this country? Am I only a true patriot if I am prepared to take the life of another to protect this place or to lay down my life to protect this place? Does true patriotism have to do with the willingness to shed blood, my own or someone else's? Is that what a true patriot is? Or is true patriotism the courage to call my entire culture into the evolution which will spearhead a quantum leap in the experiment homo sapiens. Am I truly patriotic to the extent that I am trying to create a kind of democracy in which there is indeed freedom of expression, freedom of worship, freedom of all of the things that the Bill of Rights guarantees to us? Am I truly patriotic by trying to create a country where there is true democracy and a nation in which we are spearheading global enlightenment? Does that make me more of a patriot? Obviously, I lean very heavily towards this viewpoint. True patriotism has nothing to do with the notion of "my group right or wrong." True patriotism has nothing to do with the blind following of anyone under any circumstances and true patriotism has nothing to do with the willingness to shed human blood, mine or theirs. True patriotism, to be a true American at this stage, is to ensure that our democracy survives and continues to develop and that we become the spearhead for global evolution. Then I am truly an American.

It is painful to me to watch how the bible has been high-jacked by fundamentalist Christians. They have high-jacked it, they have eviscerated it and they have ludicrously reduced it to its literal content. They have claimed it as their own and the rest of us main stream Christians have abandoned the field to them as if, in deed, the bible is theirs to do with it what they will. They have high-jacked it. We need to recover the bible and we need to mine it for its mystical teachings, not its literal interpretations but its deep mystical core. By the same token, is seems to me, the hawks have high-jacked the notion of patriotism and they are equating patriotism with the willingness to engage in an agenda of violence against anyone that doesn't agree with them. Why are we ceding to them the notion of patriotism? Why do we not have the courage to recover this notion; it is our birthright as native born or naturalized Americans. It is our birthright to take this notion of patriotism and to make it a shining example of a nation. When the history of America comes to be written, will we just be one more arrogant super power in a lineage extending back from Egypt to Assyria to Babylon to Persia to Greece to Rome and then to England? Or will we indeed be a light for the edification of all nations? We are being called to an extraordinary destiny.

Generations of Americans who have died before us both naturalized and native born have bequeathed to us the most extraordinary patrimony that any people have ever inherited. They left us with resources to do something extraordinary on the planet. Are we going to turn self-righteously to violence and war or are we really going to be the generation that turns planet Earth on its head? Will we put it on its knees so that it will bow its head and worship the God that is really Father and Mother?

In 1850 B.C., Abraham was willing to sacrifice his first born son and then allegedly God relented. Six hundred years later, in 1250 B.C., Moses was willing to sacrifice the first born of the Egyptians both man and beast; allegedly this time God consented.

In 33 A.D., God allegedly sacrificed his own first-born. I don't believe it for a minute. Today we are being called upon to sacrifice the first-born: our first-born here in America and their first-born in Iraq. Do you really believe that the ineffable ground of our being, the ultimate mystery of all there is, has ever been, is now, or will ever be, calls for the death of the first-born, or a second-born or a fifteenth-born?

Any God who needs the death of the first-born is a false God. And any religion that preaches that it is acceptable to sacrifice the first-born is a false religion. And any political regime that mandates the death of the first-born is an illegitimate regime. They have nothing to do with God. It is no accident that in this stage in human history 6.5 billion souls stood before God and volunteered for a mission on planet Earth. We stand at the most extraordinary time in human history and we are here by choice. No other generation of Americans or generation of human beings since the time of Jesus has stood at a crossroad that is so decisive in which we can take a step that will create the destiny of enlightenment of our entire planet. Welcome to your mission.

CHRISTIANITY AND CHRIST CONSCIOUSNESS

"We know the divine and become the divine because we are that already in our secret nature."

Sri Aurobindo

"ALL THE WORLD'S a stage and all the men and women merely players. They have their exits and their entrances; one man in his time plays seven parts; his act being seven stages." Shakespeare outlines that the seven stages of life are culminating in a return to childishness with, "Sans teeth, sans eyes, sans taste, sans everything," i.e., without teeth, without taste, without everything. It came from "As You Like It," a play he wrote in 1598.

I think Shakespeare was possibly one of the greatest social commentators of all time. I agree with him that life unfolds in seven stages. I have my own idea on what the seven stages are. I will part company with Shakespeare at this stage and while I agree with his numbers, I do not agree with his outline.

Jesus became the Christ in seven stages: Conception, mission, death, hell, resurrection, ascension, Pentecost. The very first stage is conception: the movement from pre-incarnation into incarnation. It is most beautifully and poetically captured by Saint Paul. He said of Jesus. "Have that mindset in you that was also in Jesus because although he was God, he did not cling to his divinity with God but he took on human form and was found in human likeness." Paul then goes on to talk about how he further humiliated himself by the kind of death he died.

The first piece is the conception of Jesus as the movement from relinquishing the trappings of divinity and accepting incarnation. That is the first stage of the journey.

The second stage of the journey of Jesus was the mission. The mission of Jesus was not primarily about his teaching. He did not come to deliver wise sayings or to do a lot of healings or raisings from the dead; this was not his primary mission. His primary mission was to be the prototype of the evolution of the experiment of homo sapiens. It is the evolution of all of us. Jesus was meant to be the prototype of where we are headed. He was the ultimate exemplar of where this experiment is supposed to wind up. That was the main reason for his coming. More importantly than what he said, more importantly than the healings he did was who he was. What he exemplified by way of being the prototype of where this entire experiment is meant to be headed; that was his mission.

Stage three then is the death. What did the death of Jesus mean? I do not believe that the death of Jesus was payback for the sins of humanity. There was no distant, demanding deity in the sky calling for a blood sacrifice to satisfy his pain for being sinned against. It had nothing to do with that. I believe that if Jesus had lived to be a man of 80 his life would have been no less effective. But Jesus died because he had to die because the teacher always needs to die.

In order to reach enlightenment we have to become serial killers. Every one of us needs to commit four murders in order to become an enlightened being. The first murder is that I have to kill my father. This means that I have to let go of all the traditions that keep me bound to the past. The second murder I have to commit is: I have to kill my ego. The ego is that thing that thinks it is me, which is not me, and prevents me from understanding who I really am. I have to kill my ego. The third murder is I have to kill my teacher. There is no teacher who can bring me all the way. At some stage I have to let go of the teacher or the teacher needs to let go of me. And finally, I have to kill God. Any theology that I construct is made up. There is no way that any theological system can understand God. With Meister

Eckhart I have to say, "I pray daily to God to rid me of God." With the Buddhist I have to say, "If you meet the Buddha on the road, kill him." The reason that Jesus had to die was that in order for the disciples to grow into who they were meant to become, they needed to let go of the teacher. Because they couldn't let go of him, he chose to let go of them.

Hell is the fourth stage. There is a very strange phrase in the Apostles Creed where it says, "Jesus died and descended into hell." What does it mean to say that Jesus descended into hell? Traditionally the church teaches that this descent into hell was Jesus liberating the trapped souls. According to this teaching from the time of Original Sin with Adam and Eve, God closed heaven. Not only did he kick us out of the Garden of Eden, he closed the doors of heaven. This is the teaching and I don't believe it for a moment. I do not believe that the Buddha, who died 500 years before Jesus and Lao-tzu who died 600 years before Jesus and Socrates who died 400 years before Jesus were all locked in some kind of limbo waiting for Jesus to reopen the gates of heaven. I don't believe that for a moment, but there are souls that get trapped after death. There are people at the moment of death who are so afraid of facing the light and so addicted to life on planet Earth and so attached to their ego that they can't move forward. These souls need the example of a fully evolved soul. Jesus' descent into hell models to this group of souls what the journey from darkness to light to full liberation is.

The fifth stage is the resurrection. Jesus demonstrated that we don't get just one shot at this life. We come back as often as we need until every single one of us gets it, not just in our heads, but in our hearts that the only thing that works is love. Jesus came back. He remanifested over a period of 40 days which is just a biblical magical number for completeness. He came back to demonstrate to them that we too have the opportunity of coming as often as we need to until every single one of us gets it no matter what our gender, ethnicity, social-economical class, IQ level or religious affiliations are. All of these things are meaningful only in so far as they offer us other opportunities to be able to love in that particular configuration of circumstances. That is what the resurrection of Jesus means as far as I am concerned.

The sixth stage is the ascension. What did his ascension represent? It represented the fact that this phase of his mission, this particular incarnation was complete. He had done what he had come to do and now he was going back; he was disincarnating.

The seventh stage was the Pentecost event. The Pentecost is the ultimate movement in human evolution. It is the movement from soul into Spirit. It is the movement from even great soul, mahatma, into great Holy Spirit. Everyone has to do it. Human evolution, broadly speaking, happens in five stages. This planet consisted of just matter for millions of years, and then 3.8 billion years ago the first life forms emerged. The evolution was from matter to life form, from physics to biology. At some stage, just a few million years ago life created mind. We then moved from physics to biology to psychology. The fourth stage was the evolution of individual souls and that took us from physics to biology to psychology to theology. But that is not the end of the process. The end of the process is the movement from soul into Spirit, from even great soul into Holy Spirit. It is the final movement. It is the movement from theology into mysticism. Pentecost represented that. Jesus could only release and let Spirit come once soul had done its work. Only when we move from physics to biology to psychology to theology are we ready for mysticism. Jesus completed his great work. He moved from being Jesus of Nazareth to being the Christ conscious being that he became.

I want to examine in seven stages why the Jesus movement fails to become the Christ carriers. We have gone through seven stages as well. I want to emphasize that this is true not just of the Christian churches but it is true of all religions. We go through the same kind of phases. We have the same obstacles. We start off with great intentions. We start off like Jesus did with conception. Again the seven stages are: first is conception, second is mission, but where there should be death instead there is institutionalization as stage three, stage four becomes the development of dogma and stage five becomes dealing in death and then stage six becomes reluctant reformation and stage seven becomes infallibility.

This is not true of just the Christian churches; it is true of all religious movements. We've all stepped ourselves through this process. The conception, in the case of the Christian churches, started off beautifully. It lasted for a period of about three years; and occurred during the public ministry of Jesus as he was moving from religion into spirituality. It was an extraordinary time for everyone associated with him; they were totally enamored by what this man was creating.

The second stage lasted for about a 40-year period. This was the young Christian community that totally embraced Spirit and was trying to become the prototype of how religion is meant to transform into spirituality. In the same way that soul is meant to evolve into Spirit, in the same way that theology is meant to evolve into mysticism, religion is meant to evolve into spirituality. This young group became the prototype of how that might happen and they maintained it for a period of about 40 years from the death of Jesus up to the fall of Jerusalem in the year 70 A.D. Then at stage three where death should have given birth to spirituality and then relinquished the mission; it formed institution instead. There were historical circumstances why this might have been so. It was a pity that it happened, but it happened and we have to face the consequences.

The first reason why this happened was the fall of Jerusalem, the conquest of Israel by the Romans, the destruction of the temple and the end of the priesthood. At this stage, normative Judaism disassociated itself from the Jews who believed that Jesus was the messiah; this later movement was regarded as a superstition and kicked out. They created institutions in order to maintain some semblance of togetherness and battle against the persecution by Rome. The institutionalization happened from about 70 A.D., with the fall of Jerusalem, up to about 312 A.D. Christians spread throughout all of Europe and tried to institutionalize their movement and so the Christian religion got set in concrete. That which should have birthed spirituality got bogged down in the concrete detail of creating institution.

Then a very significant event happened in the year 312 A.D; the conversion of Constantine. Constantine saw a sign in the sky and interpreted it as the Christian symbol of a cross and he legalized Christianity for the first time. This began a new development; the fourth stage. This phase developed dogma and it lasted from 312 A.D. up to about 700 A.D. At this stage, the great parabolic teaching of a great Jewish story-teller was run through the grinder of Greek, philosophical, rational thinking. Semitic idiom was reduced to theological conundrum. Beginning very shortly after the conversion of Constantine was the great council of the church at Nicaea in 325 A.D. This council hammered out a totally esoteric statement about how the father gives birth to the son and the son proceeds from the father and the Spirit proceeds from the father and the son. They used extraordinary phrases like homeostasis and words that were totally meaningless because they were stuck in religion when they should have birthed spirituality. They were stuck in that stage, the development of dogma, for about 400 years and then stage five came. It dealt in death and happened in three phrases.

The first phase in European history is called the Dark Ages and Spirit got lost by a religion reluctant to give birth to spirituality and darkness hung over Europe like a cloud. This gave birth in the second phase; the Crusades. Paranoia identified the enemy as Jews, Greek Orthodoxy and Muslims. And beginning in 1099 A.D., crusaders swept across Europe in a paroxysm of paranoia killing Jews, Greek Orthodox and Muslims. This was kept up for hundreds of years and then the paranoia went where it always goes; against itself. Having destroyed all of the enemies outside, the church invented the Inquisition and destroyed all of the enemies inside. That third phase lasted down to about 1540 A.D.

Stage six was reluctant reformation. Beginning in 1517 A.D., Martin Luther nailed his 95 theses to the cathedral door and all hell broke loose in Europe. Within a 40-year period, the Catholic Church admitted that there was some need for renewal and created what it called, not the Reformation, but the counter-Reformation; the anti-renewal movement to heal itself. That movement lasted in one form or another until 1850 A.D.

Beginning around 1850 A.D., the Catholic Church that maintained huge holdings all over Europe that had nations of its own and armies of its own, finally began to crumble and the Italian army came in and wiped out the Papal States. In this seventh stage, as the theocracy began to crumble, a petulant Pius IX insisted on some recompense. The recompense was the Doctrine of Infallibility. Grudgingly, the fathers of the church gathered in council at Vatican I and ultimately agreed that; "The Pope, in certain circumstances, can speak infal-libly." That is the stage where we still find ourselves today. Those are the seven stages where the Jesus movement failed to become carriers of Christ consciousness and instead became just a religion.

During all that time, of course, there was an underground move-ment. The mystics have always been among us. The trinity in action, I call them, those attempting Resurrection, Ascension and Pentecost are always bubbling through and they will always be countered by what I call the bureaucratic triangle; institutionalization, development of dogma and "death dealing." You have two trinities against each other i.e., the trinity of Resurrection, Ascension and Pentecost that the mystics are promoting countered by the trinity of institutionaliza-tion, development of dogma and dealing in death. It happens in all religions. For every Vatican II, prompted by John XXIII who threw open the windows for the Spirit to come in, there will be a fearful Paul VI who will close the windows, put his foot on the brake and be followed by John Paul II who will put us into reverse. It will happen in every movement and in every religion again and again. But you can no more hold back spirit any more than water can be contained. No matter what kind of dam of dogma you erect, the water of the spirit will find a way under it, over it, around it or through it, but the evolutionary spirit will not be stopped. We will finally get there; all of us will get there. Ultimately all Christians, Jews, Muslims, Hindus, and Buddhists, etc. will go beyond religion into spirituality.

This is an invitation to you to develop Christ consciousness in seven stages. I invite you to emulate what Jesus did in his movement from being Jesus the Carpenter of Nazareth to being the Christ. Every one of us is meant to go from who we are into carriers of Christ consciousness. For each one of us it will happen in the same seven stages.

The seven stages will again be conception followed by mission followed by death followed by hell followed by resurrection followed by ascension and followed by Pentecost.

What do I mean by conception? I have a belief system from my meditations that the scariest part of life is conception. Souls freak out when they find themselves confined in these tiny, dense little bodies with only three pounds of brain to try to channel the extraordinary wisdom of Spirit. There are two reasons why women suffer miscarriages. I think that sometimes the body is capable of creating a host for a soul but the host itself is defective in some way physiologically or biologically: it is not an adequate container for the soul to perform its mission and the embryo is shed. Upwards of a third of all pregnancies will end in miscarriages. Others create a healthy host body but finally the spirit that occupies it changes its mind and it departs. I am convinced that for the first few months of a pregnancy the soul comes in and out until it makes a final decision. That is what conception looks like to me.

What is mission about? Mission is the breaking of the illusion of separate identity; that we are separate from each other and that we are separate from God. It is the ability to embrace fully my own awakening so that I can help you awaken and that together we can help the entire world awaken. Mission is threefold: it is waking up so that I can help you wake up so that together we can wake our planet. That is the mission of every single one of us. We constantly misidentify it. We think our mission is our job, our vocation or our addiction.

Mission is never vocation, job or addiction. It is waking up so that I can help you to wake so that together we can wake up our planet.

Where conception is the scariest part of the journey for a soul coming in, death is the scariest part of the journey for the ego going out. There is nothing that scares the ego as much as death. It is not just the final demise when we slough off our mortal coil, but the death that happens in relationships or when your idea is overruled at a board meeting. The ego goes through death again and again and that is the hardest part of the journey for the ego. Ultimately we have to face it that every one of us has to kill the ego and finally let go of the spacesuit itself.

Just as Jesus experienced hell on the demise of the spacesuit, every one of us is faced with the choice of going back to the light or staying addicted to planet Earth. We want to hang on desperately because even then we can't let go of the ego. We experience hell to the extent that we cannot relinquish ego even at death. At some stage though we will all break through. There will be a resurrection for every single one of us. Resurrection, in my cosmology, will be the reincarnation or possibility of coming back onto this planet as often as I need to until I finally get it in the core of my being that the only thing that works is love. God has infinite patience with us and lets us come back as often as we need to until every one of us gets it not just in our head, but in the heart that the only thing that works is love.

What is ascension? Ascension is the final journey into total enlightenment and every single one of us will reach that at some point. It doesn't matter what ethnicity we belong to, gender we are or what religious affiliation we have in any particular incarnation, every single one of us is guaranteed to finally come to the realization that only love works because all that exists is God. All of us are merely articulations of the divine.

That leads to the Pentecost experience for every single one of us. The Pentecost experience is one of two possibilities. Either the final relinquishing of all ego so we merge back into the divinity never to be separated again from Her or we take the Bodhisattva vow.

The Bodhisattva determines to keep coming back on planet Earth, even though enlightened, until every single sentient being becomes awake. Pentecost was not just a one time event orchestrated by a departed Jesus, it happens again and again and again. Are you ready for Pentecost?

Signs, Symbols, and Sacraments

"Unless we see or hear phenomena or things from within the things them-selves, we shall never succeed in recording them in our hearts."

Matsuo Basho

A SIGN HAS BOTH feet in physicality. A sign is just one physical object standing for another physical object. A road sign is just a painted sign standing for some tarmac a few hundred meters farther on. It is one physical thing standing for another physical thing.

A symbol is very different from a sign. A symbol has one foot in physical reality and the other foot in non-physical reality. For instance, a kiss is a symbol. It is not a sign; it is a symbol. The physical part of the kiss is two pair of lips meeting. The non-physical part of it is that it communicates a much deeper truth; I love you.

A sacrament is a very special category of symbols because it causes to happen the very thing that it symbolizes. The difficult thing is that they can all be made to tell lies. A sign can tell lies. Someone can take a signpost and swing it around and you think that San Jose is this way because it says San Jose when San Jose is in the opposite direction.

Symbols can be made to tell lies. The archetypal symbol that told a lie was the kiss of Judas to Jesus in the garden of Gethsemane, which was about affection for Jesus but, in fact, was a sign to the soldiers that this was the man they needed to arrest.

Strictly speaking, a sacrament can never tell a lie if it is a true sacrament. Often what passes for a sacrament isn't sacrament at all be-

133

cause sacrament is predicated upon mindfulness. You cannot receive a sacrament mindlessly because it is the mindfulness and awareness that turns this symbol into a sacrament. It is something that creates the very thing that it symbolizes; otherwise it is a dead symbol. If a person approaches the sacrament of Eucharist in a mindless manner, all that person gets is the wafer and there is no Eucharist "in it." Eucharist is about the mindfulness of the encounter otherwise what appears to be a sacrament is turned into a meaningless sign. It is extraordinary to me that when Jesus gave us the sacraments, that this most masculine of men finally gave us the most feminine of symbols as the final gesture of his love. This man who had the courage and the decisiveness and the intellect of a true man also had the sensitivity and the love of a complete woman. This was a pure symbol of the mother feeding her child from her own body. This is pure symbol and pure sacrament. Jesus, the most masculine of men leaves us the most feminine symbol as his final gesture of love to us.

We assume that a mystery is something that cannot be understood. I do not believe that a mystery is something that cannot be understood. We may not be able to understand mystery with our minds. We have to transcend mind and sense in order to come into the experience of mystery. Mystery can be understood at the level of soul far deeper than when we wrestle with a problem and understand it purely intellectually. Once we have experienced the mystery we can then use the mind to articulate the experience. It cannot capture the experience; it cannot give us the experience, but subsequently, it can help us wrestle with and make sense of the experience and hold on to it. Epi-genesis is the system by which all subsequent stages transcend but incorporate all the previous stages. Nothing is left out. So this is an epi-genetic model in which the soul having the experience of the mystery doesn't lose the mind in the process of subsequently understanding the mystery that the soul has experienced. The mind is very important and the senses are very important.

I heard of a little four-year-old who managed to lock himself into the bathroom while playing with the lock on the bathroom door.

When he realized that he couldn't get out, he became anxious and began screaming. The mother on the other side of the door said, "Open the door, open the door." The mother became frantic and began rushing at the door with her body to push the door open, but to no avail. It was then that she had an extraordinary moment of clarity. Very calmly she slid a piece of newspaper under the door and then with a pencil she pushed the key out and it fell on the newspaper which she pulled out with the key on it and unlocked the door. She was not able to deal with this problem physically, she had to transcend the physicality in order to wrestle with the physical problem. It was by going to the mind level that she was able to transcend the physical obstacle. She still had to use her body to accomplish it but without the mind jump the physical thing would have been useless.

The same thing happens to us in Eucharist and in mystery. In order to experience the mystery we have to totally transcend mere intellectuality. Once we have had a real experience as human beings, spirits in spacesuits, we have to then use our minds to try to understand the experience that we just had. We have to transcend the mere literalness of the encounter to the deep mystery of the encounter. We get stuck constantly. Theologians and religions are constantly getting bogged down by thinking that the literal interpretation is the key to the mystery. It never is. I came across this a lot in the seminary.

When we were preparing for the celebration of mass and the understanding of Eucharist, many different scenarios were used to help us understand the Eucharist. One scenario was: If a priest is consecrating the bread saying the words, "This is my body," and just at that instance a bread van passes by, has he just consecrated the contents of the bread van? Of course, they would tell us, "No, no, no, only the material on the corporal gets consecrated."

Then suppose there was a large crowd at mass and there is not enough room on the corporal to hold all of the hosts and one of them accidentally gets pushed off to the side and you say, "This is my body," is Jesus going to say, "Me too, me too?" Of course they said,

"No, no, it is the intention of the priest that is important not just the physical location of the corporal but the intention of the priest."

At one time, at the back door of the sacristy in every church there was a special container called a sacrarium: a metal pipe that was stuck in the ground outside the sacristy. If there was any water left over from saying mass, this water was poured down the sacrarium. Or when something needed to be destroyed perhaps when one of the altar cloths got soiled and was no longer fit for Eucharist, we couldn't just throw it out, we had to burn it and then put the ashes into the sacrarium because these cloths were considered sacred.

I remember one day in class the professor said, "Suppose you are saying mass and you have just consecrated the host and you place the host on the altar and suddenly a mouse runs up onto the altar, grabs the host and runs down a mouse hole and there is no way you can catch him. What are you going to do?" One smart ass said, "Father, I would burn down the church and put the ashes in the sacrarium."

Is that what it is about? Is Jesus really stuck in a mouse hole? Is that what we mean by Eucharist? Or is it that the consciousness, mindset and intentionality of the encounter create Christ consciousness? That is the difference between the literalness and the mystery.

There is an ongoing struggle between real scientists and people who practice mere "scientism" and between theologians and mystics as to what ultimate reality might be about. Those who practice scientism have a belief system that the only reality is what is physically apprehensible; what I can apprehend through my five senses or by extension through the instrumentation developed for the senses. People who practice scientism, as distinct from science, claim that the only reality is the phenomenological or the physical world. They claim that it is brain that creates consciousness. I think it is consciousness that uses brain. For instance, they say; "When you kill a brain, consciousness ceases and therefore that proves that brain comes first and consciousness comes out of brain; it is just a biochemical process. It is an epiphenomenon or an illusion created by neurons firing." I would say when you are watching a ballgame on TV and the Forty-niners are playing and suddenly the TV breaks down and you no longer have a picture or sound, has the ballgame ground to a halt? Of course it hasn't because the TV was not creating the ballgame. The TV was merely a medium taking in electromagnetic activity and translating it into visual and auditory signals. That is all the brain does. The brain is merely a medium for consciousness. If that is true, what then is ultimate reality? Ultimate reality is some form of spirit or some form of consciousness that uses the physical world as an expression of its inner self.

For instance, the physical world is to the real world what a photograph is to the subject of the photograph. When you look at a photograph and see yourself you know that is not you at all. It is a small two-dimensional photo image of the front part of your body. The photo cannot capture your essence because the physical world is to the real world as the photograph is to you. You are much deeper and much more essential than the photograph of you might suggest. The real world is much more complex, beautiful and mysterious than the physical world would suggest. You are much more than that. Unfortunately, the Native Americans got it wrong. When you take a photograph of someone, you can't capture his or her spirit.

If I really understand what Eucharist is about, then I have to know, even if I hold onto the realization for a short period of time, that I am intimately and essentially connected to all living beings. To the extent that I can sit in the middle of that mystery, I am in a Eucharistic experience. The moment that experience begins to dissolve, Eucharist is also beginning to dissolve. If I am in a deep Eucharist experience it is impossible to be angry or prejudiced or lonely because I am totally connected to all living things. I can't be disconnected from anything.

If the only difference between the communion that we receive and the cookies that we receive later is that the latter tastes a whole lot better than the former, we have not understood Eucharist. If we are still concerned about getting Jesus stuck to the roof of our mouths, then we need to meditate some more on the mystery. Eucharist is primarily about ridding ourselves of the illusion of a separate identity.

DREAMS WITHIN DREAMS WITHIN DREAMS

"Every act done in the sunlight of awareness becomes sacred."

Thich Nhat Hanh

THERE IS NOTHING the gods like better than dressing up in human clothes and visiting us on planet Earth. If the gods happen to have a Trinitarian aspect, as some gods do, it is always the second person of the trinity who gets to incarnate. For instance, within Christianity, which has a triune god, it is the second person of the Christian trinity who gets to incarnate. The son gets to incarnate in the person of Jesus the carpenter from Nazareth.

The Hindus have a triune god as well: Brahma, Vishnu and Shiva. It is always the second person of the Hindu trinity, Vishnu, who gets to incarnate. Unlike the second person of the Christian trinity, who only managed this feat once, Vishnu managed it many times.

One of my favorite incarnations of Vishnu is Krishna. Vishnu came as Krishna at one time and there are some great stories about what happened in the course of this particular incarnation. On a particular occasion, Krishna and one of his followers were walking along the banks of the Ganges. It was a very hot day so they found a large Banyan tree and they sat beneath it. Krishna asked his follower to go to the water and bring him a drink. The follower went down to the river and as he knelt to dip his jug into the water he saw an island in the middle of the river. On the island he saw a village with a beautiful woman and he fell instantly in love with her. He abandoned the jug, dove into the water and swam out to the island. But, before he could begin to woo this beautiful woman, she said that he had to meet her father. When he met her father, he told him of his love for his daughter. Her father told him that before he could marry his daughter he would have to work for him for seven years. He worked for seven years and finally they were wed and lived together for fifteen years, had three children and were very happy.

One night there was an extraordinary storm and a deluge flooded the entire village. One child was swept out of the house, and as he grabbed the child another child was swept away. One by one all his children and his wife were swept away and drowned. He was tumbled through the rushing water and awoke on the banks of the river the next morning. As he looked back he saw that not only the village was gone but the island was gone as well. He was absolutely disconsolate. He dragged himself up from the river and wandered about for an hour until he came upon Krishna. Krishna said to him, "Did you fetch me my water?" "Are you serious? Have you any idea what I've been through for the last 22 years?" Then he told Krishna his sad tale. With patience, Krishna listened to him relate his story. Krishna then said, "I have two pieces of bad news for you. First, this never happened to you. It was a dream you had. And secondly, you don't exist; you are an element in my dream."

This is a great story and it is the story of the psyche. In some sense, Krishna represents the soul and the follower represents the ego. The ego is merely a dream that the soul is having. Life is merely a dream that the ego is having. Life is a series of nested dreams; dreams within dreams within dreams. What we take to be life is simply a dream the ego is enjoying and what we take to be the ego is simply a dream the soul is having. What we take to be the soul is merely a dream that God is having.

I'm sure you have come across the notion while reading that people will sometimes dream lucidly. When you are asleep at night and you are having a dream, you suddenly realize that you are having a dream. Some part of your psyche says to you, "This is only a dream." Sometimes it happens in a very upsetting dream and you say to yourself this is only a dream I'm having, I don't have to believe this and you wake yourself up. Other people develop this skill to actually enter the dream and steer it where they want it to go.

Typically when we are dreaming, it is very difficult for us to activate the major muscles in the body. There is a substance called non-epinephrine which is released into the system to immobilize our major muscles so we don't act out our dreams and get in trouble. But some minor muscles are still under conscious control. When some people dream, they can become lucidly aware that they are dreaming and if they are hooked up to an electroencephalogram which shows the brain-wave states, they will move a finger to tell the researchers that they are dreaming. Lucid dreaming is the ability to know when one is dreaming. Some people develop this extraordinary gift.

There is a more important skill than that and it is called lucid living. It is the ability to realize when we are living that this too is a dream. Very few people come to that realization. Most of us buy so totally into the dream of living that we don't realize that this too is a dream. When we come to that conclusion, then we too can lucidly live and we can know that this too is an illusion. At that point we can take control of the process and we can steer it where we want. The ultimate reward for lucid living is lucid dying. When people come to a stage in life when they are ready to exit, then even that process is done lucidly with full control and management of the process. They know that they are not their spacesuit and know that a transition is about to occur and do it with full awareness and full consciousness.

Many people have claimed to have done this. It is said that when their time comes for transition many of the great enlightened beings within the Tibetan system sit down in the lotus position and exit leaving behind their spacesuit. This is sometimes called the rainbow body. But it happens to ordinary people. I have come across many old men and women who prepared day by day for their own dying. They did it without fear realizing that this was just a safari that they were on. When the time came to let go, they let go lucidly. We can have lucid dreaming, lucid living and lucid dying.

During all of these stages the most important element is lucid killing. If I have the courage to enter my dream lucidly, to live my life lucidly and to die my death lucidly it involves lucid killing. It means that again and again killing the illusion under which most of us labor most of the time.

The dream has three levels to it. The deepest part of all is the illusion, and in some sense the most ridiculous part of the illusion is the persona. The persona is the person I pretend I am. It is so ridiculous that I don't even believe it myself. When society asks me to put on a different masks depending on whatever role I'm meant to be playing or whatever responsibility I'm meant to be adopting, I'm going to present a mask or spacesuit. It is so ridiculous I don't even believe it myself. That is the most ridiculous part of the dream and as low as we go. The next part is the most dangerous part of the dream or illusion and we call that the ego. It is dangerous because we totally believe that that is who we are. None of us believes we are our persona so it is ridiculous but it is not dangerous. Believing that I am my ego is really dangerous. But that is not to say that the ego is not important. It performs a very useful function.

It takes a child 12 or 15 months to develop an ego and it typically builds around the notion of a given name. At some stage, every child comes to the realization that his/her name is who s/he is. Ego allows us to tie our shoe laces, have jobs and so it is very important. But when we identify with it, it gets us into all kinds of trouble. Almost every ego, at some stage of its evolution, becomes paranoid. It becomes a kind of Herod. Herod was so paranoid that his throne was going to be overthrown that he killed his favorite wife, his mother-in-law and three of his own sons. He killed all those nearest and dearest to him. So fearful that it will be overthrown, the ego is constantly on a campaign to wipe out the opposition. That is the most dangerous part of the illusion and the dream.

We have the persona which is the most ridiculous part, we have the most dangerous part which is the ego and we have the most subtle part which is the soul. But the soul is not the full thing. Soul is to Spirit as Hamlet is to Shakespeare. Hamlet is just a particular work of the genius, Shakespeare, and soul is just a bite-size piece of God. When the soul masquerades as the totality of the divinity, we get into trouble. The soul is the subtlest of all of the parts of the illusion. It is the first stage of the devolution from divinity down into incarnation and it is the last stage of the illusion as we walk back, evolutionarily speaking, to total merging with God. It is the first stage of God playing Hide and Go Seek with God. The first way that God plays Hide and Go Seek is by breaking Herself into bite-size pieces that we call souls and then hiding Herself in illusion. The last part of the journey back to God is the wiping away of all the illusions of separate identity until we merge totally back into divinity. That is what happens when we plumb the depths of divinity.

The practice of dying daily means, paradoxically, that you never have to die. If you practice dying every day, you never have to die. If you are in fear of dying every day, then you die every day. Shakespeare said at one stage, "The hero dies only once, the coward dies a thousand times." When we have the courage to practice dying daily, then we never die. When we have a fear of dying then we die every day. In either case, are we dying every day? Yes and no. If I practice dying daily, what is dying daily is merely the ego and the illusion, because there is no such thing as death. There is no death of God. When I am constantly afraid of dying, then I am dying daily and what is dying is the ego fearful of losing its grip on consciousness. It is a very different kind of dying. The truth is death is the ultimate illusion; there is no such thing as death. What we take to be death is merely a particular phase of life. Life is a continuum that has both incarnation phases and non-physical phases. What we take to be death is merely the transition between these phases. What we take to be birth is merely the other transition. Birth is the transition from the non-physical phase of life into physicality and death merely the transition from the physical phase of life back into the non-physical phase of life. There is no death as there is no birth. There is just weaving in and out of the tapestry of life in its physical and its non-physical format.

In this process, we have to learn, not only how to face death, but how to face murder. To be a truly spiritual person, you have to become a serial killer. You have to commit four murders. You have to murder your ego. You have to murder the father. You have to murder the guru and you have to murder God. What do I mean by that? You have to murder the ego because the ego is the most dangerous part of the illusion. If you don't kill the ego, the ego will kill you. The ego is the illusion or attachment to the persona. What I mean by killing the father is we have to kill the cultural ego. The father represents the ego of an entire culture. It represents the power of the group. We have to kill our attachment to the power of the group or else the group will kill us and lots of others in the process. We have to kill the guru because the guru is the effort to be attached vicariously to power, because I can't have enough power myself, I will attach myself to someone who is a powerful figure and I will live through that person. I cannot complete my spiritual journey as long as I am fastened to a guru. There is a point at which the guru can help me walk part of my journey just as there is a point at which the ego can help me walk part of my journey and a point at which my father can walk with me and my culture, but there comes a time when I have to slough off all of these.

Then the fourth murder is: I have to murder God because all theology is made up. Any effort to ascribe any kind of category to God is totally a human invention and will get me in trouble. Buddhism will say, "If you meet the Buddha on the road, kill him." Christian mysticism says: "I pray daily to God to rid me of God." The ultimate murder that has to be committed is the murder of God.

The hardest murder for most of us is the murder of the ego. How do we go about murdering the ego? When we realize that the ego has its importance and it has its dangers, the simplest way I know to begin to murder the ego is by learning how to listen. I can detach from my own personal viewpoint by listening to someone else. Listening carefully to another person is a great beginning to letting go of the ego and eventually murdering the ego. The second best way of murdering the ego is compassion. When I can empathize and feel another's pain, I begin to disengage from my ego. Ultimately, if I can touch my own essence, my soul, then my ego will no longer have power over me. When someone said to Jesus, "I will follow you wherever you go," Jesus said, "The foxes have lairs and the birds of heaven have their nests, but the Son of Man has no place to lay his head." Do you think Jesus was advocating homelessness? Was he glorifying being without shelter? It has nothing to do with having a place to live or a place to put down one's head. What he was saying was: You cannot afford to go back to sleep. The laying down of the head is a metaphor for going back to sleep. Jesus said, "Once you have begun to wake up, you cannot afford to go back to sleep again. You have to stay awake. "

When someone said to Jesus: "I will follow you, but first let me go and bury my father." Jesus then makes what seems to be a very cruel reply: "Let the dead bury the dead. You come and follow me." This is not a story about someone whose father had just died. Rather, it is a story about a man saying that his father is old and that he wants to hang around and look after him, then later he will follow Jesus. What Jesus was saying to this man was that the Kingdom of Heaven is now. You have to find the Kingdom now. You can't wait for some event to happen in order for it to be appropriate for you to begin your quest. The quest for the Kingdom of God has to begin now and only now.

A third man said to Jesus: "I will follow you but let me go home and say goodbye to my parents." Jesus replies: "Anyone who puts his hand to the plow and then turns back is not worthy of me." Jesus is not saying to this man: you have no permission to go back and say goodbye to your parents. What this man is really saying is that his parents are old and have a different belief system. Let me go back and explain to my parents what I am about to do so they will let me follow you. Jesus tells this man that he can't do that. If you need permission from anyone to be different, then you stay the same as you always were. No one can give you permission to be different. It is your birthright to be different. No one can liberate you but yourself. If I have to ask someone to set me free, I will always be in chains. Jesus was saying, "The Kingdom of God is like this: It is not only within, it is now." It is not about asking permission of old systems in order to erect new systems. It is not asking permission from old gurus in order to follow new gurus. The Kingdom of God is about following your soul, liberating yourself and asking permission of no one in the process.

One of the greatest illusions of the scientific models through which we conduct most of our activities is that consciousness is an epiphenomenon of matter. Consciousness is merely an illusion created by the firing of neurons that consist of physical substances. It is not matter that creates consciousness; it is consciousness that manifests as matter. Consciousness manifests in many different guises among them the ability to appear as matter. It is consciousness that creates matter.

The mind is merely a tool to recognize the fact. The mind is not some mapping organism that allows us to have a relationship with a preexisting reality and to construct accurate representations of it. That is not the function of the mind. The mind doesn't map or model onto preexisting reality, the mind is the instrument through which consciousness creates these things. We need to come to that realization. Propaganda is not a political or religious tool that reminds us of preexisting truths, it's an artifice that makes up perceptions and perspectives that if uncritically accepted, become the "truth." Something that wasn't the truth to begin with, becomes the truth because we have uncritically accepted the perceptions of some other group as to what reality might be. Mind does this unfortunately. Mind acts as if its function is merely to relate to a preexisting reality and create maps and representations of it.

If consciousness is so powerful that it can actually create reality in a physical format, imagine what it can do in merely an emotional and mental format. Consciousness has the ability to create whole universes that are non-physical. Given that it has the ability to create a physical universe, imagine what it can do in creating emotional universes and mental universes. We do this regularly. We do it every night. Every night when we dream, we create a brand new universe in which we travel in our astral body. Our dream has an emotional and mental aspect. When we die, we are doing the very same thing. We are creating a brand new universe. As we transition from this physical spacesuit to a non-physical condition, we are literally creating other heavens and other hells within our emotional and mental state. If only we could remember, then we wouldn't have to create and we wouldn't have to imagine anymore.

The other illusion we labor under in developmental psychology is that little babies are too young to have memories, so all they have is imagination. Whereas adults who have lived long enough to generate many memories don't need imagination. It is absolutely the opposite; they are 180 degrees off. It is not the imagination of little babies that connects them to reality, it is their memory. They are so newly come from the ultimate source of "all that is" that it is their memory that serves them. What they appear to be imagining is what they are actually remembering. For the rest of us, we are so jaded with life that what we take to be memories is merely our own creation. We have imagined stuff with such clarity and consistency over such a long period of time that we have actually managed to manifest it. We have imagined prejudice, warfare and differences for so long that we have actually managed to manifest our imaginings. Wouldn't it be an extraordinary development if we could remember our original state? What a difference it would make if instead of creating imaginary worlds of heaven and hell we could begin to remember where we actually came from in the first place. If we could do this, every one of us would have a different experience.

The Kingdom of God is among you and within you. What did Jesus mean by that? The Kingdom of God within you means this: we have the ability as individuals to discover the Kingdom of God "within" because we are articulations of the divine. When we answer the two final questions, we can answer as the Buddha answered. When the Buddha began his public ministry, the Brahmin class was outraged that a mere Kshatriya was attempting to preach about spirituality and they asked him, "Who in God's name do you think you are? Are you a prophet?" "No." "Are you an angel?" "No, I am not." "Are you a sage?" "No, I am not a sage." "So who are you?" "I am awake." The word or title, Buddha, means the one who is awake. The only answer to the two questions, who are you and why are you doing what you are doing is: "I am doing it because I am awake."

FREEDOM AND INDEPENDENCE

"Only in God and by the supremacy of the spirit can we enjoy a perfect freedom."

Sri Aurobindo

ANIEL O'CONNELL STRODE across the pages of Irish history like a colossus dominating the first half of the nineteenth century and was known as the liberator. He was born in 1775 and died in 1847. He went to a college in France and became an eloquent lawyer, returned to Ireland and got involved in Irish politics. He tried to appeal the penal laws enacted by colonial regimes that made it illegal to practice Catholicism and illegal for a Catholic to own a horse valued at more than five pounds. In 1829, he ran for a seat on the Westminster Parliament and was elected by an overwhelming majority. Although he was elected, he couldn't take his place at Parliament because he was Catholic. It was illegal for a Catholic to be a member to the British House of Commons. Another election the following year gave him an even bigger majority. He went on to become the Mayor of Dublin and he led an entire movement that resulted in Catholic emancipation. For the first time in 150 years, it was no longer illegal to be Catholic.

He formed a movement for Irish independence which culminated in an extraordinary march of over one million people in Dublin in 1843. The British ordered him not to address the marchers or be arrested. He was encouraged to go ahead and address the meeting and let happen what might. Daniel O'Connel, a firm believer in non violence, said: "The cause of Irish freedom is not worth a single drop of Irish blood." This was an extraordinary pronouncement by an extraordinary man in an extraordinary time. He died four years later during the Irish famine that reduced the Irish population from eight million to four million people. In some sense he died a broken man.

The first great liberation movement in scripture took place in Egypt when a group of slaves escaped into the desert. For the first 40 days after their escape all they really had was physical freedom. They had escaped as a group of slaves, but they still had the slave mentality. It was only after Moses when up on Mount Sinai and got the new constitution that would bind them into a new people and give them a new understanding of their covenanted relationship with God that they would be free psychologically and spiritually. They continued to not believe in themselves because they still didn't fully grasp the notion of freedom. They wandered in fear for forty years in the desert before they believed in themselves enough to enter the Promised Land.

Then those who had been oppressed for 450 years and gained their freedom marched into a country and took it over by force. There is no group of people on planet Earth today that has not taken by force land belonging to others. It is human history that we constantly push each other out. Ever since we began migrating out of Africa we have been displacing the aboriginal people of other lands to replace them by more powerful regimes. That is the trajectory of freedom today, unfortunately.

Fast forward about 700 years and those people will in turn be oppressed, enslaved, colonized and brutalized first by the Egyptians then the Assyrians then the Babylonians then by the Persians then by the Greeks and finally by the Romans. About the year 721 B.C., ten of the twelve tribes of these people will be taken into exile by the great Assyrian Empire and they were never heard of again. About the year 587 B.C., the two final tribes of Judah were taken off by the Babylonian Empire and they will barely cling onto life. Only when the Persian Empire displaces the Babylonians in the year 529 B.C., will a remnant be allowed to go back to Israel. Only a small group, less than 24 thousand people, actually chose to go back. They knew what lay ahead. They knew that they would possess a devastated land where the city no longer existed, their temple destroyed and a priesthood that had been annihilated. They would also be living with their half-brothers, Samaritans, their deadly enemies. They were the result of the interbreeding between the colonial forces of occupation and the remnant that had been left behind to see to the farm work. The free slaves became disheartened and wanted to give up, but eventually they built up their spirits and created a New Jerusalem with a new temple and a new notion of priesthood.

At the time of Jesus, the people wrestled again with the notion of freedom, independence and holiness. When you live in a theocratic society, holiness, freedom and independence are the same thing. It was interesting also that people at this stage, having suffered occupation by the Romans for almost 100 years, were wrestling with a new response. There are several different versions of that response. The Pharisees claimed that the way to achieve true independence and true sanctity was through a much more fastidious observation of the 613 laws of Torah. The Zealot party claimed that the only answer to Rome was through violence. The Essene response was opting for salvation, holiness and freedom through separation i.e., going off into the desert to make themselves more holy. In the year 742 B.C., Isaiah had an extraordinary vision of God and his train filling the temple while the seraphim proclaimed, "Holy, holy, holy is the Lord God of Israel." Thereafter, Israel created a holiness code based on separation. During the Babylonian exile, 587 to 529 B.C., they maintained their integrity and independence by a holiness code based on separation. They separated the holy day of the week, the Sabbath, from the unclean day, the clean food from the unclean food, the infidels from the gentiles by an act of circumcision and themselves from table fellowship with anyone who was not Jewish. This allowed them to survive, but at the time of Jesus, it was fracturing the community. Jesus, having been invited to holiness and freedom by way of the law, rejected it. He also rejected freedom and holiness by violence against the Romans and he thoroughly rejected freedom and holiness by separation. He opted for freedom and holiness by incarnation and association. Jesus' model of freedom and holiness was to incarnate into the human condition and associate with the lowliest of the lowly. We can see throughout scripture very different models of what freedom began to look like.

Physical slavery is being in prison in some way. Almost two million of our citizens are having this experience. America imprisons more of its citizens than any country in the world. That is the experiment of slavery in our society today. Emotional slavery is being locked in relationships in which one's self esteem is constantly devastated by the other party. Mental slavery is being stuck in a mindset that will not allow someone to realize his/her full potential as a child of God and a spirit in a spacesuit. Many of us walk with a mindset of slavery and do not believe in ourselves because we have not been taught to believe in ourselves. Spiritual slavery is the mistaken identity where we think that dogmatic, fear-based religion is actually transcendent soul experience. They are totally different phenomena. Political slavery is having no right to exercise democratic human rights. In many countries in the world that is the case. Some people who have the right to exercise democratic rights, don't have the will to engage their democracy. There will possibly be only 40 percent of the voting population that will vote in the next election. We do not exercise the responsibility of living in a democratic society. Media slavery is where our news and reporting of what is actually happening in the world is in the hands of a small group with a specific agenda as to what we need to hear and how we need to hear it. Financial slavery finds mother and father holding down two jobs in order to keep a roof over their heads, put food on the table, education their children and provide medical attention when needed.

What is the evolution of freedom and what does it look like as it evolves? There is a difference between freedom and free will. Free will is the ability to choose to do whatever I want and freedom is the ability to choose what God wants or to choose the good. To the extent that I do not choose the good, I am not free. I am merely exercising free will. I am only truly free when I am not subject to the addictions of consumerism, fear or propaganda. I am only truly free when I continue to opt for what is good, true and beautiful.

There are three stages to the process of freedom and evolution. We go from slavery to independence to interdependence. Or in a slightly more complicated model of freedom and evolution there are five stages to the process. There is slavery, violent rebellion, independence and then colonialism where the newly independent people become the oppressors themselves and then finally there is interdependence. The blight on the second half of the 20th century is that country after country, particularly in Africa and South America, violently wrested their independence from colonialist regimes. In the act, they became violent people and created on-going civil wars which pitted tribe against tribe and most of the resources of the nation were wasted in the war effort. All this was aided and abetted by armament makers who are very happy to supply arms to both sides and keep the conflict going so there would be a ready market for their product. All violence births further violence.

What would be the blight of the first half of the 21st century if we were to start importing the same thinking into the Middle East? If the only way we can dismantle the non-democratic systems in the Middle East is to advocate forms of violence where we divide them against each other, then we will look forward to another 50 years of what we witnessed in Africa and South America for the last 50 years. There has to be a different way, and there is a different way. It is the notion of moving toward interdependence not independence or bloody rebellion as a modality of reaching human unanimity.

There are three factors that will drive this process. The first process is the inexorable law of evolution. Only that system that is really adapted to the human conditions and problems will ultimately survive. Any system that does not take cognizance of the rights of all the people on planet Earth is destined to ultimately fail. Natural selection and survival of the fittest will guarantee that only that system that truly benefits everyone equally will ultimately survive. We can try other systems for as long as we want, but they will not succeed and they will only lead to further bloodshed.

The second driving force that will benefit everyone is all of us being fully awake human beings. We need to be people who are spearheading the evolution of our species and who realize that the hit and miss, trial and error way in which natural selection and survival of the fittest operated in the past is no longer valid, because the movement of evolution, for the first time ever, becomes aware of itself. The participants become aware of and are fully able to consciously participate in the ongoing process.

The third force that has always driven evolution is the presence of Spirit. Spirit has breathed life and creativity into the process of evolution since the very beginning and will manage to salvage spirituality from the wreckage of religion. As Americans we are in an extraordinarily privileged position to spearhead this movement. Because of our resources and our freedoms there is no other nation on planet Earth that has both the resources and the ability to drive this movement.

When I became an American citizen five years ago I remembered a preconception contract I made long before I incarnated this time. It was a contract to be part of the culture and nation that would have the resources and freedom necessary to spearhead the movement to create Christ consciousness and Buddha nature for all people. Why did you decide to be born American? Did you just want the privileges of freedom? Did you want the privileges of consumerism or do you remember that you too, in a preconception contract, signed on to become one of those people who is awake and move this extraordinary nation with its extraordinary resources to be the spearhead that will allow Christ consciousness and Buddhahood to be the next phase of the evolution of the entire planet.

"No Child left Behind," is a beautiful phrase; unfortunately, it is much more honored in the breach than in the observance. It is a very catchy political slogan that subsequent legislation has totally eviscerated. We will make significant progress only when every American child has equal access to adequate housing, ample food, a full education and proper medical care. We will know that we have made the ultimate progress when every child on planet Earth will have equal access to the same things.

I dream that finally the United States of America, as the only super power left on planet Earth, willingly, compassionately and lovingly rejoins the family of nations as an equal member and puts itself under exactly the same ethical checks and balances that are imposed on other nations. I also dream that this extraordinary country will look at our bloated military budget and reorder it so that those resources are put into the quest for Christ consciousness and Buddhahood for the entire planet. I dream that it would be the radiant faces of the children of the planet and not some faded piece of parchment from 1776 that reminds us that we all have the right to life, liberty and the pursuit of happiness.

I dream that Jesus will no longer need to die on the cross in agony in order to pronounce the words, "It is finished." I dream that Jesus, having cuddled the little ones and given the high-five to the older ones will be able to sigh contentedly and say, "Now, it is finished."

HOSPITALITY

"God whose boundless love and joy are present everywhere cannot come to visit you unless you are not there."

Angelus Selesius

Y FATHER WAS an archeologist and he is one of the founding members of the Mizzen Archeological and Historical Society. Mizzen is an area of west Cork on a famous peninsula that divides Cork from Kerry. Every year this society puts out a journal of the archeological findings, history and folklore of the area. I get a copy of this journal every year. I remember in the 1995 copy there was a story about an old man, Bernard O'Reagan. He was born in 1896 and was a lifetime honorary member of the Mizzen Archeological and Historical Society.

There was one story that stood out from this interview. Bernard told my father: "When I was a young boy about eight-years old there was an old beggar who came to our farmhouse. My mother would take him to the kitchen and feed him and they would sit down and talk for a few hours. When he got up to leave, I'd run down our walkway before him and hide behind the bushes and watch him because he had a strange way of walking. From the knees down, his legs were bent out sideways, almost at right angles and he wobbled back and forth which fascinated me. One day, I asked my mother, "Why does that old man walk so strangely?" My mother said, "I'll tell you why. About 60 years ago there was a great famine in this area and people were dying like flies. There was a big pit in the graveyard and every morning a horse and cart would come along gathering up all the bod-

156

ies of the people who had died during the night and take them out and put them into this big pit. Then in the evening, the cart would go around the village again and it would take all the bodies of the people who had died during the day and put them on top of the bodies buried that morning. There was a family living in this area; a mother, father and two little boys. One boy was five and the other was two. The little five-year old died and was taken on the cart and put into the ground with all the other bodies. A few weeks later, the little two-year old died and the mother was absolutely heartbroken. She held the dead child to herself and refused to give it up. She held it for two or three days and the father pleaded with her to bury the child and the mother said, 'No, I can't let him go.' Finally she agreed on one condition. 'You have to make a little box for him. I'm not going to let him go into the pit with all the other decomposing bodies. Find a little box and we'll put him in the box.'"

"The father searched for little pieces of timber and he found enough wood to make a small box. But the child was too big for the little box. They had to dislocate his legs at the knees in order to fit him into the box. Then the mother said, 'In the morning, take him around and put him in the pit.' So they did. That evening when the cart came to the pit, they heard someone crying. They listened and looked around and they found that the crying was coming from the little box. When they pulled the box out and opened it up, the little boy was still alive. And that is the man that you saw walking down the lane today."

I believe that there are possibly four versions to the story of Mary and Martha. According to Luke, when Jesus came to the house of Mary and Martha, he saw Martha preparing a meal for Jesus and his followers while Mary sat at the feet of Jesus listening to Jesus. Martha became upset because she wanted Mary to help her prepare the meal. Jesus looked at Martha and said: "Martha, you are busy about many things. Mary has chosen the better part and it will not be taken from her." John's version of this story is about the raising of Lazarus who was the brother of Mary and Martha. In honor of what Jesus had done for their brother, Mary and Martha invited Jesus and his followers to a feast at their house. In this story by John, we read that: "Martha waited on the table, Lazarus reclined at table and Mary knelt at the feet of Jesus, anointed his feet with oil and dried his feet with her hair." There is another possible version: Jesus came to this village to be entertained by the family of Mary, Martha and Lazarus. Jesus was tired from his journey and Mary gave him her undivided attention while Martha was in the kitchen preparing dinner. Martha came into the room and she said to Jesus, "Don't you see my sister! I'm doing everything, tell her to help me!" Jesus then looked at Martha and said: "Martha, you are busy about many things. Only one thing is necessary and Mary has chosen the better part." Martha angrily said to Jesus, "Okay, cook your own bloody meal." Jesus got no meal and he continued on his journey and when he came to a fig tree with no fruit on it, he cursed the tree and it withered. It's called displaced aggression.

The real story however is the relationship between Jesus and Mary. While Mary sat at the feet of Jesus listening to what he had to say, his disciples sat around waiting for food. It was forbidden in those days for a woman to sit at the feet of a teacher. It is written in the Talmud that it is better for a Jewish father to allow his daughter to go into whoredom than to attempt to teach her Torah. Torah was only for the men. Mary broke this law by sitting adoringly at the feet of Jesus, looking into his eyes and listening with her heart to every thing he had to say. Mary was in the inner circle of Jesus and his disciples. Mary was probably closer to Jesus than any of his disciples. The women with Jesus were on an equal footing with the men. That has all changed. Today, 2000 years later, women are back in the kitchen with Martha while celibate males decide what is best for them. Some things change for only a little bit and then they go back to business as usual.

Another story of hospitality is the story of Abraham and the three strangers who are actually angels of God. Abraham didn't know that they were angels. Abraham was a nomad and greeted anyone immediately as guests. It is interesting in this story that it was Sarah who was listening and it was Abraham who was rushing madly about. Because Abraham was busy doing stuff and Sarah was listening to their guests, Sarah conceived and a year later gave birth to Isaac. She conceived because she wasn't busy. Abraham was into the busy stuff.

In the story of Bernard O'Reagan, his mother did both. She wasn't someone who just made food for this wandering beggar and then spent her time in the kitchen with her pots, she sat down and ate with him and they swapped stories together. That is a different kind of hospitality. In the story with Jesus, it is the same notion. Young Bernard listened to his mother and conceived an extraordinary compassion for the downtrodden and would spend the rest of his life looking out for poor people. Because Mary listened intently to Jesus, she conceived Jesus in her heart and she conceived Christ consciousness in her soul.

With good hospitality something miraculous happens. There is one form of hospitality that attempts to merely address the specific physical needs of someone else. There is another level of hospitality that meets the soul of the guest. In that dialogue, extraordinary things happen. The word of God goes backwards and forwards between us when we meet at that level of hospitality.

There is a saying in Ireland that the way to a man's heart is through his stomach. That may be true, but the real way to a man's soul is through his eyes. When we look deeply at someone and listen and look with our soul, we enter the soul of someone else. That is much more important than merely feeding someone. Martha still had not gotten that. The greatest hospitality of all is to attend to the physical needs of your guests and then listen and connect soul to soul with your guest. Mary managed to do that. Mary conceived Christ consciousness because she sat at the feet of Jesus listening to him. Mary conceived Jesus in her soul while Martha was busy attending to his physical wants.

The song, "I Did it My Way," is the song Jesus heard many times, I did it my way except there was a byline that said, I did it my way, you need to do it my way too. People in the life of Jesus who had done it their way wanted Jesus to not do it his way but to do it their way. The Pharisees' way was the way of law and they wanted Jesus to do things by law. They wanted a model of salvation by law. The zealots, the guerrilla fighters at the time when Simon was a member, were trying to throw the Romans out by force. Their way was violent and they wanted Jesus to do it their way. Essenes, the monks of the desert, wanted to save themselves by being extra pure in their following of Torah. They invited Jesus to do it their way. There have been many historical reenactments of those three productions. Roman Catholic Canon law is the same effort to try to force people into love. You cannot force people into love. You cannot bring people into salvation by imposing laws. Most organizations don't understand this. We still manage to work violence. Throughout Christian history the Crusades, Inquisition and the Conquistadors for instance, tried to brutalize people into God. You can brutalize people into religion but you cannot brutalize them into God.

There is a secular version of that and we call it warfare. We invade Iraq or someplace else and try to brutalize people into capitalistic democracy. You cannot brutalize anyone into taking responsibility for his/her own destiny. The flip side of this is that throughout history we have also tried to abandon people and to leave them to their own devices and go off and save ourselves. You cannot do that either. Abandonment of others is not the path to individual spirituality.

We find Jesus in this extraordinary dance of the spirit between the poles of these three possibilities. On the one hand, Jesus knew that he couldn't force people into loving God while at the same time saying, "I have come, not to abolish the law, but to bring it to fulfillment. Therefore, I tell you; until every letter of the law has been fulfilled it will not pass away." Which laws was he talking about? He was not talking about the 613 man-made precepts. He was talking about the ultimate law of the universe; how the universe works. Not just in its physical manifestation, but most importantly, its underlying mystery, the laws of karma and the laws of love. It is only by bringing ourselves into alignment with that kind of law that spirituality happens. It is a balancing act because there is a need in each community to have some kind of rules of engagement. We do need some kind of rules of conduct. While rules will not save us, they keep us from chaos, but they do not bring us into spirituality. It is only by being in complete alignment with the ultimate law of the universe that true spirituality emerges. Jesus danced an extraordinary dance between the laws and between violence because while he was eschewing physical violence on all occasions he said, "Since the time of John the Baptist, the Kingdom of Heaven is being subject to violence and the violent are taking it." What did he mean by that? He meant the violence of over throwing old ways of thinking and the courage to adopt brand new paradigms. Jesus was moving into the Shiva mode. In Hinduism, Shiva is the destructive aspect of God. Not in the sense that God demolishes and destroys out of anger, but that God is constantly inviting more complex configurations of existing material. Jesus danced the extraordinary dance between complexity on the one hand and entropy on the other. The two great forces of the evolution of the physical universe are entropy on the one hand and complexity on the other. Science teaches that all systems left to their own natural devices run down into chaos. This is the second law of thermo dynamics. How then can more and more complex organisms arise? Ilya Prygogine won a Nobel Prize for his theory of dissipative structures which claims that the system that escapes from entropy comes to a higher order of complexity by dissipating the entropy into the larger system, (Order out of chaos). Jesus was doing precisely that. He was walking an extraordinary line between complexity theory and chaos theory. He realized that salvation is by association. You have to reach out and touch the people who are hungry and who need healing and who need good news. Then you have to draw aside and spend quality time in silence and solitude in the desert of your ego self. That has to be done again and again. That is how spiritual evolution proceeds.

I have a metaphor of the Father aspect of God and the Son aspect of God and the Holy Spirit aspect of God. The Father aspect of the metaphor represents the Isness or the Ultimate Ground of our Being. The Son aspect of God represents God's total self understanding and the Spirit aspect of God represents the love that God has for whom She knows Herself to be. So it is being, knowing self and loving self and the journey back to spirituality is the reverse of that process. It is going from loving to knowing to being. It is a process back to God. If the devolution of God has been from being to knowing to loving so that it participates in human history, the return journey back into God is the reverse of that process. It is first loving so that we may understand and be free to be who we are.

It is a mistake to think that you can only love someone when you know them. The opposite is the case. You can only know someone when you first love him. The first stage back is not knowledge or understanding, it is love. To the extent that I love someone, I can truly know him. If I love someone unconditionally from my soul out then I can understand him from the soul in. The journey back is loving someone so that I may understand him then he is free to be who he really is. We mistake this journey many times. The difficulty about loving is that in order to love I have to really see and this is the difference between prophets and the rest of us. Prophets are not people who prognosticate or foretell the future. The prophet is the one among us who sees very clearly what is. The prophet has learned to listen not just with the eyes and ears of the body, but to listen with the eyes and the ears of the soul.

The followers of Jesus often complained that Jesus always spoke in parables and riddles. They wanted him to speak plainly to them. Jesus answered, "I talk in parables so that seeing you may see and not understand and hearing you may hear and not comprehend." As long as we just look with our eyes and listen with our ears, we will not understand. We have to cause the heart to hear and cause the heart to see. It is only by really seeing and hearing at that level that we can extract the true essence.

162

When we listen to someone merely with our mind or eyes or ears, then we are putting filters on the process. These filters are our fears, expectations, prejudices and pathologies. All we manage to do is to put these blocks in the way. When I really listen with my heart, and see with my soul then I circumvent all of these filters and my soul reaches your soul. If you're speaking from a place of truth or from your soul then my soul recognizes that immediately and remembers that immediately. If you are not speaking from your soul and are only speaking from your ego, my soul will recognize that as well and it will realize that it needs to move on to the next phase.

In order to understand, we need to love and in order to love we need to really listen with our souls. I defy any political or military hawk to look deeply into the eyes and souls of the little Iraqi girls and then order their village to be bombed. It cannot happen. We have to create this distance between us. We use mind to create distances. We use terminology so the "smart bombs" are merely the latest in a long list of lies that we employ in order to put distance between the perpetrators of the violence and the victims of the violence. It is a modern form of idolatry where we attempt to dialogue with people by a meeting of minds rather than a meeting of souls.

There were people in the life of Jesus who merely listened with their ears and saw with their eyes and then there were those people who listened with their souls and heard with their hearts.

Herod met Jesus just as really as Mary met Jesus, but Herod was a jaded human being who merely wanted to be entertained. Herod was only prepared to see Jesus and to listen to Jesus at the level of his physical sensorium and in response Jesus remained silent. The Pharisees were fearful men who wanted to listen to Jesus via the notion of salvation through legislation. They were lost in old ritualistic laws and they attempted to listen to Jesus' message through that filter and it didn't work. The priestly castes, at the time of Jesus, were arrogant men who tried to shore up the oligarchy so they listened through a political agenda. They could not hear him. The crowd, for the main part, was suffering humanity who listened to the words of

Jesus through their own physical hunger and their own physical suffering and that became the filter by which they related to him. Peter was a bumbling serf wanting to be a prince so he listened to Jesus through his own personal ambition. He tried to regulate the teachings of Jesus. On one occasion he said, "God forbid that this should happen to you." Jesus said to him, "Get behind me Satan." No matter how hard Peter tried to understand Jesus nothing happened because he still had not learned to love Jesus.

There is a beautiful story where Jesus appeared to the disciples for the last time. They were fishing and Peter saw Jesus on the shore and jumped into the water and swam to shore and they had breakfast together. Jesus said, "I have one final teaching for you Peter. Peter do you love me"? Peter was shocked by this question because Peter had spent many years trying to understand Jesus. He was expecting the question, do you know who I am. Peter responded, "Yes, I do." Jesus then said, "Peter do you love me?" Peter said, "Yes." Jesus then said, "Peter do you love me?" At that stage Peter got it. Peter had stopped listening with his ears and looking with his eyes and for the first time ever his heart and his soul opened and then he realized that he was in love with Jesus. Only then could he understand who Jesus was and only then could he understand who he, himself, was. Until we truly love, we can't understand. Until I love myself, I do not understand what I am about and I cannot be free to be who I am. Until I love someone else, I cannot understand that person and he is not free to be who he is. That was Peter's filter.

Martha was the proper matron attempting to be the perfect hostess and she listened to Jesus through the filter of propriety and convention and that didn't work. With her hand on Jesus' knee Mary looked through his eyes into his soul and listened with her heart into his heart. Mary is the first person to really hear Jesus. She is the first person to really see Jesus and therefore she is the very first person to really love Jesus. Because she was the first person to love Jesus she is the first person to understand Jesus. Because she understood Jesus, then Jesus was free to be who Jesus was to complete his mission. And Mary was free to be who she was and complete her mission. Among Jesus' disciples, Mary was the first person to put on Christ consciousness. In deed, Mary had chosen the better part.

The "Our Father"

"The spirit is not called me; it is called all of us."

Nikos Kazantzakis

H E WAS WORKING really hard in a little rocky, rain washed, wind swept field behind a stone fence trying to eke out a meager living for himself his wife and eight children when the priest rode up on horseback. It was 1850 in a remote area in the west of Ireland. The priest said, "Hello and God be with you, Patrick." And Patrick replied, "God and Mary be with you father." And the priest said, "The blessing of God on your work." And the farmer said, "The same blessings be on you Father." They continued to chat and the priest looked over the fence and he said, "Between yourself and God, you've made a mighty job of that field." And Patrick said, "Humph, You should have seen it Father when God had it on his own." And the priest said, "It can't be that bad, Patrick, farming can't be that hard." Patrick said, "You have an easy life riding around on your horse all day long just saying your prayers." And the priest said, "You think saying prayers is easy, Pat?" "I know God helps you say prayers, Father." "Okay, I'll put a bet with you. Here's the bargain, if you can say the Our Father for me from beginning to end without getting distracted, I'll give you this horse." "Are you joking me?" "No, I'm deadly serious. If you can go from beginning to end of the Our Father without one distraction, I'll give you this horse." The farmer took off his cap, closed his eyes and he clasped his hands and he said, "Our Father, who are in heaven, hallowed be

166

thy name. Thy kingdom come, thy will … By the way Father, are you throwing the saddle in as part of the bargain?"

The version of the Our Father that comes from Luke's gospel is different from the one that we normally say. The one that we normally say comes from Matthew's account. Both of them divide the Our Father into two main parts. There is the first part which is praise of God and then the second part which is prayer of petition. Matthew has three parts to the prayer of praise: "Our Father who art in heaven, hallowed be your name, your kingdom come, your will be done on Earth as it is in heaven." Luke doesn't say anything about God's will being done. He just says, "Hallowed be your name, your kingdom come." Luke is also missing the petition: "Deliver us from evil." Matthew says, "Give us this day our daily bread and forgive us our trespasses as we forgive those who trespass against us and do not lead us into temptation but deliver us from evil." Where there are seven pieces in Matthew's version there are only five in Luke's. Then the clincher at the end of Matthew's account of the Our Father is that he has Jesus focus only on the phrase, "forgive us our sins as we forgive those who sin against us." In Matthew's account, Jesus goes on to tell a few different parables about how this in fact may be the most important line of the Our Father. If you are reading Luke, he takes a different tack. Luke insists that the main thing about prayer is persistence. There are seven instances of Luke insisting that if we stay on God's case long enough, we get what we want. There are two different versions with different emphases. One has an emphasis on forgiveness and the other is an emphasis on persistence.

I don't believe that God has a will for planet Earth. I am not terribly disturbed that Luke left out the piece about thy will be done on Earth as it is in heaven. I do not believe that the ultimate, ineffable ground of our being has a program in mind for planet Earth and that he is really bent out of shape when it is not happening and he is trying to force us to make it come out the way he wants it. I am totally convinced that when we pray, "thy will be done," what we are going back to is trying to remind ourselves of what I call the preconception

167

contract into which we entered long before we incarnated. I think that we create the agenda for our incarnation experience as a cohort group long before we come onto the planet. We make an agreement with a whole coterie of souls who will inhabit planet Earth at the same time. We have an agreement about how to learn to love and how to learn to forgive and how to learn to be compassionate in this lifetime. That is the will. It is the will of the cohort group who understands compassion and love. That is the will that we want to visit on planet Earth. When we pray, thy will be done, it is not the ineffable ground of our being who has been bent out of shape or insisting on a particular outcome, it is us trying to remind ourselves of the agreement that we entered into before we came onto planet Earth. I'm not particularly upset Luke left out the phrase, "thy will be done on Earth as it is in heaven."

The Our Father, as Matthew and Luke have said, is indeed arranged in two significant parts. The first part is prayer of praise. It is about alignment with God because the essence of all prayer is to bring one's Self into total alignment with God. Prayer is not about forcing God to do my purpose. It is about me coming into total alignment with the ultimate ground of my being. The very first part of the prayer for both Matthew and Luke is the realization that there is no point in going to prayer and just straight up asking for stuff. It is bad manners in the first place. Even if you believe that God was the giver of boons to people who ask, it is very bad manners to say, "I want $5 to go to the movies." If your child came to you and just straight out made a request, you would get upset.

If you are lost in Nairobi, you would never come up to someone and say, "Where is Kenyatta Avenue?" It is extremely bad manners. You would never go up to anyone and make a request of them for information. You first greet them and then you ask them how their children are and how is their home and almost as an afterthought say, by the way could you tell me where Kenyatta Avenue is?

There are many kinds of prayer, i.e., praise, gratitude, thanksgiving, formal, communal and silent prayer etc. To reduce all the many forms of prayer to prayer of petition and then to reduce prayer of petition further to twisting God's arm to one's own pursuit of luxuries is a total misunderstanding of what prayer is about.

The first and most important dimension of prayer is to bring myself into alignment with God by praying, "may your kingdom come, may your will be done, may your name be held holy." It is not that I am praising some kind of transcendent entity who is other to me, but I'm bringing myself into alignment with my core identity. That is the first part of the prayer and then they both go on to the second part and make the petition. But it is interesting to me what Jesus teaches us to ask for after we have brought ourselves into alignment with God. If you take Matthew's version, there are four requests. Three of the four requests have to do with the fact that we are spirits in spacesuits and only one of them has to do with the fact that we are spirits in spacesuits. In other words, only one of them has to do with incarnation and three of them have to do with our spiritual essence. Matthew has Jesus say, "Give us this day our daily bread." Indeed, we are incarnated and we are in spacesuits therefore, we have needs, i.e. physical, emotional, and intellectual and relationship needs: we need to ask for those. We need to ask for those because it is part of our mission. Then we need to realize that we're spirits in these spacesuits and there are basic spirit needs; there is the need about forgiveness, about temptation and about evil.

When Jesus said, "Forgive us our sins as we forgive those who sin against us," of course, he is not speaking in English. He is not even speaking in Hebrew; he is speaking in Aramaic which has been translated into English which in some sense, spiritually speaking, is a very impoverished language. The translation we have in English is totally inadequate. When we say, "forgive us our sins as we forgive those who sin against us," that little word "as" is totally inadequate to the task. I truly learned what forgiveness meant while I was in Africa. I had the opportunity of learning to pray in four different languages. What I learned in Swahili meant, forgive us our sins in exactly the same fashion that we forgive those who sin against us. It is not that

God is some kind of cosmic CPA who is keeping score. It is the realization that only to the extent that I can forgive and only to the extent that I can love, only to that extent can I experience forgiveness and only to that extent can I feel loved. Not in a quid pro quo fashion, but who I become will determine what I allow in and what I put out. Therefore, to the extent that I can offer forgiveness and only to that extent can I accept forgiveness. To the extent that I can love and only to that extent can I experience love.

In another language, Kipsigis, it was totally different. In this language the word for forgiveness comes from their greeting. When Kipsigis people meet on the road there is a ritual that goes, "Hello, do you love yourself? Does your wife love herself? Do your children love themselves? Do your cattle love themselves?" From the 1880's on when the agricultural revolution hit Africa I would then have to ask, "Does your maize love itself?" This is like a linguistic incarnation of a mystical insight. It's trapped in the very language itself; encapsulated in the very words spoken is the understanding that true spirituality consists in being in total alignment with Self; not with ego, but with Self, the God within. The world, when it is at peace, is in alignment with God. Then they would use that very same phrase: forgiveness means "Come and greet me." Come and ask me if I am in alignment with my Self, the God within. Forgiveness is not about dispensing largesse to other people. It is about bringing my Self into total alignment and wishing for you and all that is yours to be in total alignment. That is my understanding of the phrase, "forgive us our sins as we forgive those who sin against us."

Jesus goes further in saying, "do not lead us into temptation." It seems a strange thing to ask of God. Why would God even think about leading us into temptation? My understanding of that is this. It is reminding ourselves not to bite off more than we can chew. Lead us not into temptation is a reminder to myself during my lifetime that I shouldn't attempt to bite off more than I can chew and get myself into trouble. More importantly, it is a reminder of the time when I was scripting my next lifetime in the state between lifetimes. When I and my cohort group, mentor figures and angelic advisors were creating a drama for my next lifetime, I would often forget how tough it is on planet Earth, the boot camp of the galaxy. I would create these grandiose scripts that would call for me to be born in a handicapped body in a poor part of the world and I would think that I was going to make great progress with that script. They would tell me, "Back up a little bit. You don't remember how hard it is." This prayer is a reminder to ourselves not to create unrealistic scripts between lifetimes and not to create unrealistic expectations of our spiritual journey in this lifetime. This is not to say we must not dream our dreams and stretch ourselves, but at the same time not to be too unrealistic in pursuit of spirituality. The ego can hijack any human activity including the quest for spirituality.

When I look at the phrase, "deliver us from evil," I must ask myself, what is evil about? I have three different ideas on what evil is. I think that there are many dimensions to these universes of ours and in particular there is an astral plane to our universe. It is a place that is divided into two subsections: a lower astral plane and a higher astral plane. The higher astral plane is the place of angelic beings and ascended masters. In the lower astral plane are less evolved beings some of whom are still wrapped in their own selfishness and their own egocentricity. They are disincarnate and they are quite powerful and some of the evil comes from messing in that realm without knowing what one is getting into.

A second part of the evil is what I call projected shadow. We know that in interpersonal relationships much of the difficulty that arises between us is because in you I see parts of myself that I don't recognize as being in me and because I can't see them in myself, I project them onto you and then I beat up on you for having these qualities. We do this not just as individuals, but we do this as communities, as nations, and even as a species, homo sapiens. This projected shadow material of the entire species becomes an energy force in our interactions with each other and with the planet.

The third understanding of evil is the notion of the illusion of separate identity: we are all different and separated by gender, ethnicity, socio-economic status, IQ, and education. The worst part is when we apply it to intercultural activity and we create a God who is a partisan God. We create a God who is on our side and is pursuing our particular political or economic agenda. When we have sunk into the abyss of separate identity as cultures not just as individuals within the culture, that is as low as it gets: that is real evil.

In 1992, I had the privilege of conducting what was at that stage the largest, clinical, randomized, controlled double-blinded prayer experiment. Since then it has been surpassed by a group at Duke University. It was a prayer study where we brought in 496 people, 90 of whom were going to do the praying and 406 who were going to be prayed for. We divided the prayer groups into two sections. One group was to pray in a directed prayer fashion and one group was to pray in a non directed prayer fashion. The 406 subjects were randomly assigned to one of three conditions; a control group which was not prayed for during the course of the experiment and two experimental groups one of which was prayed for by directed prayer and the other by non directed prayer. No one knew which group anyone was in. We pre-tested everyone on a host of psychological parameters particularly self esteem, anxiety and depression levels and three months later, retested them on the same parameters as well as how they physically improved or how their creativity developed. The prayer experiment went on for 15 minutes every day for twelve weeks. I gave everyone doing the praying a sheet with nine photographs and the names of the people for whom they were to pray and they were to keep a log of their prayer. I collated all of those so that I knew to within a quarter of an hour how much prayer each person had done and how much prayer each person had received. At the end we analyzed the data. Some interesting results came out.

The first result was that there was a significant improvement both for those doing the praying and for those being prayed for. In fact, there was a bigger improvement in the people doing the praying than

172

in the people being prayed for. People who prayed over the 12-week period experienced a greater increase in self esteem, and a greater reduction in depression and anxiety than the people being prayed for. One question I asked of everyone was: "When God acts in your life do you think that God acts from the inside out or from the outside in or both; or you don't believe in God or you have no idea how it works?" I correlated the responses to that question with what happened to the self esteem, anxiety and depression levels of the participants. The people who believed that God acted from within or people who believed that God acted both within and without had the most improvement. For the people who believed that God acted only from the outside, there was very little change and the other two groups didn't experience change at all.

I also asked people, "Do you believe in the power of prayer for others? When you pray for other people do you think it works, doesn't work or you have no idea?" I collated the responses to those questions and the result was that for those who believed that prayer worked, it worked. When they didn't believe that prayer would work, it didn't work. Then I asked people who had no idea which group they were in: "Which group do you think that you were actually in? Do you think you were in the experimental group or in the control group?" For those who replied that they thought they were in the control group, nothing happened for them. For those who thought they were in the experiment group, whether they were or not, improved significantly.

Finally, since I knew within a quarter of an hour exactly how much prayer each individual had offered and how much prayer each one received I found out that as far as those being prayed for, the amount of prayer did not matter. There was no correlation between how much prayer each individual received and how much improvement was experienced. But there was significant correlation for those who were doing the praying. The more prayer done, the more improvement experienced. That was some of the very interesting information that came out of this experiment.

I began looking for models that could explain this. How does it look? I came up with a few different models. The first model is the placebo effect. You could say, for instance, if you really believe in God and God is omniscient and knows the final outcome, then prayer of petition is merely chatting about the inevitable and it doesn't work because God has already factored your prayer in even before you prayed and he has decided on the outcome and therefore praying is a waste of time, but I don't believe that is a good interpretation of the results.

A second model is what I call the satellite dish. It is as if I'm going to pray for someone who lives at the other side of the world and, because of the curvature of the Earth, I can't beam my prayer straight at him so I have to hit this satellite dish in the sky that I call God and God is going to redirect my prayer down to that someone. I don't believe that that is how it works either.

Then there is the great model of Moses. I call it the Mosaic model. It is the notion that there is some kind of trick and if you can figure out what the trick is you can get it to work every time. There is a story of Moses shortly after the children of Israel had escaped from slavery into Egypt and were wandering in the desert. They came across a tribe called the Amalekites and go into battle. Moses went up on the hill and prayed to God, "God, please, please give victory to the Israelites." And as long as he could keep his arms in the air the Israelites were winning. But his arms began to get tired and droop and as they did, the Amalekites began to win. Two of Moses' friends noticed this and they propped up his arms and the Israelites won. There are versions of this in all religions.

In the Catholic religion, it's the nine first Fridays. You can go to mass and communion on the first Friday for nine consecutive months and say an "Our Father," a "Hail Mary," and a "Glory Be to the Father" for the Pope's intentions and you are in like Flynn; you will go to heaven! God can't stop you. You can have a ball for the rest of your life as long as you do these nine first Fridays. The Buddhists' version for that are prayer flags. If you don't have time to meditate and pray, you can put flags in the wind and as they flap in the wind they are praying for you and you can continue with your business. The Islamic version is a trip to Mecca. Go to Mecca once in your life and God will take you into heaven no matter what you do for the rest of it. There is a version of this in every religion.

Another model is Abraham bargaining with God. Abraham pleaded with God for the fate of Sodom and Gomorrah after God vowed, "I'm going to wipe out the good people with the bad people." Even the notion that God had to come down to Earth to verify for Himself whether the stories He was hearing were true or not is ridiculous. How anthropomorphic can you get if you think that the omniscient, ineffable ground of our being had to come down to check if these stories were accurate! The stories apparently were true, terrible things were happening there and God decided to wipe out the two cities. So Abraham said, "Suppose there are 50 good people. Are you going to kill 50 good people?" And God said, "Okay if there are 50 good guys, I won't do it." And Abraham said, "Suppose there are 5 less than 50 suppose there are only 40 or 30 or 20 or only 10?" He kept bargaining God down, down and down. And God said, "That's my last offer. If you find 10 good people for me, I'll save the two cities." As it transpired there were not 10 good people and God wiped them out anyway.

The same model can be found in Luke. Luke emphasized the persistence of prayer except Abraham did it like a business trader and Luke did it like a nag. Luke said, "Keep nagging at God and you'll finally wear him down. It's not bargaining down; it's just nagging. You don't have to offer him any bargain at all just stay in his face and finally if you keep knocking at his door he'll get up and give in to you."

We think that if we stay in God's face long enough we can get our national agenda visited on planet Earth. In the old days, God was a monarch with whom you could bargain in your typical Middle Eastern fashion. Now we regard God as a cosmic CEO who blesses rampant capitalism and the World Bank, the I.M.F. sweat shops and child labor. It's just a modern version of the same thing.

I don't believe in any of these models of prayer. If I were to use a metaphor for how prayer works, it seems to me that the best metaphor would be a sprinkler system in a lawn. You have a large underground network of pipes all connected to a central faucet. What is coming through the faucet is water which is the grace of God or love. It is permeating the entire system and there are particular nodules all over the lawn which have been spaced to nourish the lawn. If one of these gets stuck or congested, then a large area of the lawn gets desiccated. Every single one of us is such a nodule. You are made to be sprinklers in the lawn of God's existence. We are made to be dispersing this water of love and compassion, but when we are congested, (and we get congested mainly through not forgiving,) there is an entire area of lawn that gets desiccated. In some sense, God has nothing to do with the process of who gets saved or forgiven. It is up to me. Am I dispensing water from my nodule? Is the area around me green with the love of my compassion or is it desiccated through my hardness of heart? Therefore, I come down very heavily on the side of Matthew rather than Luke with his emphasis on forgiveness over persistence. This is the most important aspect of it. This is the key to the whole thing. This is how prayer works. It is not some distant God bending to my purposes and ultimately granting my requests. It is the inner divinity in every one of us being freed up by our forgiveness and our compassion to sprinkle the lawn of the human experience.

All prayer requests are granted, but not all prayer requests are successful. What do I mean by that? Who grants prayer requests? Not God. God is not intervening and changing the intended outcome to satisfy the prayers of the persistent. That is not how it works. We grant our own prayer. That is how prayer works. We have to be very careful about what we pray for because every request is going to be granted, but not every request is going to be successful. There are consequences to every outcome. If I pray for something, I have to deal with getting that thing and the consequences of getting it. If I pray that I win the Lotto and finally I win the Lotto, then everyone wants to be my friend and I wonder if it is only because I won the Lotto. I wonder if they would be my friends if I was poverty stricken. I haven't heard from some friends for years and now all of a sudden I get emails from them. Did they hear that I won the Lotto? I start getting paranoid and I lose all my friends. There is a consequence of getting my request granted. It was granted, but it wasn't successful. It didn't turn me into a loving person. There are always consequences to having prayers granted. What is successful prayer as distinct from prayer being granted? Successful prayer is that which aligns me with God.

In fundamentalist Christianity, at the end of every request you tie on this magic formula, "In Jesus' name I pray," as if somehow it is a computer password that allows me to hack into God's program.

The Catholic version is, "This we ask through Christ our Lord." Unfortunately, very often the Church doesn't understand what this means. The church thinks when you end a prayer by saying, "This we ask through Christ our Lord," you are regarding Jesus as a mediator or a intercessor between the ineffable ground of our being and us and that is not how it works. These two phrases properly understood mean the following: "In Jesus' name we pray" and "this we ask through Christ our Lord," only have meaning if what they do for me is bring me into Christ consciousness; the same kind of relationship to the father and the same understanding of my own inner divinity. When I get in that space and I am in alignment and then I pray, I will only ask for what is good. I'm not going to be asking for stupid egotistical things. I will ask for that which makes me a very adequate sprinkler on God's lawn. Praying in "Jesus' name" and finishing our prayers through, "Christ our Lord," has nothing to do with tacking on a formula to an intercession. It has everything to do with coming into alignment with my own divinity so that I too can be a freed sprinkler on the lawn of God's love.

WHAT DOES THE ASSUMPTION
OF MARY MEAN?

"It is my belief, for the world in general, that compassion is more important than religion."

Dalai Lama

RYAN O'CONNOR IS four years old and he is a mystic and like all mystics, he remembers. One day Ryan declared to his Daddy, "Daddy, you know a long time ago before I was born I came down here to check you and Mommy out to see if I wanted to be part of this family." Ryan's father was astounded.

Is mysticism merely a naïve throwback to the infancy of our species? Or is mysticism the prototype of where the species is meant to be headed? When we celebrate the Feast of the Assumption, is this a meaningless myth? Is it merely a metaphor or is it a mystery? What does mystery mean? Is mystery something that cannot be understood? Or is mystery something that cannot be understood by the mind, but can be understood by the soul? If the soul understands the mystery, subsequently the mind can attempt to make sense of it. But the mind, left to its own devices, cannot understand mystery. What does the Assumption of Mary into heaven really mean? The 15th of August has been celebrated since the fifth century as the assumption of Mary in the Eastern and Western churches. The church teaches that Mary went to heaven, body and soul.

Have you ever wondered how you can take a huge tree in the forest, use a chain saw, cut it down, chop it up into pieces, break it into firewood and then burn it and all you are left with from this huge tree is a few buckets of ashes. What happened? What happened, of course, is that the vast bulk of the tree is carbon that comes directly from sunlight. When you burn the tree, you shrink its volume and weight enormously because the bulk of the tree goes back as light and heat. You have reduced this extraordinary thing to a few buckets of ashes. Because the vast bulk of the tree wasn't stuff at all; it was light and heat.

What happens when you cremate a human body? You take 160 pounds of human being, cremate it, and you get about 15 pounds of ashes. Why is this? The why, of course, is that we are not stuff. All life on planet Earth comes from sunlight. It comes in one of three guises. First, the planet is literally a spin-off that was gestated by the sun 4.5 billion years ago. All the nine planets in our solar system are all chunks of the sun. Literally, everything on the planet came from the sun originally. Over the next 4.5 billion years the sun has continued to interact with us through light enhancing all the life forms that began to develop on the planet. Having birthed us, it has continued to be the source of our life. Moreover, information theory tells us that sunlight continues to help the evolutionary process of the planet. Carl Sagan estimated at one time that if you take all the information in all of the archives and libraries on planet Earth and reduce it to bites it would total 10 to the power of 17 bites of information. That is a lot of information. But there are 10 to the power of 21 bites of information beamed onto planet Earth every five minutes by sunlight. Some evolutionary biologists think that part of what is happening in our evolution and part of the reason that there are these quantum leaps in evolution on our planet is that the sun continues to act as a medium for incoming information that is necessary to complete the jigsaw of evolution. So the sun not only birthed us 4.5 billion years ago, not only has it continued to sustain life on the planet in the interim, but it is sending these snippets of a jigsaw puzzle to allow the process to continue to unfold. All life on the planet comes from light.

In fact, the universe in which we live is one million parts of light to one part matter. Matter is a minor contaminant in the universe of light. There are about 10^{38} photons of light in the human body. If we had some way of releasing those photons there is enough light in the human body to light up a baseball stadium at one million watts for three and a half hours. We are basically beams of light. Dying is merely the shrinking process until we get down to our core essence. I call it dying in order to down-size.

What might science say about the assumption of Mary into heaven? It seems to me that when we come on to the planet every one of us comes on with an exit and recycling strategy. For most of us our exit strategy is disease or accident. Every one of us has an exit strategy that is one of these two modalities. Secondly, we have figured out what our recycling strategy is going to be. Having exited, what are we going to do with this spacesuit? We have one or two recycle strategies for our space suits. One of them is cremation. Cremation is faster for this reason: in cremation we give back directly to the sun what we took directly from the sun and we give back indirectly what we took indirectly from the sun. A lot of our life comes directly from sunlight and then a lot of it comes indirectly through the nutrients that the sun helped grow and we take in as our food supply.

Our second recycling strategy is burial. Burial is much slower. In burial, we give back to the sun indirectly everything that we got from it. That which we get directly and indirectly we give back to the sun indirectly. It takes much longer because the Earth's metabolism is much slower than the sun's metabolism. It takes the Earth much longer to metabolize the same information. Basically we have all of these strategies.

There are stories throughout human history of sages, extraordinary individuals who manage to have a different exit strategy and a different recycling strategy. There are stories in mystical literature of great sages in all the great world religions from Buddhism, Hinduism, Islam and Christianity who didn't need an exit strategy of disease or accident in order to let go. They were people who could literally sit down in the lotus position and meditate mindfully and release their spirit and abandon their spacesuit. So the exit strategy is very different in that instance. It didn't take death through disease or accident; it merely took mindfully letting go. There are stories that in some of these cases the spacesuit managed to be preserved. There are cases in Catholic tradition where there are still bodies extant after hundreds of years after the entities have left. Their recycling strategy was different.

Then there are stories in the Buddhist tradition, particularly from Tibet, of great Bodhisattvas who sit in the lotus position and meditate and then release their spirits and suddenly all that is left is what they call a rainbow body; no body, colored light is all that is seen.

Then there is the story of the burial wrapping of Jesus, now known as the Shroud of Turin; how do you account for the impregnating of the image of Jesus on this garment? Was this the combustion of an extraordinary light source? Was Jesus releasing his protons so fast that they burned his image onto this cloth? Where was the body? It appeared that the body was gone. Great sages have a different exit strategy and they have a different recycling method. Why might this be? It might be that physical life is merely a hard-copy of on-line, continuously edited programs created by cosmic consciousness and mediated by light. The operating system is light. The creative consciousness of the cosmos is behind it and every one of us is merely a hard-copy of the ongoing, on-line programs which cosmic consciousness is constantly editing and adapting.

What is birth? Is it merely that the "programmer" has hit the print command. What happens with twins: someone hits print twice and you have two copies? What happens when we die: someone hits the delete button? What happens at a near death experience: someone hits the delete button and then hits the undo edit button? What happens in reincarnation: someone hits change the format and re-print button? Every one of us, in a sense, is merely a hard-copy of the extraordinary on-line programs created by a cosmic consciousness and mediated by light. If that is the science behind it, what then might have happened when Jesus rose from the dead or when Mary allegedly was assumed into heaven? If they took their physical bodies with them it must mean that heaven is an actual location in this space-time continuum, and maybe it is. The cosmos is certainly big enough for such a place to exist. Maybe that is what it is. It is much more likely however, that the assumption into heaven of Jesus or Mary was the ability of these extraordinary sages to hit the delete on the hard-copy but to save the original on-line version. What is then happening is that they are just releasing the spacesuit back into a light body and disappearing as pure light and the soul is released to be back in the on-line program. Maybe that is what it comes to.

When someone has a vision, it seems that one of three things may happen. Either some over-active imagination in some gullible human being is dreaming up the vision; that is one possibility. The other possibility, for instance, in an apparition of Mary, is that this entity that was known as Mary, the mother of Jesus, chose to appear to someone, and for the purpose of the appearance, manifests a spacesuit in order to be recognized by the one having the vision. Why not? Or it may be that Mary or Jesus or anyone else appears on a non-physical plane in the soul of the visionary and for all its non-physicality it is no less real. The problem that happens is this: all visionaries are human beings and have to unpack their experience. They have to bio-physiologically mediate the experience and thus it will pass through a lot of filters, some of them biochemical, some physiological, some cultural, some theological and some pathological. Visions are difficult to explain because they have to be articulated in language and language is a notoriously leaky vessel to express any kind of a mystical experience. No articulation of a vision is ever going to be absolute truth. It will always be mediated through the person who is having the vision.

What was Mary's mission? I'm convinced that 2000 years ago Mary, mother of Jesus, made a preconception contract with an entity who would be known as Jesus and an entity who would be known as Joseph and an entity who would be known as Mary Magdalene and twelve other entities who would be known as the disciples of Jesus and countless others who are lesser known beings.

Mary made a preconception contract to come onto planet Earth to create a drama to introduce Christ consciousness into the evolution of our species. Mary and her cohort group got off to a brilliant start but within 100 years the effort got hijacked by orthodox religion and within 300 years it had been further hijacked by the political agenda. It had to go underground and it has continued to bubble through the great religions as the mystical core of all the great religions. It is waiting for a time when a critical mass will be reached or when enough of us wake up enough to remember our own preconception contracts so that by embracing this reality the planet itself will make a shift. And then, for the first time ever, planet Earth will have fulfilled its destiny of throwing up a species capable of recognizing its own divinity and living from its own divinity. Then planet Earth will graduate and move to the next level, a fifth dimension level. It will subsequently attract only those souls who are prepared to live at that level and at the Christ conscious level. The rest of us will have to find other planets on which to reincarnate so we can continue to indulge our illusions of separate identity, religious affiliations and national identity.

I am convinced that these great souls known as Jesus, Mary, Joseph, Mary Magdalene, Peter and all the rest have come back onto this planet many times. They continue to be the yeast allowing this mystical movement to continue to bubble up onto the planet. They have always been held under suspicion and they have always been persecuted because the truth is that within every religious tradition these people are dangerous. Within the Christian tradition, the followers of Jesus have always persecuted the followers of Christ. Those who are stuck in their intolerant exclusive, fundamentalist Christianity will always continue to persecute people who are aiming at Christ consciousness. But the job must go on. If we really honor Mary, the honoring of Mary is not about pilgrimages to Lourdes and it's not about saying the rosary daily. It is by attempting to put on the same kind of

Christ consciousness that she came to initiate on planet Earth. When Mary had the encounter with the angel in which she said, "May your will be done," for the first time ever her amnesia was rolled back and she remembered why she had come. With that mantra, "May your will be done," the extraordinary drama of the Christ event began to unfold.

It is hypocritical and futile to claim that we honor Mary when we continue to ignore her message. It is hypocritical to continue to embrace religions that discriminate against women so that women have no ministry in the unfolding drama of creating Christ consciousness on the planet. To claim that we are honoring Mary when we indulge in that kind of religious intolerance is hypocritical and meaningless to me. To continue to claim that we can build basilicas to Mary or say rosaries in her honor while espousing a narrow identity of nationalism or affiliation with particular ethnic groups is to totally miss the message of Mary. When I have finally managed to dissolve the body of my prejudices, then I too, like Mary, will have been assumed into the heavens of the light body of Christ consciousness.

THE BANQUET OF GOD'S LARGESS
FOR PLANET EARTH

"The whole world is held in the embrace of the God of unconditional love."

Diarmuid O'Murchu

EVERY OCTOBER THEY meet for five days in San Rafael, California. They look to nature to find clues as to how we can solve our problems. They call themselves the Bioneers. They bring highly disciplined scientists in agriculture, psychology, physics, consciousness studies, etc. from all over the world to brainstorm together. Some extraordinarily inspiring stories come out of these meetings and occasionally some very upsetting stories.

For instance, last year a farmer from Canada told a story that was really upsetting. This man has a little farm that is completely organic; he grows produce without any insecticides of any kind. A few years ago Monsanto, one of the five great food organizations on the planet, bought a large piece of land around his farm. They planted genetically modified food in their fields. Over time, the wind blew seeds into this man's farm and contaminated his organic produce. Monsanto took him to court and sued him for "stealing its technology." The worst news is that they won. The lower court agreed that this organic farmer had "stolen" the technology from Monsanto. It has since gone to a higher court.

The equivalent of that would be if you were a non-smoker all your life and you contracted cancer through second-hand smoke and the Reynolds Tobacco Company sued you for stealing its nicotine.

There has been a weapon of mass destruction on this planet for about 5000 years. This is the oldest weapon of mass destruction we have created. It all happened about the year 3000 B.C., with the agricultural revolution. There were two great breakthroughs in technology; the ox-drawn plough and glazed pottery. The pottery made it possible to store food without water spoilage or rodent infestation. We were able to produce and store food in large quantities. We no longer had to struggle on a daily bases to provide food for ourselves. But now, for the first time, food could be hoarded or hijacked. The people controlling the food supplies controlled the group. In this way they could use food to destroy their enemies. All they had to do when they marched into another culture was to burn their grain supplies. At home, they could dole out food to those who believed in their policies. For the first time in human history this weapon of mass destruction was created and has been used very successfully ever since.

I have pretty much divided my life into two parts. The first 26 years I lived in third world countries; Ireland, in my youth, was a third world country. Then for 14 years I lived in Kenya which is also a third would country. And for the last 17 years I've lived in the United States which is definitely a first-world country. When I look at the third world countries, two things strike me about food: the extraordinary generosity of the poor and the extraordinary naiveté of the poor. When guests come for a visit in any third world country, people share from their meager sources almost all they have with their guests. The second thing is that paired with this extraordinary naiveté they believe whatever you tell them. One day, I watched in horror as a young Kenyan mother came into our village with 12 eggs. She sold the eggs and bought a bottle of Cocoa Cola to feed to her child who was suffering from malnutrition. She did this because a local advertisement claimed that "Cocoa Cola brings you health and energy;" and she believed it. It was written in the printed word and therefore it had to be true. That is an example of the third world naiveté coupled with extraordinary generosity. My experience of leadership in first-world countries is that its two great traits are hypocrisy and cunning.

Many of the great food producing companies like Monsanto would like us to believe that they are developing the kind of technology in agriculture that will feed the ever burgeoning human population. Nothing could be further from the truth. There is no need for better technology to provide more and more food faster and faster. There is more than enough food on the planet right now to set a banquet three times a day in front of every human being on the planet. It is not a question of producing more food; it is a question of how we distribute the food that we have. There are mountains of butter and lakes of milk that have been held under lock and key in order to artificially inflate the prices of these commodities on the world market. This extraordinary hypocrisy and cunning of the West allows us to pretend that we are really out to make more and more food available to more and more people on the planet. It is not true and it has never been true.

I read a book by a brilliant Indian woman, Vandana Shiva. She has a reputation as a great physicist, but about 20 years ago she left her science in order to devote herself to the plight of the women of India who are being brow-beaten by great multi-national corporations in their food production. In her book, she quotes a statement from a large corporation: "Weeds are stealing sunlight from us and therefore the weeds have to be blasted with some chemical that will devastate everything." The man making this statement was not concerned that food was being taken out of the mouths of the starving masses. He was primarily thinking that dollars were being taken out of the pockets of the multi-millionaires: that was his chief concern. Groups like Monsanto are managing to starve the masses more and more effectively. They are creating technology and they are creating agreements with the government that make it illegal for local farmers to harvest their crops and use the seeds from last year's crop to produce the seeds for next year's crop. A seed technology that has taken India 10,000 painstaking years of research and painstaking farming evolution to produce is now patented by Monsanto. If you want to set the seed, you have to buy it from Monsanto.

One story in the documentary, "The Corporation," is about a town of 10,000 people in Guatemala whose water supply was totally polluted. The government invited the Bechtel Corporation to come in and clean up the water supply. Bechtel agreed on condition that thereafter all of the water of this town would belong to Bechtel and therefore it would be illegal under this agreement for a householder in this city to put a bucket outside the door and trap the rainwater because all the water in the town belonged to Bechtel. It led to riots and finally it lead to the overthrow of the government. This is the banquet, allegedly, at which we are all sitting as equal partners in God's sight.

When I look at the teaching of Jesus, the parable that most upsets me is a parable in which he talks about a man who owed his master a lot of money and because he couldn't pay his debt to the master, the master threw the man, his wife and children in jail until he paid the last penny. Is this what Jesus is advocating? Is Jesus saying that this is how God deals with us or is Jesus, as a social commentator, saying this is what happens in human society? Increasingly, a man, his wife and his children are being thrown into jail. In some instances, entire communities are being thrown into jails in order to squeeze from them the last penny to fill the coffers of the multi-national corporations. It is true and it continues to happen and we brand anyone that objects as an agitator.

The very famous and saintly, Cardinal Archbishop Dom Helder Camara of Sao Paulo, said at one stage, "When I give food to the poor, they call me a saint. When I ask why is it that the poor do not have food? They call me a communist." Food is the oldest weapon of mass destruction on planet Earth.

When I look at what has happened to food production on our planet over the last 10,000 years, I see that more and more we are beginning to impregnate the entire process with some horrific practices. I see mass doses of pesticides used for the production of vegetables and I see that animals are conceived and birthed and raised in the most horrendous of circumstances and then slaughtered in a torturous fashion. I also see that our food is mindlessly harvested in huge masses, cooked and served without any kind of blessing or any kind of intention. We also eat our food with this same lack of intention. How many of us even bother to bless the food before we eat or to think about where it came from? The carbon, hydrogen, oxygen and the nitrogen of which our bodies are composed we get from our foodstuff, so physically we are what we eat.

Sociologically we are those with whom we eat. Anthropologists did a study of people's eating habits. They looked at how, with whom, and when people eat and they said that you can tell everything you need to know about people just by looking at their eating habits. They claim that this tells us the basic set up of the entire culture.

Psycho-spiritually we are how we eat. The mind-set, mindfulness and awareness which we bring to our eating are most important; that is who we become psycho-spiritually. If I can bring gratitude, mindfulness and awareness to my eating because I see it is the final stage in a long process that literally involves the entire globe, I will eat my food in a totally different fashion. If I plunk down in front of the TV while mindlessly stuffing my face with French fries, then psycho-spiritually I'm a big zero.

Are we cursing or blessing the land? In older societies, every phase of this process was blessed. When seeds were sown into the ground, there were big blessing rituals. There were mindful intentions that went into the sowing of the seeds. The seeds were mindfully watched as they grew and mindfully weeded thus aiding God in the process of evolving the next food stuff. There were mindful, prayerful rituals around the harvesting of food. There were mindful, prayerful rituals around the cooking, serving and eating of food. Most of that seems to have gone by the wayside. Today, at no stage of the process is food impregnated with prayer.

There was an experiment done in a city in Belgium about 15 years ago to celebrate its 1000 year anniversary as a chartered city. The city fathers commissioned a musician to write some music for the occasion. Instead of writing music the musician decided to invite a few bakers, divide them randomly into two groups and have them bake enough buns so that everyone who came to the celebration got two buns. The only difference in the two buns was that half of the buns had a symbolic O and the other half had a symbolic triangle shape. One group of bakers was asked to chant over and bless the food as they were baking it and the other bakers were told to make the buns without the chanting and blessing. As people came to the celebration they were given two different buns and invited to eat them. Then they were asked to tell which bun they enjoyed most. With statistical significance the buns that had been prayed over tasted much better to people. Food is not just the physical and chemical ingredients. It is the energy with which it gets impregnated in the process of sowing, growing, harvesting, cooking, serving and eating. All of these are part of the process.

Was Jesus obsessed with food? Either Jesus was anorexic or bulimic or he was a wannabe Yiddish speaking bubbe who kept telling everyone, "Eat, eat, eat my child." So much of what Jesus had to say was about food. His parables are constantly about sowing, weeding, harvesting, cooking, eating and having banquets. At one time, Jesus was having breakfast on the lake at Galilee and at another time there was a huge feast for 4,000 people. Jesus frequently talked about food. Why did he speak so much about food? For Jesus, food was the widest cultural articulation of the symbol of inclusivity or exclusivity for his time. Table fellowship was the ultimate criterion of inclusivity for the times in which Jesus lived. Table fellowship was used to discriminate against the sinners and to invite in the like-minded. Jesus was at pains to point out that every one of us by birthright is equally beloved of God. Every one of us is called with equal affection and love by the God who is the Father of all of us. When the time came for Jesus to let go and to die, the final symbol he gave us was of the motherhood of God. It was the symbol of feeding us from his own body; we call it Eucharist; the essence of Jesus.

When you find Eucharist mentioned in the New Testament there is always a key. There are four sacred code words that go with it.

Whatever the context, whether there were 5000 people involved or a little group of seven at the lake of Galilee, when you find the words "He took, he broke, he blessed and he gave," you are always talking about Eucharist. What do they mean? When he took the food it was the grateful acceptance from God of the gift of food. Then he broke it and breaking food was the intention to share. The intention comes before the practice. It is the intention that of its essence; food is meant to be shared. It is broken to symbolize that it is for more than just one. The third part is that he blessed the food. We constantly misunderstand what this means. It is not that Jesus was taking an inert substance called food and blessing it or breathing God into it. The blessing of food is the recognition of its inherent blessedness. It is God's way of gifting us. We don't bless food by putting into it what was not there before; we bless food by recognizing what is in it before we receive it. Then we share our food. Having had the intention to share, we now actually share our food. This is what Eucharist represented for Jesus. It was the ultimate weapon of inclusivity; a banquet table to which everyone was invited without any discrimination.

What have we done with it? We have used Eucharist as the ultimate weapon of discrimination. In the Roman Catholic tradition, if you are gay you may not receive with us. If you are divorced and remarried, you may not receive with us. If you are not an orthodox Roman Catholic, you may not receive with us. We have taken the ultimate weapon of inclusivity and turned it into the ultimate weapon of discrimination. Not only that, we have the nerve to extend it into the afterlife. It is not bad enough that we will say in our churches you cannot come to the table of the Lord if you are gay, divorced, or not Roman Catholic, but not only that, at the heavenly banquet you will also be denied participation because heaven is only for Catholics who are straight or never divorced.

On behalf of Jesus, I say to you straight, never-divorced Roman Catholics, move over and make room for the gays, the divorced and the "separated brethren" who are just as beloved of God as you are.

WHAT DOES THE CROSS MEAN
IN CHRISTIAN COSMOLOGY

"Happiness comes from the Self and can be found in the Self only. Find your real Self and all else will come with it."

Sri Nisargadatta

H E WAS UTTERLY incorrigible. They couldn't bribe, threaten or cajole him. He was a very bright fifth-grade child who refused to work at school and was failing in every subject, especially mathematics. This little Jewish boy was very much loved by his parents. They tried their best to persuade him in every way they could to apply himself at school, but he wouldn't. He was put in several different schools. He went to public, private and remedial schools and continued to fail. They sent him to the East Coast Academy for Young Gentlemen and he failed. Finally, in desperation, although they were Jewish, they put him in a Catholic school run by nuns. He returned home the first day from school, went straight into his room studied furiously for three hours, came out at dinner time took some food and went back and studied for four more hours. This went on for the entire first week of school. Finally, on Friday, at the Shabbat meal his father said to him, "I'm really impressed and very happy with what you are doing, but what is so different about this school? Why are you applying yourself in this school when you didn't apply yourself in the other schools? The boy said, "Are you serious? The people in charge of this school, the nuns, they are ferocious. They don't make idle threats. Every classroom has this huge color photo of another Jewish kid who was nailed to a plus sign."

Jesus said that unless you get nailed to a plus sign you can't be my disciple. What did Jesus mean by being nailed to a plus sign? What does the cross mean in Christian cosmology? What is the connection between wisdom and the cross?

When Jesus said, "Unless you are prepared to carry your cross, you cannot be my disciple," what do you think he had in mind? Two thousand years later it is very difficult for us to figure out what he meant when he said; you have to carry your cross. Crucifixion is probably the single most disgusting execution method every devised by human beings. It was devised by the Romans many years before Jesus and it was in use at the time of Jesus. There were two forms of crucifixion. One form had a seat on the cross for the criminal to sit on as he hung on the cross and this allowed him to die slowly from dehydration and exhaustion over a period of about seven days. There was another form without the seat so the person would hang with pressure on his hands or on his feet. When the pressure on the feet got to be too much, then he would hang from his hands and then his chest would get constricted and he couldn't breathe. That is a very cruel way of killing someone.

Is Jesus advocating this kind of death for all of us? Is he so pessimistic about life that he is suggesting that this is what life involves? Two thousand years of Christian misrepresentation has painted Jesus as advocating that everyone has to take this cross on his/her shoulder, proceed to Golgotha and get crucified. It has nothing to do with that.

This is not an injunction to a masochistic addiction to pain and suffering. Rather, it is the embrace of the total human experience. It is only tangentially related to suffering. Of course, life sometimes involves suffering as it also involves successes and joys of various kinds. In any human lifetime there will be good experiences and tough experiences. Jesus is not advocating that we zone in and embrace only the suffering. The cross represents the total embrace of the incarnation experience of being a human being on planet Earth and experiencing everything that incarnation brings with it. He is not just focusing on the negative or the persecution; Jesus is not advocating that. He said at one stage, "I have come that you may have life and have it to the fullest." In 2000 years of Christianity, the church has proposed a model whereby we are nailed to a plus sign to keep our heads in our books until we get a passing grade in mathematics. Of course, it has nothing to do with that.

The horizontal beam of the cross represents our relationship to all living things and reminds me that I am connected to all sentient life forms; not just on planet Earth, but in the entire cosmos. It is my relationship to all that is.

The vertical arm of the cross represents my relationship with the transcendent; the ultimate ground of my being. The horizontal element connects me to all beings and it connects me to the feminine face of God. It connects me to God as evident in creation. The vertical arm of the cross connects me to the transcendent aspect of God or the masculine aspect of God. The intersection of these two pieces where the vertical and the horizontal meet is my connection to myself. I cannot be meaningfully in connection with myself unless I am in connection with God and in connection with all of my brothers and sisters. To attempt only one of these is to miss the point. People who attempt only a connection with each other and do not create a relationship with God are merely secular humanists and humanism is fine, but it is not the whole picture. People who only have a relationship with God are on an esoteric ego trip unless it is balanced by the connection to everything else. Unless I am prepared to walk my talk in my relationship with my brothers and sisters, I have not understood what the cross is about. When I bring these two meaningfully together, then and only then can I meaningfully believe in my relationship to my own core identity. We constantly misunderstand what these are about. We constantly focus on one element or the other element and forget that the two must come together. We then continue to reinforce this mistake by insisting that the cross means persecution or suffering. It has nothing to do with that. It is only tangentially related to the fact that every human life will experience all the facets of what it means to be a human, including pain.

The cross is the ultimate illusion buster. The cross is the place that grounds me firmly in my physicality and my humanity and allows me to reach for the transcendence of my inner divinity. It breaks through the illusion of a separate identity that my brothers and sisters are ontologically discrete entities totally different from me. The cross is the ultimate breaker of all of these illusions because when I put the two pieces in place and I am truly in contact with my core essence, I find that the core essence with which I am in contact is the same core essence that manifested you or the daffodils or the butterflies. When I am in contact with that there are no separations anymore and the illusions go.

I think it was Yogi Berra who said at one time, "When you come to a fork in the road, take it." He was right. When you come to a fork in the road, take it because every cross is a crossroads. What it means is this: it affords you a choice not between A and B, it affords the opportunity of embracing both A and B. When you meet Yogi Berra on the road don't kill him, follow him. When you meet Yogi Berra on the road it is an invitation to embrace the horizontal dimension of the cross which is the embrace of my humanity and to embrace the vertical arm of the cross is the embracing of my divinity. Yogi Berra was right.

Finally, there are two very interesting versions of the cross that come through in Christianity. There is the Catholic cross with the corpus on it; the figure of Jesus. Its focus is on the historical character that developed Christ consciousness so there is great value in the cross with the corpus on it. It really allows us to look at evidence for at least one other human being who developed Christ consciousness by embracing the totality of his human experience. Then there is the Protestant cross which has no corpus on it. It means that there is a vacancy. Would you like to apply for it? It means every single one of us is being asked to accept the invitation to also experience life in its totality right across the board connecting ourselves to all that is and to our own divinity.

How would you know if you are wise? There is a large distinction between knowledge and wisdom. They are both important but there is a big distinction between them. Knowledge is the ability to manipulate the external environment and that is very important. It allows us to create cars, build and heat our homes, tie our shoelaces and therefore, knowledge is very important. In fact, we have much more knowledge now than Jesus had. Your average university student today has ten times more knowledge than either the Buddha or Jesus had. If you put the Buddha, Socrates and Jesus together then your modern student will have three times the knowledge that the three of them had. Knowledge is merely about manipulating the external environment.

Wisdom, on the other hand, is that which connects me to my inner source. It is that which brings me into total alignment with my Isness; they are both very important and are both arms of the cross as well. The horizontal arm of the cross is knowledge or my ability to manipulate and be at home in my environment. The vertical arm of the cross is my connection to my inner wisdom. Wisdom and knowledge are both very important. One can be taught and the other cannot be taught. Knowledge can be taught. You can fill an empty head with lots of facts some of which are important and some of which are only used for Trivial Pursuit. You can fill up someone with lots of facts and knowledge, but you can't give him wisdom.

You can't give anyone wisdom because wisdom is our birthright. Therefore, only of wisdom can we truly use the word education. Because the Latin phrase, *educare,* means literally to lead out from. It is to draw out what is already inside. You can draw wisdom out from someone because wisdom truly resides at the core of our being. If you attempt to draw knowledge out of someone, you are merely taking out what you previously put in. Most education merely draws out in tests and examinations what has previously been deposited. But wisdom is not so. You can bring wisdom out of yourself because you are at your core truly a wise being. We are eternal entities who have always lived in the palm of God's hand knowing at our core who we really are. True education is about uncovering all of the membranes that have caused amnesia in us for our true origin, mission and our true destiny. That is the difference between wisdom and knowledge.

Knowledge deals with facts and facts are important, but wisdom deals with truth. What is the difference between truth and facts? Facts are our attempts to make maps of the phenomenological world which then allows us to navigate through the experience of being in spacesuits and so are very important. Knowledge is about creating maps or models that allow us to navigate easily through the labyrinth of the experience of being grounded in a spacesuit.

Wisdom is very different. Wisdom doesn't give us facts, it deals with truth. What is truth? Truth is that which transforms. Ultimate truth is that which transforms radically. Truth is not something to be verified on the internet. These two pieces fit together. They are both important. They are two arms of the cross and they are both important for the experience of being spirits in spacesuits. Since we have spacesuits, knowledge is very important otherwise we wouldn't know how to use or inhabit the spacesuit. If we didn't have wisdom, we would forget that we are Spirits in spacesuits but rather think we are just spacesuits and then we would spend our entire lives just merely chasing factoids and getting nowhere. Knowledge is the ability to navigate the journey to a rendezvous with my long lost lover. Wisdom is the ability to recognize her/him when we arrive at the meeting place. There is a very big difference. One allows me to get there the other one allows me to recognize the face of my beloved when I finally encounter her/him at the meeting place.

What happens in the practice of the present moment? If I know that I am wise, how do I know that I know what I know? If there were one practice that allows people to evolve most quickly, one spiritual practice that I would advocate above all others I would say that it is the practice of the present moment. I don't know of any other symbol that more accurately captures and signifies this than the notion of the cross. The intersection between the connection to God and the connection to others is the ultimate invitation to live totally in the present moment.

The practice of the present moment unfolds in four stages. The first stage is that I have to <u>recognize</u> that the situation in which I find myself is not just some kind of coincidence or an accident. There are no coincidences and there are no accidents. All of us at every stage of our lives find ourselves in relationships and in situations that are the inevitable outcome of all of the preconception contracts we have made and all of the free-will choices we have made during incarnation. There is no relationship in which I find myself that is not the result of all of the choices that I and my entire cohort group have made and all of the preconception contracts that we have entered into. When I recognize that, a lot of pressure comes off. There is no situation you find yourself in that just happens to you. You weren't "lucky" or you weren't "unlucky" and it wasn't a coincidence. It is the inevitable outcome of all of the choices and all of the preconception contracts that you and the others in your cohort group have made. That is the first stage of the practice of the present moment. The second stage is that I have to <u>accept</u> that. I have to believe that to be the case. It is a reality and I accept it.

The third stage is that I now have to <u>work with</u> it. There is no way beyond working with it. I can try working with what is not. I can try working with what I prefer were there, but it doesn't lead to success. The only way through is to work with what is.

The fourth stage of the practice of the present moment is the *belief system* that ultimate liberation and true enlightenment lie in the total embrace of the present moment. It is only by embracing the present moment that enlightenment is a possibility or that liberation lies ahead. If I go back to the Hebrew Scriptures and I look at the great story in Exodus, Chapter 3, I find an extraordinary encounter between God and Moses in which Moses asked God to identify Himself. God said, "I am who I am." It is only by embracing the present moment and by being on the cross that I can subsume all of time into the intersection between the divine and immanent. Only by dwelling in that present moment can I say, I am who I am. If I know that, I can say just as truly as God did, I am who I am. If I have really understood the cross, I can say with Jesus, "The Father and I are one."

Who then am I? I know that I am okay, but I am not so sure who I am. What do I mean by that phrase? To speak very simplistically in psychological terminology there are basically three components to it. There is the persona that I put on i.e., who I want you to believe I am. I don't believe it myself, I know that I am not that, but I'd like you to believe that this is who I am. I offer you my persona because I want to make an impression on you. The second stage is my ego. This is who I think I am. This is the CEO of waking consciousness; this is who I think I am. Then the third stage is the Self who, in fact, I really am, but I am not aware of it. The word self has been used very differently in many psychologies. When you read how Freud, Adler or Jung used the word self, you realize that there are many different meanings for the word self.

The persona is just the image of myself or the fancy dress I put on in order to impress people. The ego is merely the executive of waking consciousness, but the soul is my true essence. It is the bite-size piece of God-stuff that each one of us is. When Jesus said, "Unless you are prepared to hate your father, mother, spouse, children and your self, you cannot be my disciples," he was not talking about soul. He was talking about persona and ego. Unless I am prepared to shed ego and persona, I am not able to reach my Self. That is another function of cross. Jesus died naked on the cross. It was the Roman custom to make the victim totally naked and thus further embarrass him. We all have dreams where we are either inappropriately clad in public places or completely naked. In psychological parlance, these dreams always translate into some kind of an issue with my persona. The image I want to portray to people is somehow being interfered with and I am being embarrassed.

When I can dispense with persona then I'm free to dwell in ego, but the ego too needs to be stripped. Therefore, crucifixion in the real sense of the word is having the courage to strip myself not just of my clothes and therefore shed my persona, but to strip myself of ego as well so that I can reveal the soul within me. That is what I mean. I know that I'm okay, but do I know who I am? With what level of myself do I constantly identify? Am I identifying merely with my persona, the costume and the impressions I want to make on people? Am I identifying merely with the CEO of waking consciousness? Do I think that I am my ego? Am I identified with the job I do or with the relationships I am in? Am I identified with body image? Am I identified with my mind and my thoughts? Am I identified with my reputation? With what do I really identify? Anything less than identification with the soul means that I have still not fully understood what the cross is about. The cross is the ultimate instrument not of the torture of a human being, it is not about the persecution of incarnation, it is about having the courage to strip away first the persona, then the ego so that finally, with Jesus, there is only Christ consciousness locked in an extraordinary dance between my divinity and my humanity.

ILLNESS AND ACCIDENTS

"It is by losing the self that God is found."

Guru Nanak

BOUT TWO MONTHS ago, someone sent me a joke that I thought was hilarious. The source assured me that it had actually happened last year in Australia. Some weeks later, during the all-night party following my brother's wedding, I told it. There was a polite ripple of laughter. Then my brother told me that this "recent actual occurrence" was the storyline of an Irish ballad dating back some 40 years. He then proceeded to sing it for me! It was an exact musical version of my joke.

But, on the odd chance that you have heard neither the song nor the joke, here it is for you: A man applied for Worker's Compensation as a result of an accident. His written report of the incident went like this: "I was working on the top floor of a new six-story building. When the job was done, there was a pile of bricks weighing about 500 pounds left up top. Rather than lugging these bricks down six flights of ladders, I got a brainwave. I found a 50-pound barrel on the ground, rigged up a pulley system and with myself on the ground, pulled until the barrel was at the sixth floor then attached the end of the rope securely to a tree. I climbed the ladders and piled all of the bricks into the barrel then down the ladders I came and untied the rope. I got yanked upwards by the 550 pounds of barrel-and-bricks and we encountered each other at the third floor and it broke my left shoulder, but I held on for dear life. Upwards I rushed for three more stories and jammed two fingers into the pulley, breaking both of them, but I kept my wits about me and, in spite of the pain, I held on. Just as I was losing two fingers to the pulley, the barrel hit the ground, causing the bottom to break and the bricks to spill out. Now there was only a 50-pound weight below while my 180 pounds was at the sixth floor, so down I began to plummet. I renewed my acquaintance with the barrel at the third floor and this time it broke my left leg, but I still held on. I hit the ground with a ferocious wallop and broke my right leg. By now I'd had enough, so I let go of the rope. Then the barrel made its final descent and fractured my skull. Any financial assistance you can render me will be greatly appreciated."

With that said, let me speak then of accidents and illnesses and their place in the human drama. To do so I want to address the relationship between consciousness and the unconscious. By way of analogy, their relationship is that of a rider and horse. The horse provides the power of the system, while the rider exerts the control. Consciousness can very easily be overtaxed. For instance, if I give you two sheets of paper and two pens and instruct you to, simultaneously, draw a circle on one page and a triangle on the other, you can't do it. The best you can manage is either two triangles or two circles, or, more likely, two mangled polygons. In computer-speak, consciousness can only handle about five bytes of information at a time.

The unconscious, on the other hand, is the ultimate expert at multi-tasking. At the same time, it monitors and regulates all your vital functions; blood pressure, heart rate, body temperature and 2,000 different bio-chemicals. And it does all this while also orchestrating conversations between all 100 trillion cells in your body. But evolution decrees that consciousness and the unconscious be in a loving relationship with each other, with the unconscious providing the horsepower and consciousness giving it direction. Left to its own devices, a horse won't necessarily take a rider where the rider wishes to go, control is necessary. Consciousness and the unconscious need each other like a rider and horse do.

This relationship, however, exists on a continuum. At one end are people who totally ignore the unconscious. At the other end are those who see it as an omniscient oracle.

Carl Jung claimed that the unconscious is constantly trying to get our conscious attention in order to forge a healthy working connection. And, he claimed, it speaks more and more insistently until we finally give heed. Initially, mainly and least obtrusively it speaks to us nightly in our dreams. If we pay attention, it is happy and the result is a balanced set of data from unconscious and conscious viewpoints on all the major issues of our life. Mostly, however, this attempt by the unconscious is ignored and the night's downloading is dismissed with, "It was only a dream." The next ploy is the manipulation of mood. We wake up in the morning in a bad mood (depressed, anxious or angry) and can't think of any good reason why it should be so. Or, perhaps, such an irrational affect can manifest in the middle of a perfectly ordinary day without apparent cause. It is the unconscious saying, "Please listen up!" For the main part, we explain away such instances as, "Maybe 'twas something I ate?"

Since we haven't listened when the unconscious used our minds or when it used our emotions, it now uses the body as a wake up call by somatizing the breakdown of the intended connection between consciousness and the unconscious. Mostly, this merely triggers a visit to an allopath, who will do blood slides, X-rays, MRI's and CAT scans, and then offer medications, surgery, or, if you're really lucky, advice to go see a shrink.

What, then, of the theories of illnesses' origins? These, too, lie on a spectrum. At one end is the biblical explanation: all sickness is of demonic etiology. The solution, then, is some form of magical incantation. At the other end, is the allopathic explanation: all illness is the result of microbes. The father of this hugely successful theory, Louis Pasteur, is said to have recanted this model on his deathbed and accepted that the defeated model of his adversary, Claude Bernard, was more accurate. Bernard pointed out that the human body, at any stage of life, is unwitting host to over 2,000 different forms of bacteria. Why then, he asked, are we not always ill? The answer, he averred, was that the "terrain" is a more important factor than is the "invader" in trying to understand illness. The general vitality of an organism determines whether or not it will succumb to an always-present parasite. Those who accept the microbiological etiology respond to sickness with "magic bullets"

I believe that the truth is somewhere in between, and I hold that the success of either response is due, in no small measure, to the placebo effect. Modern medical research has shown that about 35 percent of the effectiveness of any treatment is placebo, the belief of the patient in the power of intervention. There is a truism that you had better use a new medication within the first five years of its coming on the market because later studies will inevitably show that it is not at all as effective as the initial studies indicated. Why? Because, I believe, the intervening years will provide evidence that it is not all it was cracked up to be and then the placebo percentage falls significantly, further reducing its effectiveness. Whichever etiology you subscribe to, then, placebo will be a major player.

In 1992, I conducted a double-blind, controlled, randomized study with 506 participants on the effects of Intercessory-prayer-at-a-distance on self-esteem, anxiety and depression. Two of the most interesting results had a placebo flavor. I asked the participants during the post-testing, "Do you believe you were in the experimental group or in the control group?" Those who answered, "I believe I was in the experimental group" whether or not they were, enjoyed very significant improvement on all measures. Those who answered, "I believe I was in the control group" whether or not they were, did not experience significant improvement on any measure.

Another question was, "Do you believe that praying for others is effective?" Again, a positive response to this correlated with significant improvement, while a negative response correlated with no significant improvement.

This leads to a discussion of theories of symptomology. Before leaving Ireland in 1972, to spend 14 years in East Africa, I did a year-long course in a form of Community Development which taught us how to enter a remote region of the third world, analyze who the leaders were, what the needs of the people were, what project might address those needs, what short-term objectives and long-term goals might be appropriate, what obstacles might be expected and the best solutions to those obstacles. It was a very scientific approach. About three years into my East African stint, I was sitting, literally, on the equator in a semi-desert area of Kenya in temperatures of 125 degrees Fahrenheit, at a meeting of the elders, delivering my answers to the region's problems.

One of the old men interrupted with a question. He asked, "Can you tell me why it is that for you Europeans your only response to a problem is to want to solve it?" This sounded to me like a Zen Koan. What the heck does anyone do with a problem except try to solve it! I was baffled so I threw the question back at him, "Well, what do you do with a problem?" I have never forgotten his answer. Essentially, he said, "A problem is an invitation to self-transcendence. And if all you do is solve it, why, life will just give you another problem. And if you merely try to solve that one, then it will give you a bigger problem. No, problems are God's way of making us grow. When we understand that, most problems solve themselves!" This proclamation drew wise, knowing head-nods from the others. I have carried that gem in my heart for the last 30 years.

When I came to the USA in 1987 and began to study psychology, I applied this insight to symptoms (the medical-psychological equivalent of "problems") and what I found was the following: Freud saw symptoms as evidence of childhood trauma; Jung saw them as evidence of the frustration of archetypal intent; Behaviorism sees them as learned actions that need to be extinguished, and Process Oriented Psychotherapy sees them as evidence of a creative process about to happen. Homeopathy tends to agree, saying that symptoms are evidence that the body-emotions-mind are doing exactly what they need to do to bring about healing. Like Behaviorism, however, allopathy sees symptoms as the villains that need to be suppressed.

205

Me? I'm on the side of Process Oriented Psychotherapy and homeopathy. How we view symptomology determines how we treat illnesses. I have an equation of my own that pithily expresses my theory: $Ax_1 + Bx_2 + Cx_3 + Dx_4 + Ex_5 + Fx_6 = $ illness. In this equation x_1 stands for Genetic Predisposition. Each system, whether it be an ethnic group, a family, an individual or an organ, has a weakest spot. When pressure comes on, that's where it will break. X_2 stands for Environmental Influence, by which I mean the full context of the organism's experience from in utero, to the childhood food, clothing, shelter, to family and cultural dynamics. X_3 stands for Personal Lifestyle, by that I mean adult practices around diet, exercise, sleep and work. X_4 stands for Personal Beliefs, since I find that one's mindset, i.e., anxious, relaxed, open, intolerant, forgiving, grudge-bearing etc., significantly impact health. X_5 stands for Karma, or the larger lessons that tend to span several lifetimes because of their importance to one's growth. X_6 stands for the Bodhisattva dimension. In Buddhism, the bodhisattva is that enlightened being who has worked off all of his personal karma but takes a vow to keep reincarnating until all sentient beings are awake. Illness, I believe, is an equation where these six factors are weighted differently for different people and for different illnesses.

We all get ill, but what is our response? It very much depends on our model of illness. I believe the question needs to be extended and it is important to ask, what is the purpose of this illness rather than what caused this illness. There are both etiological and evolutionary aspects to each incidence of sickness. Furthermore, both the genetic predisposition and the environmental influence factors are the ideal domains for science to intervene, study and resolve. The personal lifestyle and personal belief aspects, however, will not so much be solved by science as by behavioral and cognitive changes within the sufferer. And, in so far as the karmic and bodhisattva aspects are concerned, neither science nor personal effort will effect a change, because the soul will not be sidetracked from embracing its purpose and mission. Part of the gift of the true healer is the recognition of both the origin and the purpose of an illness when dealing with a sick person.

What, then, does healing prayer look like? I believe it, too, is a six-phase process. The first phase is to meditate in order to discover the origin and the purpose of the illness. Once I think I have established that, then phase two is praying for an outcome which is in alignment with the origin and the purpose of the sickness. The third phase is doing my part to effect a healing i.e., behavioral and cognitive changes. Islam has a proverb that says, "Pray to Allah, but first tie up your camel." We can't expect God or even the physician to do everything while we continue with business as usual. The fourth phase is detachment. Once I have meditated, prayed and made the necessary changes, I need to let go of my agenda and timeline and accept and work with the outcome, even if it is only a temporary outcome. Persistence of effort is not antithetical to detachment, but annoyance and frustration are. In stage five, I cycle back to meditation to fine-tune my understanding of the origin and purpose of the illness, in light of the outcome. Stage six is, possibly, the most important stage of all. It is the recognition that I can't lose. If I am truly in alignment with my core Self and with my purpose, then whether I live or die, whether I go into permanent remission or deteriorate significantly, I cannot lose.

Who do I thank if I am healed? There is what I call the "Auntie Mary" response. Imagine a precocious kid who just got a $20 bill from his aunt for his birthday. He figures it will only take him ten minutes and a 37-cent postage stamp to write a thank you note and that will probably guarantee another 20 bucks next year. That's a pretty good return on an investment. Of course, that is not true gratitude. True gratitude is the total embrace of the mission. It is the full recognition that nothing happens to me by chance, and that everything is grist for the mill of spiritual evolution.

People can be thrown off track by either success or failure. Success is devastating if it leads to arrogance or entitlement, but excellent if it leads to real gratitude. Failure can be devastating if it leads to despair, but can be great if it wakes me up. Neither success nor failure is important, but embracing the lesson of both is vital

One of the most enigmatic parables Jesus ever told was a story of a rich man who had a steward that was in charge of all of his property. Eventually he found out that his steward was embezzling his money. He called him in and said, "What is this that I hear about you? Are you embezzling my money?" The steward thought, "My God, I'm going to lose my job," so he called in all his master's creditors and said, "Juan, how much do you owe my master?" Juan said, "One hundred bushels of wheat." He said to him, "Take your bill and change the 100 to 80." Then he went to the next man and said, "Bob, how much do you owe my master?" Bob said, "Eighty barrels of oil." He said, "Here is your bill, write down 50."

Then Jesus said a very strange thing. He said, "The rich man praised the unjust steward in so far as he acted wisely." What was Jesus praising? Was he praising the duplicity of this man for his embezzling tendencies? Of course he wasn't. What he said was, "Here is a man who could turn every situation to his own economic advantage. When things were going great and he had full access to his master's property he was stealing from him. But even when things turned against him and he was going to lose his job, he turned even that situation to his own economic advantage." Jesus meant that what is important is to be able to turn any situation to your own spiritual advantage. Gratitude is the ability to turn every life situation into an embracing of your mission.

There is a story in the Hebrew scriptures of Elisha the prophet and Naaman who was a general in the Syrian army which had invaded Israel. Now Naaman happened to be a leper. Naaman was a good commander and totally fearless in battle. His lack of fear came from the belief that he was going to die from leprosy anyway. Then he heard that there was a prophet in Israel who could cure him. He went back into the country that he had just conquered to ask if Elisha would cure him. He was told to go down to the river Jordan and bathe seven times and then come back. He did and was cured.

He came back to Elisha and said; "Now I know that there is no God except the God of Israel. Moreover, with your permission, I'm going to take two mule loads of dirt back to Syria and I will make a prayer mound out of them. I'll have my own little private prayer space because we all know that the God of Israel doesn't answer prayers unless they are said on Jewish soil. So by praying on this little patch, everything I want will be granted!"

What's the deal here? Was this the cementing of a great relationship between Israel and Syria? Not by a long shot. Within 20 years Assyria conquered Israel completely. Ten of the twelve tribes of Israel were deported and never heard of again. What kind of gratitude was this? Having been cured of leprosy, and having Israeli earth so he could continue to speak to Yahweh and get all of his requests met, he then went back and beat up on Israel and deported ten tribes and obliterated them so that they are never heard of again! Is that what gratitude looks like?

The Scripture writer unfortunately misses the entire point. The point is this. God was trying to show that there are no favorites. Healing and illnesses are not for the elect and the accursed respectively. All nations and each individual experience both. This message very strongly says: "I have no more interest in healing Israel than I have in healing Syria. I'm interested in healing everyone." But the writers of scripture totally missed it. They put a twist in the story. It wasn't good enough that the God of Israel was going to heal the Assyrian war chief; they had to somehow turn Naaman into a wannabe Jew. Naaman had to espouse two tenets, firstly, only the God of Israel is real; and secondly, God only hears prayers if they are made on Jewish turf. This happens to many of the prophets within all the major religions. Even glaring examples of God's global regard for all humans is turned into evidence of God's partisan nature in choosing only the elect and healing only the elect.

Then there is the story in the New Testament of Jesus healing ten lepers, nine Jewish and one Samaritan. Only the Samaritan came back to say, "Thank you" and Jesus commented, "Weren't ten made whole. Has no one come back except this foreigner?" Then he said to the Samaritan, "Get up your faith has cured you."

If it was his faith that cured him, what cured the other nine men? What was the difference between his faith and their faith? There is a difference between faith and Faith. There is faith, which is the placebo, and Faith, which is alignment. The faith that cured the other nine men was the placebo. It was the belief that Jesus could do it. And the only thing that changed was their skin condition. The Faith of the other man was totally different. It wasn't just a physiological change, it wasn't just a somatic difference, and it wasn't just that his skin got better. It was that his mindset, his emotional state and his spirituality all shifted significantly until he was in perfect alignment with his core essence. That is the difference between faith and Faith. He was cured by his Faith. The other nine were cured by a placebo version of faith and he was cured by an alignment version of Faith. The question I offer you then is this; if you are a person of faith, is your faith merely a placebo or is your Faith alignment?

TECHNOLOGY OF PRAYER

"God is gentle, mild and very delicate and always at the disposition of whomever desires it."

Plotinus

M Y AUNT RITA is definitely the most naive human being experiment homo sapiens has ever produced. One Friday, when she was a girl in Ireland, she was visiting a friend and was given tripe to eat. She came home that night full of excitement about the great feast she had had. My father asked her what she had eaten and she said, "Tripe." Now my father told her immediately that she was going to go to Hell for eating meat on Friday. Rita was terrorized and afraid to go to bed that night because she was sure that she would die in her sleep and go straight to Hell. She wanted to stay up all night. Finally my grandmother got a local wise man to come in and this old man persuaded Rita that the sheep was an extraordinary creature. He said, "Jesus called himself the Lamb of God. A sheep is unlike any other creature on the planet because the outside of it is meat and the inside is fish." Rita slept the night.

My Aunt Rita is also totally naïve about technology. About fifteen years ago she was visiting my brother, Páraic, whose business is in office equipment. He showed her a fax machine and Rita said, "What does that do?" Páraic said, "Well, you know, typically if you want to write a letter to your son, Paul, who lives in England, you have to get a piece of paper, write the letter, put it into an envelope, seal it, stamp it and go to the post office, mail it and a truck comes along and takes it to the boat, the boat takes it to England, a post truck takes it from the boat and delivers it to the post office at Birmingham and the postman takes it and gives it to Paul. With the fax machine, you can put the letter in this machine and within 30 seconds Paul will get it in Birmingham." Rita was absolutely flabbergasted.

About a week later, she said, "Páraic would you do a little job for me?" He said, "Sure." She handed a small package to him and said, "It's Paul's birthday tomorrow and I want to send him this shirt so could you fax it to him?" Páraic did a double take, grinned and said, "Sure." "Do I have to take it out of the package or can you fax it like this?" "No, it's fine just like this. I'll see to it in a few minutes." Rita went off happy. Páraic who was actually going to England the following day on business took the package with him, got to the airport, phoned Paul and said. "Here's the deal." Paul came to the airport to pick up his shirt and the following morning Rita rang Paul up and said, "Happy Birthday son. Did you get my fax?" He said, "I did Mom." "Did you like it?" "The shirt with the yellow sleeves is beautiful I'm wearing it right now." Rita was absolutely thrilled.

The naivety of most of us, when it comes to the technology of spirituality, is that we are still living in the spiritual technology that most of us learned in grade school. Nowhere is this more apparent than in the technology of prayer. Carl Jung had a Latin phrase over the entrance to his home that read, "Whether or not God is called upon, He is present." What is the nature or quality of God's presence? Is it a loving permeating presence? Is it the ground of our being, or is it some kind of an interfering busybody who is constantly into our stuff? When you look at the Hebrew notion of trinity, you find the God who exists, the God who intervenes in human affairs and the God who demands a covenanted response from us. The question is: what is the nature of the presence of God?

As you work your way through the Judeo/Christian scriptures you get all kinds of changes in God's job description. Sometimes God is a judge who is constantly assessing the disputes between clients. At other times, God is a king who rules with an iron fist. Sometimes God is constantly granting favors to those who ask for them. At other times, God is a tyrant or a micro manager who is into every little detail of everyone's life. There is a suggestion in the New Testament that Jesus suffered from the same syndrome. Paul said, "Jesus is both a judge of the living and the dead and he is also a king." Paul ascribed to Jesus many of the same attributes and job descriptions that applied to God within the Hebrew Scriptures. What is God's job description and why does it keep changing?

There is a very strong notion within Judeo/Christian tradition that God has an agenda or a purpose for the planet, for the chosen race, for every individual and for every event. We have this notion that God has a will for us. Does God have any concern about the forth coming election or about the Super Bowl or about whether or not I should wear a collar and tie to a reception? Is God micro-managing and totally invested in specific outcomes in everyone's life?

My heresy says that God has no will whatsoever for planet Earth, for any chosen race, for any individual person or for any event in our lives. God has no will, no agenda or no idea for any of these things. I believe it operates in the following fashion. Long before our great grandparents had spacesuits we got together in soul clusters and created what I call pre-conception contracts with each other. With our heavenly mentors, we figure out ways of creating on planet Earth or elsewhere the kinds of dramas that afford every one of us the ideal opportunities to learn the lessons that we want to learn and to grow in the fashion that we want to grow. These pre-conception contracts are what come through. It is not God's will, agenda or purpose. It is the agreements we come to as cohort groups. We build in what I call transponders into our incarnational spacesuits and these transponders act in the following fashion.

Firstly they act as conscience which guides us; secondly they act through déjà vu experiences. Déjà vu is not just a quirk of the mind, but little mementos or memories from our pre-conception contracts that try to wake us up just as the Buddha awoke to his real purpose and real agenda. A third kind of transponder is soul recognition, i.e., the way that you meet people in your life with whom you instantly bond with or to whom you take an instant dislike. This is all part of your contract group. I don't believe that the ineffable ground of our being has the slightest interest in individual events or people or even the planet itself. In God's extraordinary omniscience, wisdom and compassion, She allows us to figure out the dramas for ourselves and gives us the ability to build into these dramas ways of waking up and ways of remembering. That is how it appears to me.

Who is this God to whom we attribute job positions and who we think has a will for us? We are built in the image and likeness of this ineffable ground of our being but we constantly recreate God in our own image and likeness. The truth is that everything is built in God's image and likeness. There is nothing in reality, the universe, our imagined universe or the mental universe that is not of God. Everything is an articulation of God. Rocks are God sleeping, plants are God waking up, animals are God walking and humans are God thinking. I add to that, Christ conscious human beings are aware that they are God. There is nothing but God. Everything is an articulation of the Divine. There is nothing that is not of God including no-thing itself. Even nothing is an articulation of God.

There is a great story in the Jewish Talmud that speaks about four great sages. All four attempted to enter paradise. The first one entered paradise hoping to encounter God and because of what happened there he died of fright. The second one went into paradise hoping to meet God and because of what happened there he went mad. The third went into paradise expecting to meet God and because of what happened there lost his faith. Finally, the fourth entered paradise and he alone came back out of paradise full of peace because only he was large enough to accept that even the absence of God is God. There is nothing but God and nothing itself is God. Everything is an articulation of the ineffable ground of our being. Therefore, to force configurations on God and to continue to build God in our own image and likeness is doing a tremendous disservice to our connection to our deepest selves and to this transcendent ground of our being.

Configuring God is founded on two misconceptions; anthropomorphism and arrogance. Anthropomorphism is the tendency to try to view all phenomena in human categories. We attribute human characteristics to everything including non-human reality; we also attribute human characteristics to animals and to God. That is the foundation of so much of the misconception of God in so many different religious traditions.

The second postulate on which our relationship with God and our understanding of God is built is arrogance. We are an extraordinarily arrogant species. In the very beginning, we thought that the Earth was the center of the universe and that the sun revolved around the Earth until Galileo showed us otherwise. It was a huge shock to us that we were not the center of the universe. We were just one little planet orbiting one little star within the system. At least we could be happy we were the most important species and totally different from every other species on the planet until Darwin showed us that we are very closely related to the primates. That was also a terrible shock to us; we were not as special as we thought we were.

Then we had the belief system that at least this little planet of ours is the only place that has intelligent life. Then the second most important scientific formula of the 20th century came when astronomer, Francis Drake, postulated, $N = N^* \times F_p \times F_e \times F_l \times F_i \times F_c \times L$. The formula contains these elements: N^* is the number of stars in the Milky Way Galaxy (about 200 million). F_p is the fraction of those stars that have planets in attendance; F_e is the number of those planets that have Earth-like attributes; rocky and stable climates; F_l is the number of those planets that have produced life forms; F_i is the fraction of those planets that have evolved intelligent life forms; F_c is the proportion that have civilizations capable of developing communications and L is the longevity of such a civilization because any civilization that develops that kind of technology has the ability to destroy itself. He created this formula and the best scientific guess is that the number actually is somewhere around one million. According to this formula there are probably about one or two million such civilizations in the Milky Way Galaxy alone. Once again we find ourselves booted out of center field.

The last piece that we believed probably came from Freud who said, the ego was the center of the psyche and that was a tiny little tip of the iceberg in a huge unconscious arena. Evolution is the process of the constant conscious disidentification with the smaller or lesser holons so that we can re-identify progressively with larger and larger pictures of ourselves. We can grow from the notion of persona, who I pretend I am, to the notion of ego, who I think I am, to the notion of soul, which is what I really am to the notion of group, race, planet and universe. Evolution is the process of undoing this littleness of mind.

You have heard the story about the freed slaves coming out of Egypt and wandering in the desert and they meet the Amalekites and there is a battle. Moses went up on a hill and with his upraised arms prayed to God to give them a victory and as long as he kept his arms raised the Israelites were winning. But his arms got tired and they began to droop and then the enemy began to win. Aaron got on one side and Hur got on the other side of Moses and they propped his arms up and the Israelites won the battle. The final passage of this story is "Joshua put the Amalekites and all their people to death by the edge of the sword."

There are three misconceptions to this story. The first one is the glorification of war, violence and murder. The second one is the notion of a partisan God who chooses one people over the other. And the third is a total misconception of how prayer works as if there is some trick to it like keeping one's arms up. Every religion has developed its tricks. In the Catholic system it was the First Fridays. As long as you went to mass and communion on the first Friday on nine consecutive months God had to let you into heaven. Or if you are Muslin, all you have to do is make a pilgrimage to Mecca once in your life and then you get into heaven.

Yesterday I met two Tibetan dogs. The function of these dogs is to turn the prayer wheels. Within Buddhism there is this notion that every time the wheel turns a prayer goes up to God. Because people were busy doing their chores every day they got the dogs to turn the wheels for them. The prayers went up and God answered them. Every system has devised tricks as if somehow you can con God into granting your request. It is a crazy notion that there is some kind of trick to the trade and if you can figure it out you get your request. That is one notion of prayer.

There is another notion that prayer is merely chatting about the inevitable. Since God is omniscient, God has already factored in all of your requests into the plan long before you were born and so you are wasting your breath asking for stuff: he already knows what you want. Or there is Abraham's notion of prayer that you can bargain with God. Abraham was bargaining with God over the fate of Sodom and Gomorrah. Abraham said, "If there are 50 good people are you going to destroy them with everyone else?" God said, "Gee, I didn't think of that." Abraham said, "Suppose there only 45. Are you going to kill 45 good people with everyone else?" God said, "No." Abraham said, "What if there are only 30, 20 or 10?" He kept whittling God down as if he could bargain with God and get his way.

Jesus stressed the notion of constancy in prayer. Constancy in prayer is not about berating God until finally She bends Her will to your wishes. Prayer is about the focused intention that grows out of the fact that every one of us is God stuff. It is about helping us remember who we really are. It is about rediscovering for ourselves the preconception contracts that we made. That is the total function of intercessory prayer. It is remembering and reminding ourselves of what our contract was. That is the constancy. We are trying to remember why we are on the planet. It has nothing to do with belaboring a God, who is a distant demanding deity.

The technology of prayer is like a sprinkler system in a lawn. You have an underground system of pipes all connected to a central faucet and you have a few sprinklers in vital locations on the lawn so that the entire lawn gets wet. The grace flowing through this system is love and the faucet or source is God. Every one of us is like a little nodule; a sprinkler on the lawn. If we are congested, through anger, hatred or whatever, then our section of the lawn does not get watered. And all of those we are in connection with do not get watered. We inhibit the flow of this love and grace to other parts of the system. Prayer is the unlocking of that system. It is the dissolving of the blockages that lie deep within my own psyche so that I become a conduit for the love of God to flow through all of my relationships.

Jesus said about prayer, "Do not think that if the unjust judge listens to the widow that God won't listen to the cries of the poor and grant justice for all." Of course, he will. What is this notion of justice for all? Is it some kind of idea that there is a distant, demanding divinity that is going to come back and wreak havoc on all of us and every one of us is going to pay for his/her misdeeds? I don't believe that. I think that there are many ways in which we learn to deal with the effects of our own choices, whether they are words we speak, actions we do, thoughts we have or things we neglect to do. Every one of us gets the opportunity and we get it in one of three ways. We get it through parallel existences. I believe that every time any one of us is faced with a choice between A and B we choose both. There is the parallel probable existence in which I am acting out the consequences of the choice I didn't take. We get equal opportunity to work through all the possible choices we make and to learn from them what the consequences might be. That is one way in which we do it.

If we believe in reincarnation, then we recreate lives for ourselves in which we get the opportunities to visit all configurations of choices to learn how to love in all those circumstances. Maybe most important of all we learn to become just people by developing the ability over many lifetimes to be able to appreciate the effects of any events from the point of view of everyone effected by the event. Typically, we can only appreciate any event from our own point of view. One of the most fascinating things about the Near Death literature is that part of the life review seems to be not that there is God with a whole list of my sins written in the book accusing me, but that I get the opportunity to revisit my entire life and to re-experience each event, not from my own perspective but to literally get to stand in the shoes of everyone else effected by my choices and to experience the results and the outcomes from their point of view without any judgment whatsoever. This is the most extraordinary ability of all and this is true justice.

Justice is not a divine recompense for sins or mistakes. Justice is the ability to develop a talent to be able to appreciate and experience every event from the point of view of all those effected in the event.

I have atrocious eating habits; I tend to eat those things that taste good to me. An eating experience for me is purely about my taste buds. If I were a more enlightened being, an eating experience for me should be about the effects on my digestion or the effects on my metabolism and what will give me energy. What about my overall health? A truly mature person will adopt eating habits on the basis of the good for the entire organism rather than the effects merely on the taste buds. A just person is a person who can make a choice determined upon the effects of the choice on all the players in the drama.

I know I am truly a just person when I can experience any event from the point of view of all those effected by the event. We are not dealing with a distant, demanding deity who is going to punish us for injustice. Divine justice has nothing to do with the court system, jail or punishment. It has everything to do with evolving into the place where I can stand in everyone's moccasins and estimate the effects of my actions on every sentient being in the universe.

HUMILITY—THE KEY TO TRUTH

"When the doors of the temple of the heart are open, humility awakens upon finding oneself face to face with the living God within."

Hidayat Inayat Khan

THERE WAS A very holy Rabbi who loved God very dearly and he started a practice of sneaking into the temple early in the morning when all his congregants were fast asleep. He would go up to the sanctuary and prostrate himself in front of the Torah and he would say, "Blessed are you oh Lord, our God, of the entire universe. I am not worthy to be one of your chosen people. I don't deserve all the good things that you have given to me." He would beat his breast and prostrate himself morning after morning. Then one morning the Cantor was passing by and he noticed that the door of the temple was open. He snuck in to see what was happening. He heard the Rabbi beating his breast and thanking God and telling God that he was totally worthless and useless. The Cantor was amazed at the piety of this holy man so he snuck up beside him, knelt down, prostrated himself and he too began saying, "I am not worthy. I too am a worthless lout. I do not deserve to be blessed as I am by you."

For the next three or four days they continued side by side with their protestations of unworthiness. One day, the charwoman was passing by and as she came to the back of the temple with her mop and bucket, she saw these two holy men, listened to what they were saying and was totally struck by their piety. She put her mop and bucket down and snuck up beside them and said, "I too am totally unworthy: I am only a charwoman: I don't deserve to be one of your chosen people." Suddenly the Rabbi and the Cantor sat up and seeing this woman they said, "Such nerve! Who do you think you are to say that you are nothing?"

Viktor Frankl, a famous Jewish psychiatrist who survived the death camp of Auschwitz, wrote an interesting book and became the father of a branch of psychology called Logo Therapy (therapy of meaning). His main thesis was that people can survive any situation as long as they can impose some kind of meaning on their experience. It doesn't particularly matter what the meaning is. As long as people can impose some kind of meaning on their experience, they will survive the experience. I agree wholeheartedly with him. It is very important to create some meaning from all our experiences otherwise our experiences kill us. Imposing meaning on experience is vital, but there can be a problem with the kind of meaning we impose on our experiences. Imposing meaning on experience is very important, however there is a whole range of meanings that have been imposed on the human experience and some are good and some are not good. Societies, groups and individuals all try to make sense of what happens. Religious communities do this all the time and typically it unfolds in stages: the first stage is that God is one; the second stage is that God is just; the third stage is we are the chosen people and therefore whatever happens to us must be good so we try to reframe our experiences. This leads us in two ways: firstly, it makes us responsible for the types of society and social interaction we create. The kind of interpretation we give to our experiences as a group determines what our experiences in the future are going to be. Moreover, the interpretations we give to our experiences also help us to erect the kind of social institutions, rules and parameters that continue to propagate the present experience. It becomes a self-fulfilling prophesy. It is dangerous. Making an interpretation of my circumstances is very dangerous if it is a bad interpretation because it tends to perpetuate itself. This is where prayer comes in because the real essence of prayer, if you boil it down to its essential purpose, is that it underscores our understanding of ourselves, of others, of God and also of the relationships that exist between these three groups. Prayer underscores the very essence of that. Prayer then falls on the continuum from craven obedience to God to arrogant self entitlement vis-à-vis God.

What happens, unfortunately, is that our models of prayer are often built on poor psychology, poor sociology, poor anthropology and poor theology. Prayer has been developed and practiced by people who do not understand that they are elbowing aside others in order to get the attention of the Gods they have invented. That has been the history of prayer for the main part. We have totally misunderstood prayer. Our psychology has been atrocious our sociology has been worse, our anthropology stinks and our theology is the pits. We have based prayer on that model. When we pray, this is typically what happens: I don't understand who I am; I'm elbowing aside people to get the attention and the love of the God I have invented.

In the Judeo/Christian scriptures, there are three strands woven through Judaism's attempt to make sense of its life experiences as a tribe. These three strands don't come in strict chronological order they weave in and out of the Jewish explanation for life. In the first strand, the ideal person is Jewish, male, healthy and wealthy. In other words, if you are Jewish, male, healthy and wealthy then you are especially beloved of God. If you lack any of these characteristics you are less beloved of God. If you are Jewish but merely female, you are not the full shilling. Or if you are Jewish and male, but you are unhealthy then obviously there is something wrong with you. The same goes if you are not wealthy. This first model is predicated on a notion that suggests that there is only one God, that God is just, that there is no life after death and therefore, if God is one and God is just and there is only one lifetime, then obviously the wealthy, healthy and Jewish males are being rewarded by God for something and those who are lacking those assets are being punished by God for something. People who are not Jewish, male, healthy, or wealthy have a deadly stigma against them. Obviously they are suffering from their affliction of being merely female and moreover God is punishing them for some previous sin or some sin of a parent or grandparent from three or four generations before. That is the first strand.

The institution of prophesy is the second strand that flows through Judaism; it began about 1100 B.C. This group was called the Guild of the Prophets. They challenged the authority's injustice and spoke up for justice

Beginning about the year 800 B.C., there was a second phase of prophets. This was the time of the great individual prophets, such as Elisha and Elijah; they didn't leave any writings after them. They were very powerful individuals who challenged powerful political figures or kings. They accused individual political leaders of individual acts of injustice and sometimes they paid for it with their lives.

The next phase of that second strand was the great writing prophets, e.g. Isaiah, Jeremiah, Ezekiel, Hosea, and Amos. These prophets left books after them and challenged not just individual acts of injustice perpetrated by individual political rulers, but the institutionalization of injustice against the poor. They took as their postulate the idea that: "God is a God of justice. Although God is not partial to the poor, God hears the cry of the oppressed, looks out for the widow and for the orphan."

There is a third strand; that of victim-hood. When Judaism looked back on its history believing that it was the chosen people, it must have become obvious at some stage that God had an appalling record. Going through the Hebrew Scriptures and throughout history since the time of Jesus, I would say that since 1850 B.C., God failed miserably to deliver on his promises. It's a cycle of either the Israelites being sent into exile by a host of invaders or being colonized by a host of invaders. Judaism tried to make sense of this. The sense they made was this: We are vicarious victims who are suffering on behalf of all humanity. God is visiting his indignation with humanity on us and we are willingly accepting to do this on behalf of humanity. So you have these three strands weaving their way through Judaism to try to make sense of their experience as a people.

The Roman Catholic version has been simply that there will be pie in the sky when you die. Life is a vale of tears, don't expect it to be easy here, knuckle down, keep the commandments and obey the teachings of the church because it will be great afterwards. The extraordinary thing is that when you look at this movement sociologically and you look at the history of Europe after the Protestant reformation there is a large discrepancy between the welfare of the ordinary people in Italy, Spain and Ireland on the one hand, and on the other hand that of Germany, Norway, Holland and England. The Catholic countries continued to be oppressed and poor while the "Protestant countries" made great economic strides. But, unfortunately, this Protestant economic-welfare-of-the-masses wasn't maintained because eventually Protestantism created a different kind of hierarchy. Instead of a religious hierarchy sitting atop oppressed people you now had a class- and economics-based hierarchy that penalized those in the "lower castes." For a period of time, there was a large discrepancy in the welfare of the ordinary people. It was predicated and built upon the fact that the Roman Catholic Church operated from a model that suggested that you can't expect to be happy in this life, knuckle down, pay your taxes, listen to us, do what you are told and there will be pie in the sky when you die. That was their explanation and their model.

Protestantism followed strongly what I call "strand one" Judaism. Protestants were totally convinced that if you believe in the Lord Jesus and you read the bible every day then it was your right to expect that you would be healthy, wealthy and you would come into political and economic power and moreover you would get saved after you died. That was a pretty good deal, you had it both here and afterwards; the Catholics only had it afterwards.

The Catholic notion of life looks like this: there is no life before conception; life on planet Earth is a vale of tears, but it's going to be great when you die. Atheism, which grew out of European history, had a notion that there is no life before birth and there is no life after death; this is it; make the best of it here and now. Then the worst excesses of Protestantism came from Calvin who said, "There is no life before birth and life on Earth sucks and life after death isn't much better." So you see, people created models of their experiences that fell into these kinds of categories.

Reality is a series of nested dreams. Life is a dream that the ego is having and the ego is a dream that the soul is having and the soul is a dream that God is having. This reality unfolds chronologically in three stages. There is the embodiment of the incarnation stage when we experience ourselves in these spacesuits on planet Earth or some other place where there is life. The second stage is the disincarnated stage when we die and we shuffle off these mortal coils. Then we live in the second stage as pure soul energy.

The third stage is when we relinquish selfhood completely in order to liberate our inner divinity and then we merge with God as a wave merges back with the ocean. We give up our wave-hood in order to discover our ocean-hood. What does this look like chronologically when you break it into many stages? The first thing it looks like is cohort groups of souls. We are soul groups of disincarnate entities who do not have physicality and we make preconception contracts with each other and agree to be part of each other's evolution both in a disincarnate form and an incarnate form. We help each other out, we educate each other and we help each other to grow. Then at some stage, a group of these souls will make an agreement to plan their next incarnation together as a group. They look at possible host bodies, environments, cultures and they look at specific periods in human history when it might be appropriate to incarnate in order to have a profound experience.

Then one of two things happens. Either we live life totally forgetful of our preconception contract or at some stage we wake up and we remember what our preconception contracts were and then our enlightenment takes a huge shift. Depending on which happens to us, we live drab lives being happy if we can survive or we live very ecstatic lives because we have understood and we have remembered who we are and why we are here. Then at some stage, we die. Every one of us shuffles off this mortal coil. We undergo some kind of a life review. After the life review, there is a period of healing when our soul, traumatized by the vicissitudes of incarnation, gets an opportunity to be fully healed, debriefed of experiences and then continue with schooling and education in the disincarnate form.

At some stage we make a choice. The choice is between reincarnation and merging fully with God. We can make a choice to totally give up our selfhood which means even our soul so that the wave becomes the ocean once more and there is only God. Or we can choose to reincarnate; and we reincarnate for one of two reasons. Either we reincarnate because we still have lots of work to do and we have lots of karmic residue and we haven't fully understood how it is we are meant to love and so we come back. Or else we take Bodhisattva vows; even if we are fully evolved beings. Sometimes there is so much love in our hearts there is no way we can abandon planet Earth or there is no way that we can merge totally with the divine as long as there is a single brother or sister who is still asleep and still caught up in the illusion of the Samsara..

One of the most extraordinary aspects of the near-death research is this notion that on death we undergo a life review. It is not as if there is some kind of cosmic CPA keeping score and accusing us of our crimes. It is that we get the opportunity to experience every event of our lives but in a very different way. We get to experience it from the point of view of everyone affected by our decisions. We literally get to walk in everyone's moccasins. It is not in an accusatory fashion. No one blaming us, it is that we fully get to experience events from the point of view of all those involved.

There is nothing as pathetic as the sight of a recently deceased human standing in nakedness, having shed its pomposity, prestige and power because it was a king, a pope or a president and suddenly realizing who it really was; that it had just taken part in the "play" of life on Earth. What it had shed was merely a costume but it had identified with the costume very self-importantly and now it stands

226

in utter nakedness not being accused by anyone but by the ridiculousness of the situation.

As I look at the history of our species, during this infancy period of experiment homo sapiens I see that we have played at being kings, emperors, and presidents. It is time to give that up; it's childish. There was a subsequent time during the adolescence of homo sapiens when we played at being popes, and priests, and with hierarchies and infallibility; and it is ridiculous. It's time to give that up as well. It has long outlived its usefulness. It is time for us to begin to embrace the young adulthood of the experiment homo sapiens and come fully into the realization that all of life is a stage and all the men and women are merely players. This is not to say that it is make-believe or to say that it is not important. It is real and it is important, but the reality of it and the importance of it is that we are here to learn how to love.

I make a prediction that when the experiment, homo sapiens, comes into the fullness of maturity, it will be marked by four features. The first one will be the deconstructing of the distant, demanding deity that we have erected and feared throughout human history. The second feature will be the dissolving of the notion of chosen-ness: that any one group is any more beloved by the ultimate ground of our being than any other group. The third feature will be the realization of our own inner divinity and the inner divinity of all sentient life forms. Finally, there will be the ecstatic embrace of life as a vehicle for waking up.

MYSTICAL EXPERIENCES AND SACRED SPACE

"All of our experiences, life in the body and world, are to bring out our soul."

Paul Brunton

WHEN WE HAVE a deep experience of any kind even a mystical experience we inevitably have to force it into the nearest category or paradigm with which we are familiar. We can't encounter it on its own terms.

The truth is that all of us, no matter how unenlightened we might be, will spontaneously have deep mystical experiences. It happens to all of us. It can happen in a whole variety of guises in a whole variety of contexts and environments. All of us have these deep mystical experiences. The problem begins to arise when we begin to attempt to unpack it theoretically. How do we deal with it? How do we translate it into reality? All the mystics of all the traditions tell us that the experience goes through four phases. Firstly, there is the deep ineffable mystical experience itself. It is inarticulateable; it cannot be put into words because it is a soul experience. Secondly we attempt to foist some kind of a symbol onto it in order to hold on to the experience.

Thirdly, in order to make sense of the symbol we create ideas and concepts. And fourthly, we invent models, philosophies and theologies to explain these symbols. Of course, by the time we get to the theology, we are three stages away from the experience. Every single one of the intervening stages involves personal pathologies, group

228

biases and cultural prejudices so that the experience comes out looking very different in different cultures.

For example, suppose four different people have a deep mystical experience. A practitioner of scientism, someone who believes that the only reality is physical reality, will reduce this to just a grand mal seizure. His explanation will be that something weird happened in the brain. Since he doesn't have the paradigm and he doesn't have the container or the language or model to contain it, he explains it away in his scientistic way.

A radical fundamentalist will interpret a deep mystical experience as a command from God to become a suicide bomber. It happens. Or a less violent person may interpret a mystical experience as evidence of the exclusive choseness of his particular branch of fundamentalism i.e., there is no salvation outside the Catholic Church, or unless you believe in Jesus you will go to hell. He can have the same deep experience, but he will unpack it only according to his ability.

Whereas a truly enlightened person having a deep mystical experience will immediately recognize it as a uniting with all that is. It will dissolve all prejudices and all biases and he will understand that this is union with all sentient beings in the entire phenomenological world and with the void that lies beyond the phenomenological world. Each person will unpack even his deepest mystical experience according to the tools that he has.

Abraham Mazlow said one time, "If the only instrument you have is a hammer, everything begins to look like a nail." So depending on what resources you have, you will use those to bludgeon to death even the deepest mystical experience.

I'd like to unpack the notion of church or sacred space. Every single one of us has had encounters and experiences of sacred space. This is the space where the veil between the mystical and the mundane, between the sacred and the secular is temporarily diaphanous and we get to see through to the other side. We get to experience the reality that lies behind mere physical manifestations. Everyone has these experiences. Depending where you are coming from you will unpack it very differently. Throughout history when human beings had these experiences, they believed they had actually seen where the gods lived. The first two great effects of religion were to imitate *how* the gods lived and *where* the gods lived. All of morality comes from the notion that we on planet Earth are trying to emulate and imitate how the gods behave and interact with each other. All morality, all law, all ethical systems basically come from that. The second thing that we tried to imitate was where the gods lived. Our first efforts at building temples and sacred spaces were efforts to literally try to physically recreate where we felt the gods were living. Because people came to these places, eventually the actual locations got impregnated with the piety of generations of worshipers and they did take on sacredness. But the truth is whenever you have a deep mystical experience where two or three people are gathered together, that is church or community and the energy at these sacred spaces is created through community intention.

I believe that there are particular places that have special energy much like specific parts of the human body have particular sensitivities. The skin is the biggest organ of the body and there are parts of the skin that are more sensitive than others and more amenable to human touch. The skin of the planet has zones that are more sensitive, areas where energy consulates in an extraordinary fashion and very amenable to human touch. We call these places the sacred spaces.

Jerusalem, Mecca or Sedona may be for some, sacred spaces. We begin unpacking the notion of church and sacred space according to the paradigm from where we are operating. Some people think that you have to build shrines and actual physical constructions on these spots. We have built huge facilities where we think Jesus was born or where we think Jesus died. This is an effort to try to contain the energy in some way, so we try to unpack this experience that everyone has of encountering a sacred space. We unpack it according to our mind-set.

For the first 300 years of the Jesus movement, Christians were persecuted by Rome, because Rome considered Christians a danger to the state. Rome believed that if a group of citizens was not worshiping the gods of Rome, the gods got really angry and they would visit horrible things upon the group and the state. Christianity was considered a dangerous superstition that took people away from honoring the gods who were looking out for the welfare of Rome. In the year 312 A.D., Constantine had a conversion experience on the night before a famous battle. He was in a contest with another general who was also claiming to be the emperor of Rome. Constantine saw a sign in the sky that was a cross surrounded by a circle of light. He took this as a Christian symbol and he made Christianity a state religion.

A few years later, Constantine began to build a Catholic Church. It was a site donated by the Laterani family of Rome. This big basilica was dedicated in the year 324 A.D., and was called the Constantinian Basilica. After a period of time, it became known as the Basilica of Our Savior and then at some stage it became the Basilica of Saint John the Baptist and then later it became the Basilica of Saint John Lateran. The popes lived in the basilica from the fourth century until they moved to Avignon in 1309 A.D., with the exception of a short period when they lived in France. This church became known as "the mother and the head of all the churches of Rome and of the world."

The notion of temple and sacred space has been with us since we first developed consciousness. I believe that the very first temple that we worshiped in as a human species was the womb. Because the womb indeed is the first house for a soul once it begins to incarnate. It has been my experience that the most fearsome period in human life is incarnation; much more frightening than death. Death is not frightening at all, it is really going back home. The most frightening time for a soul is incarnating and coming onto this dense planet of ours to be confined physically, emotionally and mentally. And so the first sacred spaces were efforts to try to ritualize the journey into this dark cave of the womb.

The very first sacred spaces were caves; under ground caves that could only be accessed through long tortuous tunnels. The young initiate had to wend his or her way in utter darkness into these dark underground caverns. It was an experience of reentering the womb and then coming out into the sunlight. In my opinion, these were the first temples. These temples go back some 60,000 years into the shamanic culture, and all subsequent temples are efforts to recreate them.

About the year 3,000 B.C., the Sumerians, modern day Iraq, came up with the notion of building over-ground temples to God called ziggurats. The Tower of Babel really was a Sumerian ziggurat. It was an effort to build a house that went up to the heavens. There was an effort to penetrate from the immanence of the Earth to the transcendence of the heavens. The pyramids came about 600 years later. The pyramids developed special geometry that produced acoustical effects that allowed people to have transcendental experiences.

In many of these chambers, Pharaohs to-be would be subjected to an induced near-death experience. The Egyptian doctors and priests at the time had developed techniques to slow down human metabolism to a state where people had out of body experiences. In order to qualify as a Pharaoh, you had to undergo a near-death experience in such a chamber. The chambers were constructed with energy aligned in such a fashion that, combined with medications, they induced these near-death transcendental experiences. This again was an effort to recreate the womb over and under ground at the same time. They were built above the ground, but they created a womb-like atmosphere.

Moses, 1,400 years later, had his encounter at the burning bush. He stood in front of a burning bush and had an epiphany; God somehow communicated with him and said, "I am who I am." Moses then tried to recapture this encounter with God. Since they were a nomadic people wandering in the desert, he created a mobile temple. He carried this mobile temple with him for the 40 years of their sojourn. When they eventually got into the land of Canaan about 1210 B.C., their first great project was the building of a temple. This temple was built by the specifications supposedly passed on to Moses by God. This temple survived from 930 B.C. to 597 B.C., but then the Babylonians destroyed it and the Jews were sent into exile.

Ezekiel had a vision where he saw a new temple with water flowing out on four sides from 12 pillars. Released from slavery in the year 529 B.C., the Jews went back to the land of Israel and rebuilt the temple. This temple continued to the time of Jesus. Herod the Great spent 46 years adding to it. When Jesus said, "Destroy this temple and in three days I will raise it up," people thought this statement ridiculous. Jesus tried to convey the idea that temple is not a physical location where you can trap God. The temple of God is totally different. True worship is found in Spirit.

Almost 1000 years later a group known as the Knights Templar went across Europe in the first Crusade and devastated everything before them, killing Eastern Orthodox Christians, Jews and Moslems in order to recover the "holy places." The story from that time suggests that they found plans for the temple in Jerusalem buried under the rubble and brought them back to Europe. Then the great cathedrals of Europe began to flourish in the 11th and 12th centuries and were often built on old pagan caves and goddess worshiping sites and constructed according to the plans found in Jerusalem. This new movement of Christianity was represented symbolically by the building but much more powerfully by its esoteric theology.

In Ireland, the old Celtic tradition taught that it is where *people* are gathered that you have church. You can't confine God to a building; it is the place where people are gathered that is the real center of worship.

How do we recreate sacred space in our own time? There is a tendency in human beings to spontaneously do it. We have all seen evidence where people bring flowers to the exact spot where someone has been killed; erecting a sort of shrine to the deceased. When there has been a tragedy, people will spontaneously want to make it a place of pilgrimage and a shrine in memory of those who died. There is a deep instinct in us to recognize this interface between the transcendent and the immanent. How can we do this consciously?

At the community level, it is about trying to create sacred space for a period of two hours on a Sunday morning. We do it using as many of the senses as we can. We use sound through music, reading the word of God, sometimes we use incense, and during Eucharist we have a meal together. So we are seeing, feeling, hearing, tasting and touching. The hug during the Kiss of Peace is the God in me reaching out to the God in you through the medium of this spacesuit with which we have been gifted. A hug is not just a, "Hi how are you?" A hug is literally the transcendence of God in me reaching the transcendence of God in you through our two spacesuits. We appeal to all the senses so as to engage the emotions and then, hopefully, we get swept up in the ritual and the experience. That leads to an intellectual involvement. The readings and the homilies stimulate us to think more deeply about who we really are and ultimately it engages the soul. We start with the senses that feed the emotions that lead to the intellect that finally goes right to the soul. That is what good liturgy should be about. That is what creating sacred space as a community is about on a Sunday morning on a regular basis.

I recommend that we find a place in our homes where we can make our own "private" sacred space. We can put precious objects there such as family photographs or pictures of those we consider saints or objects from sacred places or anything that we want so that when we are in our sacred space we will be reminded of who we really are.

The human body is a temple of the Holy Spirit. When Jesus said, "Destroy this temple and in three days I will raise it up," he did precisely that. Jesus wedded the physical body with the soul because soul consecrates matter by incarnation. Matter consecrates soul by death and both are equally important. Every soul consecrates matter by incarnating. All matter consecrates soul by releasing at death, because it is the penetration of the immanent into the transcendent and incarnation is the penetration of the transcendent into the immanent. They are the male and the female aspects of God. The body is not just a house for the soul to inhabit. The body is literally the temple, a womb or sacred space that allows the soul to have a full human experience.

Without a full human experience, enlightenment is not possible. Without incarnation, enlightenment is not possible because until we have touched the depth of the illusion of separate identity, enlightenment does not make sense. It is the shattering of the illusion of separate identity that sets us firmly on the path to enlightenment. We can only experience that through incarnation. The human body is the sacred space or temple that allows the soul to have an experience that sets it on the path to full enlightenment. The human body is God the Mother manifesting as matter allowing a sacred space for God the Father manifesting as soul so the journey into enlightenment can begin.

Every single one of us is a sacred family, an extraordinary union of the Fatherhood and Motherhood of God. Your body is providing a womb for the transcendent to have such a human experience so that ultimately your path to enlightenment is assured. So the divine in me recognizing the divine in you says to you, Namasté.

SPIRITUAL AMNESIA

"One who seeks his real Self will not be afraid of any obstacle."
Ramana Maharshi

A VERY WISE OLD man with a glint in his eyes once explained to me the difference between a spinster and an old maid. He said, "A spinster is a woman who never got married. And an old maid is a woman who never got married or anything." That is a very important distinction. In Ireland, when I was young, there were lots of spinsters and old maids because of a huge male migration from Ireland. The first born son would remain to inherit the farm and all of the other boys would go. There were lots of girls left behind who became spinsters and old maids.

The O'Sullivan sisters, Annie, Barbara and Catherine, all in their 70s, lived together in my village a few doors away from my family. When I knew them they seemed very "bothered." Bothered is an Irish euphemism for senile. In other words, they were becoming very senile. Instead of using the word, senile, we tended to use softer words like bothered.

On one occasion, Annie decided to have her annual bath. She was in the upstairs bathroom and had one foot inside the tub when she stopped and said to herself, "Was I getting into the tub or getting out?" She called down to her sister, "Barbara, come up here and help me. I can't remember whether I'm getting out of the tub or into the tub." Barbara, sitting downstairs, took off her glasses with a sigh and got up and hobbled up the stairs, stopping to catch her breath at the first landing. A few moments later she sighed, "Oh my God, was I going up the stairs or down the stairs? She called to her sister, Catherine, "Come upstairs and help me a moment. Annie is in the bathroom and doesn't know whether she's getting in or out of the tub and I'm on the stairs and I don't know whether I'm going up the stairs or down the stairs." Catherine put down her knitting and looking to heaven said, "Thanks be to God I'm not as crazy as those two sisters of mine," and she carefully knocked on wood. Startled, she looked around and said, "Oh dear, was that the front door or the back door?"

There is not one of us who does not suffer from being very bothered. Life on Earth makes us very bothered. We don't know whether we are getting in or out, going up or down and where the knock is coming from.

There is a big difference between seeing and looking. In many languages they are distinguished. Because most of us grew up speaking English, we don't quite appreciate the distinction. When you have the privilege of learning another language then you begin to notice the distinction. In John's gospel, Jesus said to Andrew, "I want you to really look. I'm not just saying to glance around, really look!"

The entire function of spirituality is to make us look. Unfortunately, spirituality is too often reduced to merely having us believe stuff. The church does the looking for us and then they tell us what is there. We are supposed to sign off and say, I believe. That is not spirituality that is merely religion. Religion is telling us to believe what other people allegedly have seen and spirituality is the injunction to go see for yourself. The Buddha said again and again, "Be a lamp unto yourself." Go out and light your own light and look. Don't believe anything anyone tells you.

John the Baptist's injunction to his disciples was, "I want you to really, really look." The disciples followed Jesus; they had no idea what they were going to say as they walked behind him. Jesus realizing that they were following him said, "What are you looking for?" One of them said, "Where is your pad? Where do you hang out?" And Jesus said, "Come and see." They spent the whole day with him and they were totally transformed. That was the beginning of the Jesus movement. It is all about seeing and looking, but there are many different forms of it.

There are basically three kinds of people on planet Earth. There are those who are born and they hit the ground running. They are already on the spiritual quest from the time they are little children. They are looking because they already know; part of them never forgot. They remember who they are and where they have come from and what they are here to do.

Then there are a lot of people who at some stage in their adult life accidentally encounter a person, teacher, book, lecture and something wakes them up and then they begin their spiritual quest. Most of us spend our entire lives not questing at all: asleep, totally asleep. We are totally engaged in the pursuit of illusion. That is where most of us are. The lucky ones hit the ground running, a few more accidentally discover and the rest of us are fast asleep. Jesus told parables to illustrate all of these types of people. He told the parable about the merchant who was in search of fine pearls. He went from town to town and village to village and from country to country in search of a really great pearl. One day he found it in a little market place in a little corner of the Middle East and he said, "My God, this is what I have been looking for all my life." He told the shop keeper, "Hold it for me. I'll go home and sell all I have and I'm going to come back and buy that pearl." He went home, sold all his possessions and came back and bought the pearl. That is the person who has hit the ground running; a person, who from the time of his childhood, had been on some kind of a spiritual safari.

We don't just happen upon a great teacher or book or just happen to remember a fabulous dream that suddenly changes the course of our lives. We build these reminders into our lives long before we incarnate. As we were planning our incarnation, we thought, "Is there some clue that I can build into my life to help me remember? All of the other times, I have forgotten. I came back here kicking myself that I couldn't see the sign. I'll build some subtle thing into the next lifetime to wake me up." We build these things in and sometimes we think that they are just déjà vu experiences. They are clues I have built into my next lifetime to remind me of why I am here. These great people that we encounter or the fabulous books we read or the great lectures we hear or interesting dreams we remember have been pre-built by us into our system.

When I was in the seminary I was never interested in scripture and I had no interest in theology whatsoever. I was interested in drama and athletics and sports. I have a good memory and so on the night before any test, I would read the entire course and for each item I would make little mnemonics for myself. I would pick out ten main points for the topic, the key word from each phrase and then take the first letter of each of these words and create some kind of an anagram for myself and then remember the anagram. When I went into the test the next day and the question came up, I would write down the anagram and reconstruct it and within 15 minutes I would have the whole thing on paper.

Perhaps that is what we have done. We have created little cheat sheets for ourselves and we have built them into our lives and then we happen upon them, we are totally surprised and they begin the waking up process. There is nothing accidental about it. Because we know that we have a penchant for forgetting, we put these little reminders into ourselves.

There is a great tradition in the Jewish Talmud about the angel of night who is called Aiyella. In this tradition, just before a little infant is born, Aiyealla comes into the womb and makes an indentation on the upper lip and the two sides of its nose to cause amnesia in the baby for where they have just come from. Most of us suffer from that amnesia for our whole lifetime. But the ones who have been back here often enough perhaps have remembered when they were "up there" how much they had forgotten when they were "down here." So we put these clues or we imbed these fossils into the fabric of our life next time. These are the little things that wake us up. For the rest of us, the sleepy ones, we are too lazy even when we are up there to fossilize the fabric of the next lifetime and so we meander through the entire lifetime just buying into the illusion.

When the disciples asked Jesus the question, "Where is your pad?," and Jesus answered, "Come and see." He meant, I want you to really look. I'm not just going to show you a little cabin. I'm going to show you the house of God. I'm going to show you where you are from and where you are destined to return.

There is a beautiful phrase that we have heard for thousands of years that Jesus is the Lamb of God. Isn't that lovely! When we think of cuddly little creatures; puppies, kittens and lambs all fall into the same category. Little wooly lambs go baaa, and we love to cuddle them. There is a huge difference between lambs, puppies and kittens because puppies grow up to be man's best friend. Kittens grow up to be independent as they walk around the house and they couldn't care less about their human servants who are just there to look after them. Lambs grow up to become mutton stew.

When Saint John said, "There is the lamb of God." He was not saying; look at the cuddly little creature. Go give him a hug. He was saying, this is about sacrifice and slaughter and mutton stew except we make a mistake and we Mel Gibsonize it. The sacrifice and the crucifixion of Jesus had nothing to do with the death of Jesus. It had to do with his conception and incarnation. Moreover, it was not just about the conception and the incarnation of Jesus, it is about the conception and incarnation of every one of us. Crucifixion is about deciding to be conceived. Slaughter is about deciding to be born. The coming in is much more difficult than the exit. The decision to incarnate is an extraordinarily difficult decision. Again, there are three kinds of souls in heaven. There are those who don't want to incarnate any more anywhere and are happy where they are. Then there are the ones who incarnate on lesser planets where the negativity level is somewhere between five and ten percent and a real easy ride. Then there are those who decide to incarnate on planet Earth where the negativity is somewhere between 45 and 50 percent. It is a real tough project. Only the courageous get to come to planet Earth.

It is a really difficult place to come. But sometimes on our way we suddenly realize what we are signing up for and we say, "Know what, I've changed my mind, I can't go through with it." Over 30 percent of pregnancies end in miscarriages. Why does this happen? I'll give you a good esoteric reason for it. After a few weeks in this tiny, cluttered, dense little spacesuit where they are trying to learn how to manipulate not just the physiology of the thing but the emotionality of it and the intellectuality of it they say, "You know, I can't handle this." This is spiritual claustrophobia and they go back. The mother's body decides after a few months that there is no point in carrying an empty spacesuit and sheds it. Miscarriage is largely because the soul has changed its mind and doesn't want to go through with incarnation. One of the reasons a baby dies in the first two years of life may be that its mission is complete. Whatever this little child came to do and whatever this family signed up to do has been accomplished. But sometimes it may be that after two years in this crippling experience of this tiny little spacesuit, the soul decides that the only thing to do is to go back.

But you didn't do that. None of you decoded to make an exit by a miscarriage. We all decided to stick it out and here we are years later and we are still here. Isn't it a terrible waste of effort to have decided not to take an exit by a miscarriage but to stick it out and after all that trouble, after signing up for the toughest planet in the Cosmos and deciding to go through with the conception process and the birth process and to still be here years later, isn't it a terrible pity that we couldn't just go the extra step and wake up. We wouldn't have to come back anymore. We would have to do it only once unless we were total masochists and we signed on for the Bodhisattva vow, in which case you have to parachute back here again and again.

Someone was telling me recently about a video of a new "industry" that they had heard of where a person commits a murder while cameras record the event and they sell the video so other sick people can watch the agony of the victim. Is there anything sicker than that? There is! There is a being who has done that billions of times over billions of years. We call him God. He orchestrated the bloody death of millions of victims over millions of lifetimes. If anyone needed the twelve step program, it is he. I just invented a twelve step program called, SKA (serial killers anonymous). I can imagine God attending his first meeting and standing up and saying, "Hi, my name is God and I'm a serial killer," and everyone says, "Hi God." Is this the kind of God that we believe in? Do we really think that that is what the sin of the world is about? Is there some kind of sick divinity who needs blood sacrifice in order to feel good or in order to entertain itself? It has nothing to do with that.

The sin of the world is not about murder or rape; these are only symptoms of the sins of the world. The sin of the world is that the world is asleep. The sin of you and me is the fact that we are still asleep and we are still engaged in the illusion. We are still stuck in the illusion that we are different from God and separate from God. We are still stuck in the illusion that we are separate from other human beings and we are still stuck in the illusion that we are separate from all sentient creatures. That is sin. When we break through that sin, all of the symptoms clear up. There will be no murder, rape, lies or stealing possible when enough people have awakened. The sin of the world is that we are all fast asleep.

Wouldn't it be wonderful if we started to wake up because that is the gift of this extraordinary planet. Planet Earth is not just this molten mass of sun that was catapulted off 4.5 billion years ago that subsequently developed a kind of crush of Teutonic plates the movement and clashing of which has created mountains, valleys and oceans. It is not that at all. The real function of planet Earth is that it is a great soul meant to be the staging place for the evolution of the species which will wake up its own divinity. That is what the great soul, Gaia, signed up to do, and that is what the planet is attempting to do right now. It has created a species that is on the verge of that process, but only very few people have broken through. Only the Christ figures and the Buddha figures and a few more have managed to take the final step into Buddhahood or Christ consciousness and become truly awake. That is our function, our mission and that is why we are here. That is why we have embedded the fabric of this incarnation with dé jà vu experiences, great teachers, fabulous lectures, good books or great dreams in order to try to make ourselves become awake.

Planet Earth is groaning with labor pains trying to give birth to Christ consciousness. One of the most mystical passages in all of Saint Paul's writing, is in his letter to the Romans where he says, "Nature itself is groaning as it awaits the revelation of the children of God." It is waiting for people to wake up. This is nature's gift. It wants to birth the Christ child. But not just in Jesus of Nazareth who lived and died two thousand years ago, but in every one of us. Do you and do I have the courage to climb onto the labor table and put our feet in the stirrups and attend to the contractions and push like bloody hell until we give birth to Christ consciousness? Is this the year that you could grow up and become the Mother of God?

Staying Awake

"When we love God, we find Him in the temple of our heart and in the heart of all that lives and thus, in loving Him, we love all that exists."

Guru Nanak

MY GRANDFATHER HAD a very good relationship with the fairies of Ireland and had frequent encounters with them. When I was a small boy, he told me about these encounters. He was from the village of Blarney where the famous Blarney stone is located. One time he told me about a man in his village, Michael McCarthy, who had a very scary encounter. He was coming home late one evening and came across a little pond with a beautiful waterfall. He could hear the sound of laughter coming from the pond so he snuck up to get a closer look and saw young fairy girls swimming in the pool totally naked. He feasted his eyes on them for a few minutes and unable to contain himself he said, "Aha, wouldn't I like to have one of you come home with me tonight," and all the fairies disappeared. He continued on his way home, but before he got there he met an old bent, haggard woman who looked at him with the blackest eyes he had ever seen. She said, "Michael McCarthy you have insulted my people. I'm going to put a curse on you. From the time you close your eyes tonight until you draw your last breath on planet Earth you'll never see anything again." Poor Michael was absolutely scared. He went home and tried to stay up as long as he could but about two o'clock in the morning his eyes began to close. He splashed cold water on his face, but try as he would he couldn't stay awake and collapsed in a heap on the floor and slept for 12 hours. He never saw anything again for the rest of his life.

Imagine what the struggle was like for Michael McCarthy between the encounter with the old lady and actually falling asleep. Imagine how hard he tried and how much effort he put into trying to stay awake. That is what enlightenment is about and that is what Jesus talked about.

It is sad, really sad that the farther you go away from the Equator the sadder you get. In psychology, SAD stands for Seasonal Affective Disorder. It is what happens when the days get short and the nights get long and the skies get cloudy. It is what happens to the human hypothalamus which is responsible for our moods. When we are denied sunlight through the retina, which is where 95 percent of the photoelectric activity of the brain is generated, people's moods are affected. It is bad enough that we are experiencing this and the farther north or south from the Equator one goes this becomes exaggerated. It is bad enough that we have to experience this every year, but then the church really starts rubbing it in with the readings at this stage of the year.

The church is either a great homeopath or a great sadist. Homeopathy acts on the principle that anything that causes a disease in a well person, will heal that disease in a sick person. If you have particular symptoms, the homeopath will give you something that would have caused those symptoms if you had been well in the belief that it will accelerate the healing process. So either the church is a really good homeopath as we go through the dark days of winter and decides to try to push us through it as quickly as possible, or else, it's a real sadist and it kicks us when we are down. The liturgy readings for this part of the year contain dire predictions of what happens at the end times.

The synoptic gospels are full of this dark stuff and the church forces our faces into it at this time of year. The problem is that there are five totally different items all mixed up together in the synoptic gospels. When Luke, Matthew and Mark wrote about the end times, the signs in the sky and the dire consequences, did they mean the imminent death of Jesus or your death and my death? Was it about the fall of Jerusalem that happened 40 years after the death of Jesus? Was it about the end of the world? Was it about the second coming of Jesus? Which of these five were they writing about? The problem is that they are all mixed in together. The other problem is that we interpret them literally.

There is a very famous editor who lives in our midst who gets annoyed every time we sing the song: "Christ has died, Christ has risen, and Christ will come again." She claims that Christ did not die and she is absolutely right. Christ cannot die. Jesus died, but Christ cannot die. When we talk about the death of Jesus, we need to be really sure that we are talking about Jesus and not about Christ, because Christ consciousness cannot die. When Luke and Matthew wrote about the death of Jesus, it is true, a carpenter from Galilee died in agony on a cross two thousand years ago. Was it that death that really precipitated Christ consciousness? The important thing is not the death of Jesus; the important thing was the release of Christ consciousness. When we read in the gospels about the end of Jesus we think that this is a dire, devastating event instead of realizing that this was the ultimate liberation. It was the pouring out of Christ consciousness or the possibility of Christ consciousness on our planet.

Every single one of us is going to die some day. Does that frighten us? Is that it? Death has nothing to do with that. Death has to do with the ongoing death of the ego and the end of the illusions that separate us from God and separate us from each other. The church would have us believe that we are creatures of sin who do not merit God's love instead of realizing that every single one of us is God stuff. Every one of us is a bite-size piece of God having a human experience. Life cannot be ended; souls are eternal beings.

When I think about my own death, I'm not worried about shedding this spacesuit, I'm much more concerned with the death of my ego and the many illusions I labor under throughout this lifetime.

When I think about the fall of Jerusalem, what does that mean to me? It doesn't mean that in 70 A.D., the Romans flattened the city destroying the temple and killing the priests and that was the end of the priesthood within Judaism. It does not mean that. It means the transformation of culturally bound, nationalistic, theocratic principles so that we grow into global awareness as a species. That is what the death and the fall of Jerusalem means to me. It is not about an event that happened two thousand years ago. When I think about the end of the world, am I looking for signs that planet Earth is going to implode? It is not about that. It is about the fact that the great soul which is planet Earth, Gaia, is also bound for a transformative leap into a fifth dimension consciousness. The death of the planet would just be the death of the old way of being planet Earth. Every one of us is called to die to the old way of being you or the old way of being me in order to become the new way of being you or the new way of being me. Even the planet itself is being called upon to finally die to the old way of being Gaia and become the new way of being Gaia.

What does the second coming of Christ mean? This second coming does not mean some apocalyptic event in the future. Rather it is thinly disguised reincarnation; it is the opportunity for every one of us to reincarnate again and again until every sentient being is saved. It is not just Jesus, the carpenter from Nazareth, who is going to make his second appearance on the stage of planet Earth; it is every single one of us. It is anyone who has enough love to keep coming back until all of one's brothers and sisters have awakened; that is what it's about. That is what waking up is about.

One of the most beautiful and yet meaningless prophesies in the scriptures is that of Isaiah: "In the days to come they will beat their swords into plow shares and their spears into pruning hooks." While that scripture is poetic and beautiful, it is one of the most meaningless prognostications in all of scripture. Isaiah delivered this prophesy in 742 B.C. and since then there have been thousands of wars and hundreds of millions of people violently killed. What kind of a prophet was Isaiah? We are now beating our swords into intercontinental ballistic missiles and our spears into nuclear warheads. He wasn't much of a prophet. It's about time that he got fired if that's what he was about.

If I present you with two grandfather clocks and I say, "I want you to decide which one of these clocks is the more accurate; one loses a half an hour a day and the other loses only a minute a day; which one is more accurate?" The one that looses a half an hour a day will be right every three weeks whereas the one that loses only a minute a day will be right only once every two years. By that analogy, is Isaiah a better prophet? Is the best prophet the one who can foretell the immediate future accurately or the one who can tell the distant future accurately? We've waited 2,746 years and Isaiah's prophesy still hasn't come true. Is it because we have to live another 2,746 years and then it will be true? Does that make Isaiah a much better prophet than the one who can foretell what will happen next week? Of course, that is not the function of the prophet. The prophet is not the person who prognosticates or foretells the future. The function of prophesy is to call people into alignment with God. That is the entire function of prophesy. It has nothing to do with prognostication. Except that the prophet, because she is the person who can see very clearly what is, is much more likely to predict where it is leading. In that sense, they are prognosticators. But their function is not to tell the future. Their function is to call every single one of us into alignment with our covenanted relationship with God. And covenant is not some kind of a legalized document consisting of 613 precepts, or 2000 precepts given by an exacting, distant, demanding deity, but rather it is the God that lives within every one of us calling us into alignment.

Maybe we don't need to fire Isaiah. Maybe he was a real prophet in the real sense of the word. Either he was a long-term futurist or else he was calling us into alignment with ourselves. When we are in alignment with ourselves, we have already beaten our swords into plowshares and we have already beaten our spears into pruning hooks. Every one of us who has awakened has already done that so the prophesy proves very accurate again and again throughout human history.

What do we mean by the future? Is the future some kind of fated, inevitable outcome that is going to happen in spite of our best efforts? Or is the future the probable logical outcome because of our best efforts? Is the future going to happen without us, inevitably and against our will, or is it the logical, positive outcome of all the choices we make in the present? There is no such thing as the fated inevitable outcome. There is no future in that sense. The future is the probable, logical consequence of all of the decisions of all of us right now on the planet. We can create the kind of future we want. The best way to predict the future is to create the future. We can create it any way we want. People who are fascinated by and fixated on an apocalyptic vision of the future are in danger of precipitating just that. In fact, there is a group of Christian fundamentalists and that is its avowed agenda. These people are trying to orchestrate the world political scene and particularly the Middle East in order to precipitate Armageddon. They are in danger of doing it. If there aren't enough of us creating a different vision, a different dream or a different future then they are going to have their way. Until we can reach a critical mass of people who can think lovingly and compassionately about our future as a species, we are liable to cede the field to the others.

Throughout human history we have been fascinated by the notion that there are always signs portending what the future will inevitably bring about. What are these signs to which we are looking? As long as the signs are interpreted on postulates of fear, then we are going to create a world in which it will be very difficult to live. The signs are not meant to instill fear in us. They are intended to spur us into dreaming about a really compassionate, colorful future. We will find what we look for. If you look hard enough for anything, you will eventually find it. If you look with real intensity for something you will find only what you are looking for and you will find nothing else. If this particular regime in this time of our world is fixated on finding weapons of mass destruction and terrorists, they will eventually find them because they will have created them. If we envisage a world in which our expectation and our dream is Christ consciousness, not in Jesus coming back in anger to judge us, but the outbreak of Christ consciousness alerting all of us to our true nature and to the true nature resident in every one else, that too will come about.

Except that in order to make that happen on a global scale we first need to make it happen on an interpersonal level. To the extent that I am looking for reasons in my relationship to doubt the participation and sincerity of my partner; I'm going to find them. To the extent that I'm looking in my relationship for evidence that this could be a really great relationship; I'll find that too. I'm not going to find global Christ consciousness in the absence of finding this particular level of sharing and unity consciousness; literally love or charity begins at home. It begins where I am. It will only happen on the world stage if it is happening in my interpersonal relationships.

Hell is not some kind of spot for eternal damnation to which God consigns the evil doers. It has nothing to do with that. Hell comes in many different varieties. One variety of hell is what happens in the bardo stage when we have shuffled off this mortal coil. When we die, we are in a bardo state; a place where we are bodiless in the sense of not being somatized or physicalized. When we have shed that, it becomes increasingly easy for us to create both heaven and hell. A mindset based on fear and anger will continue to create hellish states for its own existence. It is easier to do it after death than before death, because when we are on the planet, in order to create that reality we have to put extra energy into the process by manifesting it on a physical plain. When we no longer need bodies it means there is extra energy available for creating the heaven and hell. If we are addicted to fear and anger it is much easier for us to continue to create hell after we die. When we come back on the planet again with the same level of non-evolution then we will continue to experience hell on earth for ourselves.

Heaven is not some state of bliss with God. Heaven too has many possibilities. First it is the state after we die when we can experience transformation and healing from our Earth safari. It is also where we make the bodhisattva vow or the agreement to come back onto planet Earth again and again until every one of my brothers and sisters has awakened.

What does this say about the evolution of the planet? One of two things will happen. When planet Earth grows up or planet Earth blows up, one or two things will happen. If planet Earth grows up, then this planet will continue to evolve until it creates a species capable of recognizing its own divinity and the divinity in all sentient beings, then the work of planet Earth will be complete.

If planet Earth blows up, instead of grows up, humans will be finished as an experiment and that will be the end of it. Those of us incarnated will have choices. We can seek out other planets that are commensurate with our level of evolution and we will be attracted to planets where we will continue to make war and kill people. Or, if we are a little bit more evolved, we will find other planets a little bit more evolved than planet Earth where we can live out Christ consciousness.

But if it blows up, it will eventually regenerate itself and will continue with the experiment until finally it will create a different species that will be capable of recognizing its own divinity. In the meantime, those people who have reached a particular level of consciousness, will find planets that are commensurate with their own idea of what life is really about. As long as we are driven by anger and fear we will be attracted to worlds based on war mongering and as soon as we wake up to Christ consciousness we will be attracted to planets where life is about Christ consciousness.

The final act in the drama is that every one of us will wake up. No matter how many planets it takes or how many reincarnations it takes, every one of us will eventually get it that the only thing that works is love. War doesn't work. Intercontinental ballistic missiles do not work. Weapons of mass destruction do not work. Only love works. Given enough time and given enough incarnations and enough planets to blow up all of us will finally get it that the only thing that makes sense is love. Then our work will be complete and we can all merge with God. I offer myself and I offer you, this choice, the same choice that Moses offered his people on Mount Sinai when he said, "Today I offer you life or death." I now offer you the possibility of growing up the planet or I offer you the possibility of blowing up the planet. Let's choose life.

BE AWAKE FOR THE
SECOND COMING OF CHRIST

"I am a hole in a flute that Christ's breath moves through —listen to this music."

Hafiz

ILLY KENNIFICK WAS the most prodigious sleeper I've ever met in my life. If sleep be a miniature death, when Billy laid down his head it was a major demise. Billy and I attended the same seminary. My first mission in Kenya, after my ordination in 1972, was in a little village in the Rift Valley where I spent a period of three months for orientation and to learn Swahili. There were two men in that mission when I arrived, Billy and Derry Buckley. All three of us had attended the same high school and the same seminary of the Saint Patrick's Missionary Society.

Derry was the pastor for this mission and he was a bright man with an honors degree in chemistry. Billy entered the seminary several years after graduating from high school. He was a literary man and a brilliant actor with the Cork Shakespearian Troupe. Billy taught English literature in a government high school in Kenya. But Billy had one big problem; he couldn't wake up in the morning. One day Derry rigged up an alarm system for him. He put an alarm clock in an enamel pan with a lot of forks and spoons and when the alarm clock went off in the morning it would rattle uproariously and make a terrible racket and yet Billy would not wake up. We always had to drag him out of bed in the morning and he was always late for school.

We've all heard the phrase about staying awake and the notion of, "the second coming of Christ," for which we are meant to "stay awake." What is the history of the misperception of the notion of staying awake? This notion goes back long before Jesus. It comes out of a period when the Jews had returned from their Babylonian captivity. They had all been taken into exile in the year 587 B.C. and finally after about 70 years, when the Persians overthrew the Babylonians, they set the Jews free to go back to the land of Israel. Only a tiny percentage actually chose to go back, the rest of them had settled in Babylon and its environs and they opted to stay put. Those that went back found Jerusalem in ruins, the vineyards and the temple destroyed. They became desolate and the prophets tried to persuade them to rebuild the temple of God. This was the first coming; the coming home after 70 years of deportation, but it hadn't worked. Isaiah pleaded with God to come down in a mighty show of power and make the mountains quake. So about 520 years before Jesus, you have this notion of a second coming which was going to be accompanied by earth-shattering events with mountains literally dancing in anger at the crimes of humanity. This is the beginning of the history of the notion of the second coming.

After the death of Jesus, up to the time of the young church, the disciples were totally convinced that Jesus was going to come back, maybe next week. They were sure that the second coming was imminent and it would involve the physical resurrection of Jesus and the physical presence of Jesus in their midst.

Paul picks up on this and in his letters, particularly in Thessalonians I, and in Corinthians I, he talks about the day of the coming of our Lord Jesus the Christ. Paul assures his audience saying: "Those of us who are still alive when Jesus comes back will have no advantage over those who have died in the interim." Paul is convinced that Jesus is going to come back during his own lifetime. The Thessalonians took this teaching so literally that they stopped working and there was bedlam. An urgent message went out to Paul and he wrote a second letter to the Thessalonians and said: "Those who do not work should not be allowed to eat. We don't know exactly when Jesus is coming back so get out there and contribute to society."

Throughout Christian history we had the same thing happen again and again. Every few decades there is some group that gathers around some modern day prophet and climbs up to a hilltop to wait for God to come down and devastate everyone else. It happens with great frequency, for example, there is the notion that you find in fundamentalist Christianity of the "rapture." It is a belief that God is going to come back so suddenly that we will literally have empty beds and abandoned autos on the freeways. I am not joking. This is the literal understanding among fundamentalist Christians of this notion of the rapture. They believe that there will be a sudden blast of Gabriel's trumpet and men will be driving down freeways and suddenly they will be yanked out of their cars and taken to heaven and the autos will continue down the road until they run out of gas. Or, there will be two people in bed together one of them will be chosen and the other rejected. The chosen person will be yanked out and the other person will wake in the morning and say, "What happened with my wife?" That is literally what they are expecting.

We've also had groups like "Heaven's Gate" who committed suicide because they were convinced that there was a spaceship lurking in the wake of the Haley-Bopp comet that would take them to heaven and the rest of us on the planet would all go to hell. This notion of waiting for the rapture occurs again and again. Of course, it is not about the rapture. That is a total misperception of what this event is about. These groups continue to expect traumatic times in which God is going to come back and rescue the elect from among us.

The extraordinary thing is that there is more money being poured into Israel now by fundamentalist Christians in this country than there is by Jews in this country. Not because they have any great love of Judaism, but because in their literalist interpretation of the scripture they believe that for the second coming to happen, the Jews have to occupy the biblical land of Israel in order for God to keep his promise. So they are pouring money into Israel, not because they love

Judaism, but because they are trying to force God's hand to come back and initiate the rapture.

When you read in the scriptures, "At the second coming, be awake and be aware because you do not know the day or the hour that the master will return," does that fill you with foreboding or does it fill you with excitement? What is the import of that message? What is the inference you take from this message? What is the intended message of that scripture? When you were a small child and your mother said to you, "You wait until your daddy gets home," was that a threat or was it a treat? Which was it? How would you like your child to wait for your coming home? Do you want your child to be filled with foreboding, dread and fear as s/he waits for your home coming? Or do you want your child to rush to you and smother you with kisses? Are you a better parent than God? Are you a better parent than what Jesus is offering to us when he talks about the father or the master? Which notion are you following? What is driving this theology of dread that we have been force-fed throughout Christian history?

For me it is a combination of a few different elements. Firstly, it is trying to keep discipline by making people afraid. We do this in our school systems, in our family systems and we are doing it in the country at this moment in the homeland security obsession. People are being made afraid and they give up all their rights in order to remain secure.

There are some very secure people in this country. There are only two million Americans who are really secure; they are all in jail. Everything is provided for them and they are totally secure. They don't have to worry where they are going to lay their heads, who will feed them, what they will wear or where they will exercise. They have all the security they need, but none of the freedom they want.

There are a lot of people in our society who are totally free e.g. the homeless. They are free to go anywhere they want but they have no security. So there has to be some kind of a tradeoff, someplace in between freedom and security. For 2000 years, we have been fed the notion that religion will give us the security we want, but we have to give up all our freedom. It is based on a fundamentalist understanding of the mystical word of God. It is based on anthropomorphism and it is based on a notion of elitism; that there are chosen people and there are rejected people.

Then there are the barbarians, infidels and pagans, but it is always an "us" versus "them." This kind of foreboding, threatening scriptural tradition can only survive in the presence of elitism and the giving up of freedom in order to have security in anthropomorphism and in literalism. That is what is driving this kind of theology. It is terrible theology, has no profundity whatsoever and is totally fear based.

What do I believe is the mystical understanding of this passage of scripture? I want to go back to my first statement that comes from the Buddha 550 years before Jesus. The title Buddha literally means the one who is awake. This notion of being awake is something you will find in all the great mystical spiritual traditions of the world. It is not peculiar to Christianity.

Gautama Siddhartha was born a Hindu but took exception to the excesses and corruption in the Hinduism of his time. After he became an enlightened being, the Brahmin priests asked him by what authority was he teaching. They asked, "Are you a prophet?" He said, "No I am not a prophet." "Are you an angel?" "No I am not an angel." "Are you a sage?" "No, I am not a sage." "Then what are you?" He said, "I am awake." That was how he defined himself. That is the origin of the notion of Buddhahood. The Buddha is someone who has awakened; enlightenment means being awake. It is not about fear.

The second coming of Jesus is not about fear. The second coming of Jesus is not about some kind of cataclysmic event, rapture or otherwise. The second coming of Jesus is not about the end of the world in any sense. The second coming of Jesus is not even about your own personal death. It is not about any of those things, in spite of the fact that the church throughout 2000 years has constantly been pushing this in our faces and trying through fear to lick us into some kind of shape. You can't make people become spiritual through fear. You can only make people religious out of fear, but you can never make people spiritual out of fear.

So what is this second coming? What is it about? If it is not about fear, or our death, or the end of the world, or apocalyptic events, what is it about? It is about curiosity. It is about the extraordinary sense of awe with which children are born and with which children investigate the environment into which they are born. It is a sense of awe. It is a sense of wonder at the planet. It is the ability and the daily practice of seeing the fullness of God in the most ordinary of circumstances. It is the ability to be able to see the fullness of God in a budding daffodil. It is it the ability to see the fullness of God in the face of a sleeping infant. It is the ability to see the fullness of God in our Eucharistic celebration. It is the ability to see the fullness of God in any ordinary circumstance. That is the second coming of Jesus.

What is Jesus coming to give? Is Jesus coming to dole out rewards to some and punishment to others? Is Jesus coming in order to induce fear in us? Is Jesus coming to pass some kind of judgment on us? It is none of those things.

The second coming is about the gift of Christ consciousness. We await the second coming because the second coming is Christ consciousness. The truth is that the second coming of Jesus has already happened. It has happened many times. It has happened in the hearts of every enlightened being, many of whom have never heard of Jesus or Buddha, but are filled with Christ consciousness.

How do you create Christ consciousness? How do you become awake and how do you stay awake? What are some of the tools that we might employ in order to do that? We can start by filling our minds with emptiness and silence! Emptiness is an extraordinary thing. Space is an extraordinary thing. When you look at the page of a book and you really want to emphasize the script, you create a lot of space around it between the words and between the lines and then it really stands out. If you really want to make a statement, put a single word on a page filled with lots of space around it. If you keep crowding the space with more and more words, the more words you put in it the more you kill the visual impact. You can finally cover the entire page with so many words that you literally can't read a single one of them. It is the space between the words, among the words, above, below, between paragraphs and around the edges. It is the space and the nothingness that creates the meaning of the text.

That is true in our lives. What is the meaning of the doorway? A door is not a lintel. A door is not the part that swings in and out. A door is the nothingness that allows us egress and ingress. Without that space, the most ornate surroundings in the world do not make a door. What is the essence of a chalice or a cup? When you drink your cup of coffee, what is the essence? Is it the fancy handle? It is the ceramic contours or how it is made? Or is it the nothingness in the middle that allows you to put the coffee in and to drink the coffee? Without the space inside the cup, it is not a cup. It is totally useless.

How do you define a room? Is it the furniture in it? Is it the tables, the chairs or the pictures? They don't define the room. Is it the ceiling, floor or the walls? They just put boundaries to the room. What is the room itself? The room is the nothingness. It is the emptiness inside all of it. What is the human body? The human body is 99.99 percent nothingness. The space between the atoms and the space within the atoms between the subatomic particles is so vast that 99.99 percent of us consist of nothing.

What is cosmos? If you could take a four-inch pipe and run it from here to Alpha Centauri (that is the nearest star to us, apart from our own sun, and it is millions of light years away) and gather up all the particles in between, how much stuff would you wind up with? You would have a single grain of sand. That is how empty space is. That is an extraordinary metaphor because that is what has to happen in our mind. It is the jumble in our mind that keeps us from being enlightened. The ability to create space inside our minds is the most practical way I know of coming into alignment with the Is-ness within and staying awake. We think we stay awake by thinking more and more thoughts. All we do is induce this dream-state that we take to be reality.

What about silence? Silence has the same effect. It is the silence surrounding your words, the silence out of which your words have arisen, the silence between the words of your sentences and the silence into which they finally go that gives meaning to your speech. If you try to multiply your words and tumble them out too quickly, two things happen. You sound unintelligible and you sound Irish. It is only by creating silence between the words, around the words, before the words and after the words that you really make sense and can be understood.

In 1972, one week after I went to Kenya I was sitting on the porch in the evening with a visiting 80-year-old missionary. We had been sitting in silence and after a few minutes he said to me, "Can you hear that?" Now the nights in Africa are filled with an extraordinary cacophony of insect sounds. Again he said, "Can you hear that?" I said, "Yes." He said, "If you can still hear it in a month's time, go home!" He was dead serious. He meant that if I can't learn to habituate to that kind of sound it will literally drive me crazy.

Silence has a great ability to wake people up. One night I was at a party of about 50 people and there was one man asleep on a couch amid all the conversations and loud music. So I tried an experiment. I said to the group, "Let's try an experiment, I'm going to count to three; and I want all the music and conversation to stop. At my signal, there was total silence and the sleeping man awoke and was totally disoriented. The loud noises had changed to silence which startled him.

My question is this. Do you have the courage to create the sudden silence in the soporific cacophony of your life that will allow you to wake up and stay awake and receive Christ consciousness?

REFORMATION

"All the talents of God are within you."

Hafiz

WHEN I CAME to the United States in 1987, I lived for a while at the rectory of Saint Albert the Great where I was introduced to a three-hole paper punch. In Ireland and Europe, we operate with a simple two-hole paper punch. It was amazing that for the same amount of pressure I could get fifty percent more holes in my paper and fifty percent more little dots. One night I had a very interesting dream about all these little dots. In my dream, my paper punch was full of various colored little dots and I emptied them out onto the table. I took a piece of cardboard and scooped all the little dots onto the cardboard and I was about to put them into the wastepaper basket when suddenly these dots rearranged themselves into perfect lines. There was a white, blue, green, yellow and red line. I was absolutely amazed. I went back to my desk, set the cardboard down and went to the kitchen to get some Saran Wrap so I could save this amazing thing. Suddenly a voice said, "Shake it." I said, "Are you crazy? Do you have any idea what the statistical probability is of this ever happening again?" The voice said, "Shake it." Reluctantly, I took the cardboard and I shook it and the whole thing dissolved into chaos. As I kept shaking, it began to rearrange itself into a series of concentric circles: a blue one with a pink one inside then a yellow one inside that then a red one inside that with a white dot right in the center. I was absolutely amazed. I put the cardboard onto the table and headed again for the kitchen when the voice said,

"Shake it." I said, "Are you out of your bloody mind? Do you have any idea what the probability is of this ever happening again?" The voice said, "Shake it." Reluctantly I took the cardboard back to the table and I shook it and the whole thing disintegrated back into chaos but as I continued to shake it a picture of a blond, blue-eyed woman began to emerge and then I put it down on the desk and covered my ears and I ran for the kitchen.

When I woke up, I thought: What in God's name could this dream have been about? What came to me was the following. It seemed to me that the first system of straight lines represented my first 26 years in Ireland. In my university, I had a double major in mathematics and physics: straight linear thinking. I went through eight years in the seminary which was a theological institute that taught us that outside the Catholic Church there was no salvation. It was all straight line linear thinking. That seemed to me to be the first form that appeared: mathematically straight lines.

The second formation had to do with my 14 years in Kenya where the whole thing got shaken up because Africa operates in a nested theological framework. It is the realization that there are many paths to God. That for me was represented by these concentric circles. Then recently I had just arrived in the United States to study at the Institute of Transpersonal Psychology (ITP) and my world was being radically shaken up again. For the first time in my life I was actually meeting practicing Hindus and Buddhists and I was coming across the notion of reincarnation in a way that I had never experienced.

It seemed to me that this third phrase represented the newly emerging face of God, but I was not to get stuck even in that model. Even though I wanted to put Saran Wrap to hold that impression of this blue-eyed blond forever, God wanted me to keep shaking it up. In other words, what God was saying to me was "If you meet the Buddha on the road, kill him." You have to pray daily to God to rid yourself of God. There is no fixed portrait of God that will stand for all time. The reluctance is to shake up all the pictures we get at every stage and to keep growing and keep reforming.

We can look at the word reform in two ways. Reform has this connotation of repentance in fear because God is coming and boy is He pissed so look out, get your act together, get in line and believe what you are told to believe. That is what we normally tend to think about repentance and reformation. The word actually means to re-form. It means to re-constitute. Proper reformation is not based on fear that God is going to come back and because we are out of line, He is really going to be upset with us. Reformation is not about that at all. It is more like remodeling. It is what you do with your kitchen after you've lived in it for 30 years; it is utilitarian, but you are sick and tired of looking at it. So you bring in the builders and you spend 25 thousand dollars remodeling it. That is what it's like. It is an exciting adventure bringing new joy into your life. It's about bringing excitement and a new look into your experience of life. Reformation is not about the dire consequences of being out of step with anyone. It is about the exciting possibility of having a totally different kind of experience.

Reformation is about the God, Shiva, it seems to me. The Hindus, just like Christians, have a three part God: Brahma, Vishnu and Shiva. Brahma is the creating principle of God, Vishnu is the sustaining principle of God and Shiva is the destructive principle of God. It is almost as if Brahma is the architect and Vishnu is the school janitor and Shiva is the demolition squad.

What is this Hindu teaching about? It is about the notion that there is a creative aspect to God that brings things into being for the first time. There is a sustaining aspect to God that keeps things in homeostatic balance. No matter how much salt is washed down into the ocean by the rivers of planet Earth, it manages to maintain its saline content at 3.4 percent. Then there is the ability of the cosmos to do wonderful things and destructive things. Destruction is a two-phase process. It is deconstructing old ways of being in order to reconstruct new ways of being. In order to remodel your kitchen you first have to destroy a lot of the old kitchen. You can't have the reconstruction without the deconstruction. Within Hinduism the notion of Shiva as the destructive aspect of God isn't at all negative; it is very positive. This is what Jesus talks about as well. When Jesus talks about reformation, he's not talking about an angry God who's really upset so get your act together and find out what you should be doing and get yourself back in line. It has nothing to do with that. It is the excitement of reconfiguring the pieces into a much more creative outcome.

Look at how nature reconfigures itself. Nature is the most versatile commodity in the cosmos. There is no way that you can kill nature. We can inhibit particular expressions of nature or demolish a particular articulation of nature, but we can't kill nature. Nature will always respond to every insult with something even more creative, although, to the human observer, some of what nature has to do in order to survive looks grotesque, but there is nothing grotesque about what nature does. Nature is extremely creative.

What does nature do? Nature is constantly reforming, rearticulating and remanifesting itself. Science, too, sees this. There was a controversy that raged for over 100 years in science between a force that couldn't be opposed and a thing that couldn't be moved. The second law of thermo dynamics; the law of entropy, tells us that any system left to its own devices will run itself down into chaos. However, the universe continues to evolve higher and higher life forms. For hundreds of years science could not manage to put these two pieces of the puzzle together. If nature runs itself down into chaos left to its own devices, how in God's name is it creating more and more evolved species? Ilya Prigogine, a Nobel Prize winner for biochemistry, solved this problem with a system called dissipative structures. He managed to pull these two pieces together. It was almost as if he was pulling Brahma together with Shiva. He showed that systems evolve to higher and higher stages by dissipating the entropy from their system. They dissipate it into a wider system so that in a narrower phase, life can evolve to a higher and higher format. Nature does this constantly. Nature is constantly looking for ways to refashion itself. In the process it seems to be creating chaos as a byproduct, but there is always purpose to what it is doing.

We see the same thing in quantum mechanics. There is a mathematical law in quantum mechanics that says there are 10 to the power of 27 brand-new universes called into being every second for every cubic centimeter of 11 dimensional mathematical space. That is a lot of universes. Most of them are mathematical duds, but even if the tiniest percentage of them actualize themselves as real universes, there are a lot of universes out there that we still don't know about. Nature is constantly rearticulating and trying on new possibilities.

When we look at how mutations occur on planet Earth in gene coding, we find that they sometimes happen because of toxicity and radiation. If someone is exposed to toxins or radiation, one's gene system is changed. Nature does it as well. As nature is attempting to copy a DNA sequence occasionally it makes mistakes. It is not a perfect copy. This imperfection in the copying process is what leads to all new possibilities in life. There are typically three kinds of outcomes. There are outcomes that are very negative and there are outcomes that are kind of neutral and then occasionally there is an extraordinary outcome that leads to a huge shift in evolutionary development. Nature is constantly looking for new ways to articulate itself and bring itself to whole new levels.

When we talk in spiritual circles about reformation, what are we really talking about? There are four totally different levels. We insist on concentrating on just one of them. Spiritually, when we think of the terms reform, reformation or repentance, as someone getting themselves back into alignment with the organization's teaching and belief system; that is only one level. There are four totally different levels. There are spiritual laggards who are dragging behind the rest of us and they need to be pulled forward a little bit. Reformation for those people means joining the group. It means getting into position with the group behind whom they are lagging. But the group itself needs reformation. The group needs to keep its eyes firmly fixed on the prophets who are trying to explore the territory of the mystery of God. For society and for the culture then, reformation means following in their footsteps; not roping them in but attempting to follow them.

What does reformation look like for the prophet? It means attempting more and more to dive deeper and deeper into the mystery of the God experience. What does reformation look like for God? God too is in constant need for reformation. God is in this extraordinary cosmic dance that Hinduism calls Lila, which is the dance of constantly seeking new formats to experience Her own being. When any one of these stops, problems happen. If God were ever to give up reforming Herself, then very soon through the law of entropy, the entire phenomenological universe would wind itself down into utter annihilation. God is as excited by the process as is any one of us. When society attempts to hold a homeostatic position then it too reduces itself to a kind of stagnant mediocrity. When communities and cultures try to rope in a prophet and to somehow kill the prophet before the prophet has managed to get his work done, what happens? Not only does society stagnate it actually moves backwards because now the spiritual laggards are pulling it down. It's not that it stagnates in the stage where it is, in the absence of prophets it actually begins to go backwards. There is a fix. God is reforming, communities need to reform, the prophets need to reform and the individual laggards who are dragging behind the rest of us need to reform. Reformation is not just about the laggards being whipped into shape so that they too can accept the tenets of a religious system. Religion and culture are as much in need of reformation as individuals. The prophets, themselves are in need of reformation and, heresy of heresies, God too is in need of constant ongoing reformation.

There has always been extraordinary tension in human culture between the prophetic and the princely. When kings are in charge, there is stagnation. But when the prophets get control there is anarchy. There is a kind of creative dialectic dance between these two. In the history of the Judeo/Christian bible, whenever there is a king there is a prophet to balance this dialectic. David had his prophet,

Nathan, and Ahab had his prophet, Elijah. Whenever there is a king there is a need for a prophet. Whenever there is a prophet, there is a need for a king because each of them has his purpose. The king is responsible for creating cohesion so that the culture as a whole can manage to make some progress. When everything is flying off in totally different directions, the king's purpose is to stabilize things. The prophet, too, has a purpose because left to his own devices the king favors the status quo: It worked in my grandfather's time, it's working today and it will work forever. Thus stagnation happens.

It is almost like a group of people shipwrecked on a desert island wondering where they are and how they are going to get to safety. A few things can happen. Everyone can go off in his own direction looking for the path home. In which case, if someone finds it he can't contact anyone else so everyone else is lost. Or they can stay together in fear and no one tries any new path and then surely they will all die. What needs to happen? They need to send out scouts. Society tends to send out very trusted scouts or people who have been trained by the system in the system for the system and promoted by the system. These are the scouts that are sent out to look at the new territory, but they are not really adequate to the task. The new territory needs to be explored by the rebels: those people who have the courage to bounce against the norm of society and go where no man has ever gone before. They are the only ones to lead the group forward.

When John was baptizing in the River Jordan and people were coming to reform he saw the Pharisees and Sadducees coming and said, "You brood of vipers. Who has taught you to escape the tribulation that is about to come?" Why was John so harsh with them? Because their understanding of reformation was that they wanted to come back into a full understanding and a fuller alignment with the law. John realized that the era of law was gone. He called them into a whole new place.

In its time, the insights of the Pharisees and Sadducees represented a great innovation. It was an extraordinary quantum leap in human spiritual thinking, but its time had come and gone. There was a time when Christianity was an extraordinarily insightful innovation. It was a time that took spirituality forward in a quantum leap that was almost unimaginable. But Christianity is now passé. Christianity's time has come and gone. There is a need for the human spirit to continue to investigate the next stages of the journey back into God. This is what John was doing for the people of his time. Reformation is not about pulling us back to where we were.

In our time, reformation can never be about pulling us back to where we were. All those great prophetic spiritual innovators, those characters who were the founders of new religious systems, every one was a heretic to an older religious system. For instance the Buddha to Hinduism, Jesus to Judaism, Mohammed to the Religion of Arabia, all were heretics in their own time. Unfortunately what tends to happen every time there has been an extraordinarily successful innovation in spiritual thinking, is that people think, 'My God there has never been a revelation such as this in the history of the planet. There is no place beyond this; therefore, we have to rope in anyone who attempts to go further." That is our downfall. There is no way but forward.

What we need to be doing in our time is to look for heretics in our midst. Not to burn them at the stake, but to realize that the heretics of today are the spiritual leaders of the future. Sure there will be some way-out people. There will be some people doing their own thing on ego trips. That is very true, but there will be some people who will hold the keys for the spirituality of our future. Reformation is not about licking people back into the acceptance of the dogmas of the institutional religious system. Whatever it is, it is about keeping your eyes on the prophetic figures who are inviting us as a species forward into a kind of relationship with God that is beyond fear, beyond a paternal child-like relationship into the deep mystery of the utter void out of which all possibility emanates.

WE ARE THE LIKENESS AND IMAGE OF GOD

"To identify oneself with the body and yet seek happiness is like attempting to cross a river on the back of an alligator."

Ramana Maharshi

I HAVE A LITTLE trick that I sometimes use in psychotherapy with my clients. Occasionally I will say to them, "Do you have a good photograph of yourself?" If they tell me they have I say, "Here's what I want you to do, I want you to get a full body photograph of yourself and then go to Kinko's, enlarge it onto photographic paper and then cut out the form so that it is just yourself with no background whatsoever. Then flip it over on the back and divide it up into tiny little segments with a marker as if it were a jigsaw puzzle. In each little puzzle segment, write some quality of yourself, good, bad or indifferent. Write down all the aspects of yourself that come to mind until you fill up the entire thing. Cut out the pieces with scissors and then mess them all up together. Then turn them all over so that you only have the back side up and see if you can reassemble the photograph." They never can.

No matter how unique the outline seems to be, once you have broken it up into these little segments identified only by little attributes or characteristics of yourself you can never reassemble the photograph. I tried this 40 times over 11 years as a psychologist and I have never found anyone who can reassemble the pieces. But when I say, "Flip it over so that you can see the photograph and now assemble it;" within 45 seconds they have the whole picture together.

The lesson that I am trying to have them discover for themselves is that we are much, much more that the sum of our attributes. You cannot define a person simply by putting together a bunch of characteristics; in spite of what one theory of personality in main-stream psychology would have us believe. There is one part of psychology that is called, "The 16 Personality Factors," that claims that you can reduce the personality to 16 different factors. I don't believe it for a minute. You cannot assemble a self image simply by writing down all the attributes and all the characteristics you think you have, put them together and act as if you are the sum total of all those characteristics. You need the image. Once you flip over and have the image, you can do it in seconds.

What is the image? The image is the likeness of God. The image is the reality that every single one of us is built in the likeness of God. If we try to understand who we are simply by dividing ourselves up into particular attributes; fears, weaknesses, successes i.e., characteristics; it can't be done because we are much more than the sum total of that. But when you have a picture to guide you and when you see that you are built in the image and likeness of God, then the personality can coalesce and then enlightenment can begin to happen.

Two of the most important questions that Jesus ever asked in the entire course of his ministry were when he was on the road to a little town called Caesarea Philippi. He was deep in thought and his disciples were following a few paces behind him. Jesus stopped and let them catch up with him and said to them, "Who do people think I am?" They answered, "Some people think that you are John the Baptist come back to life, and some people think you are Isaiah." "Yes, that is what the crowd thinks. What about you? You have been with me for three years, who do you think I am?" Peter then gave his famous answer, "You are the messiah and you are the son of the living God."

There is one other question that is not expressed in the gospel that is much more important than either of those two questions and it is the question I believe Jesus was actually working on for the first part of his entire public ministry. That was the question, "Who do I think I am?" Having wrestled with this question and finally figured out the answer, he then wanted to know what the crowd thought and what the disciples thought.

But in truth, it doesn't matter what strangers think and it doesn't matter what my friends think about me, the determining factor is what I know myself to be. What really matters is how I prepare myself for my mission and how I execute my mission.

The first thing I want to ask myself and have you ask yourselves is: "Who am I?" What definition and what response do you get? For the main part, we typically respond to that question with a name as if we are a name, or with a relationship, "I am such and such person's husband or wife," or by the job we do, "I'm the school janitor or I'm an anthropologist." We respond to it by some group of artifacts or characteristics where we try to assemble our image from the things we've written on the back of the photograph. Of course, none of those answers is true. How would I answer the question: "Who am I?" For me there is only one answer, I am divine essence having an incarnated experience. I'm a spirit in a spacesuit; a soul on safari. There is no more adequate answer to that question. When I understand that, then I can be in my spacesuit on safari meaningfully. But if I don't understand that, I start misidentifying who I am.

We also misidentify ourselves with our bodies; "I think I am my body." This is totally ludicrous from a scientific perspective. There is no way that I can be my body. The cells of my body are changing at a phenomenal rate. I lose about 100 million cells an hour as we dialogue with each other. I exchange them with you and with vegetable matter in my environment. I am constantly changing who I am so that in a six month's cycle, I've changed every cell on my skeleton. On a seven-year cycle, I've changed every cell in my body so that at the end of seven years there is not a single cell in my body that was there seven years before. How then can I be my body? The very same material that I am taking in to build myself, basically carbon, hydrogen, oxygen and nitrogen, are the very same elements that flowers are taking in to make flowers, earwigs are taking in to make earwigs, wolves are taking in to make wolves. If I can't be my body, I must be something deeper. I must be some kind of blueprint or information matrix or consciousness template in order for that to manifest. It is ludicrous for me to identify with my body. So to answer the question who am I by pointing to my spacesuit is meaningless.

In the '60s we had a different answer. We felt we were our feelings and had full permission to dump on everyone because we were being "authentic" by just being in touch with our selves as if our selves were our feelings. So we could dump all over anyone and our excuse was, "this is who we are and we can only be real if we let you know how we really feel." It was an excuse for all kinds of arrogance. We worked our way through that after a bit, but we are stuck in the next phase; we identify ourselves with our minds or our thoughts. We think we are our thoughts.

The academician who thinks he is his thoughts is merely an irrelevant pedant; and that is what he winds up being. A lot of us are so confused by our thinking that we don't know who the hell we are. We are following one idea of self today and another idea of self tomorrow. We can't be our thoughts either. If we are our thoughts then ego takes over and we are absolutely scared of the death of our ego.

As long as we identify with our physical being, our emotions, or our intellect we are in trouble. In fact, even when we identify with our personality, we are in trouble because the personality is merely the interface of essence with environment. My personality is not who I am. My personality is simply the masks I wear to interface with the environment in which I find myself. I am much more than my personality.

With Hinduism, I believe that I have a body but I am not my body. I have emotions, but I am not my emotions. I have an intellect but I am not my intellect. I have a personality but I am not even my personality. The truth is, I am divine essence incarnated or I am a spirit being in a spacesuit on safari. That is who I am. If I know who

I am, I can begin preparing myself for whom I am called to become. But, unless I get that piece right, I don't even have step one down.

How then do I prepare myself for enlightenment or salvation or whatever word we wish to call it? The truth is the work of enlightenment is not my work, it is God's work. It is not I who enlightens myself or finds salvation, it is God who does the work in me. This is not just about the transcendent, ineffable ground of our being; it's about the immanent image of God within every single one of us. That is who does the work of enlightenment. The work of preparing for enlightenment is the work of the spacesuit. Preparation then is our piece of it and enlightenment is God's portion of it; the God without and the God within.

How do we prepare for enlightenment if our part of the job is the preparation and God's part is the enlightenment? I think it is a one-two punch. The first one is by not misidentifying who we are. The first and most important step is to ask myself the question, who am I? The second step is I need to honor and celebrate the spacesuit as the medium through which God is going to bring about, in me, the awareness of the fact that I am already enlightened.

The fact that I am not my body does not mean that I can neglect or abuse my body, my mind or my emotions. I need to celebrate and to honor them. I need to feed them at every level. I need to look after my physical, emotional and intellectual well being. I can't become spiritually evolved while being psychologically immature. It is impossible. Therefore, the work of honoring the spacesuit and nurturing the spacesuit is a prerequisite for becoming a spiritually enlightened person. So how do we do the preparation? By acknowledging, honoring, celebrating, nurturing and feeding the spacesuit in its physicality, emotionality, intellectuality and personality as a preparation for allowing God to do the work to help us realize our enlightenment.

In Isaiah, Chapter 61, we read: "The spirit of the Lord God is upon me, because the Lord has anointed me; he has sent me to bring glad tidings to the lowly, to heal the brokenhearted, to proclaim liberty to the captives and release to the prisoners." Jesus adopted these same words as his personal job description. When Jesus was asked to read from the scriptures, he read this passage and then sat down. Everyone looked at him and he said, "Today this passage of scripture is being fulfilled in your sight." What that said very briefly is that it buys into three statements, "I have come to preach good news, I have come to heal the sick and I have come to set captives free." Those are the three parts of it. That was the job description of Jesus; to heal the sick, to preach the good news and to set those in bondage free. That is the sum total of anyone's mission. Jesus was not saying this in the synagogue in Nazareth as a proclamation of his own uniqueness or his own unique mission. Jesus was saying that this is the prototype of the reason for the fact that we are spirits in spacesuits. It is the whole point of incarnation. It is about preaching the good news to each other or being good news for each other. It is about healing each other and about freeing each other from misperceptions, prejudices and biases. There is no other mission on planet Earth. That is the only reason why anyone of us is here. We will have different vocations through which we become healers and preachers of good news and liberators of captives. Whatever jobs we do that is the mission for every one of us.

I think there are levels of souls. What do I mean by that? I mean that this work of being incarnated spirits is not just an individual phenomenon. It is also true of entire nations and it is true of the global community. There is a community spacesuit and there is a national spacesuit we call culture. Culture is nothing more and nothing less than the spacesuit of the group. The difficulty comes when you are preparing your spacesuit. Whether you are preparing for enlightenment for the soul of the community, or you are preparing for the enlightenment of the soul of an entire nation, you use the same one-two punch. The first thing you have to do is not identify with the wrong thing. We tend to identify the soul of America with the culture of America. But the culture of America is just the spacesuit of America; it is not the soul of America any more than my physical body is the soul of Seán ÓLaoire; it is not my soul it is my spacesuit.

My spacesuit is important and I need to honor it, celebrate it and nurture it, but if I think it is who I am, I am hopelessly lost. The same thing is true at a national level, and even at a global level. We constantly act as if culture and soul are the same thing. We constantly confuse them and it gets us into all kinds of trouble. Because of that, we don't know what our mission is and because of that, we are not preaching good news.

We have to constantly realize that the individual souls, for all their importance, are parts of bigger and bigger holons and bigger and bigger soul groups until we finally merge with the over-soul or God or cosmic consciousness. Those are the levels of the soul.

If no one ever comes to you and asks you, "Who are you?" maybe you don't exist. Maybe you are a figment of your own imagination. If no one ever comes to you and asks you, "What are you doing?" maybe you are irrelevant. If you don't ask yourself this question, "Who am I and why am I here?" maybe you are still asleep.

The challenge for me and for each one of you is this. How about asking ourselves this important question, "Who am I and why am I here?"

THE EVOLUTION OF SPIRITUALITY

"You must know that to be empty of all created things is to be full of God, and to be full of created things is to be empty of God"

Meister Eckhart

I'VE SEEN A lot of Christmas pageants in my 58 years on this planet. First as a child in Ireland and then over the 14 years in Kenya and for the last 17 years in Palo Alto, I've watched many different kinds of Christmas pageants. I've seen pageants where the infant Jesus was played by a little girl and in one instance the infant playing the baby Jesus was not a Christian and once the baby Jesus was played by twin baby boys. Of all the Christmas pageants I've seen, I think the least likely baby Jesus and the most obvious was in Kabarnet, my mission in Kenya. A man there had eight children and his youngest son, Stephano, was a hydro-cephalic baby. Stephano's head was bigger than the rest of his body and he could not hold his head up. His seven older siblings adored him. Stephano was the baby Jesus in our Christmas pageant. He was the least obvious and the most likely candidate to play baby Jesus. He was a sweet baby and inspired the most extraordinary devotion from his family and anyone who knew him.

Strictly speaking, Christmas did not begin until the year 330 A.D. In the year 312 A.D., Constantine, the newly crowned Emperor of Rome, decided to legalize Christianity and make it one of the state's religions. Before that, Christianity had been declared a superstition, but then it was declared an official religion of Rome. At that stage things changed radically within the Christian community. Within 13 years Constantine called the very first Council of the Church held in Nicaea. He brought the fathers of the church into conference and dictated what the agenda was to be. He wanted to create orthodoxy and there was to be no heresy or heterodoxy in the group. He wanted everyone to believe in the same thing in order to hold everything together in the center. He kept the council at their task until he got what he wanted. Before this time the emphasis had always been on the life, teaching and ministry of Jesus. Now the emphasis would be put Jesus' pre-incarnation status, magical conception and extraordinary birth. The young church and the old Empire wanted to make sure that there was a belief system that everyone held and that held everyone.

Because Christianity was only one of many religions, it set about to dominate the opposition. The biggest competitor was Mithraism. Christianity hijacked some of their ideas and quashed other ones. The founder of Mithraism was born on December 25. Christianity hijacked that date and made it the birthday of Jesus. The focus then would be the new light coming into the world, because all religions except for branches of Shamanism were birthed in the Northern Hemisphere. In the Northern Hemisphere, December 22 is the shortest day of the year and then the days get longer and longer and then the light begins anew to assert itself over the darkness. Many people had the notion that God, light and sun were synonymous ideas.

The Bushmen of Africa had the notion that every night as the sun tracked across the sky and descended in a red haze that there was an almighty cosmic battle going on and that the sun was being killed and the red in the sky was the blood emanating from this battle and they would wish it well on its way through the night so that it might resurrect the following morning. Every night they would escort it on its journey.

The Navajo People of this continent had the very same belief system. There were designated people who would sit on the roof of their houses and track the sun across the sky and pray for it and wish it all the energy for the journey throughout the night so that it might rise the following morning because they believed it had to contend with all kinds of demons in the underworld.

The people I worked with in Kenya had a belief system with many names for God. One name literally meant the nine-legged one. This name came from the image of the sunlight shining through the clouds creating shafts of light and they believed that these were the legs of God. When a Kenyan man came out of his hut in the morning he would spit in his hand and offer it to the sun; to have moisture in your mouth was very important when you lived in the desert. It was a sign of life and vitality so he offered this sign to the sun which was the source of all energy.

The Celts also had the belief that somehow light, sun and God are synonymous. In Ireland, there is a place called New Grange that is the oldest astrologically oriented human structure on planet Earth. It dates from 3000 B.C., which makes it 600 years older than the pyramids. It has an underground chamber that is aligned with the winter solstice so that at sunrise on the winter solstice, a shaft of sunlight goes down a long underground corridor and lights up the chamber at the back. To witness it now, you have to be part of a lottery system. Thousands of people sign up every year so that they may be chosen to go into this chamber on December 22 at sunrise and watch the shaft of sunlight spear the corridor and illuminate the room at the back.

This was the great shift that interested Christianity in 330 A.D., i.e., the emphasis of Jesus as the light of the world. Then in the 12th century Saint Francis of Assisi invented the notion of the crèche. We have manipulated this image of Christmas quite a bit throughout Christian history.

Spirituality happens in three stages, before story time, after story time, and during story time. As homo sapiens developed and up to about 50 thousand years ago, they were not much more advanced than the animals. They could form images and had sensory perceptions but hadn't developed the ability to think symbolically and therefore language had not developed and they couldn't communicate with each other.

That also happens with every baby. For the first several months of a child's life, a child cannot form images. If I play with a baby I can say hello until she laughs and then I move and disappear. The baby cannot hold an image of me in her head. That is why babies love peek-a-boo. Children are only able to maintain images at around the age of eight months. Thereafter if I move away the baby knows I'm still around. She can't see me, but there is an image that has been formed in her head. This is a great advantage, but she still can't manipulate symbols. The notion of a dog makes no sense to a baby. She can see a dog and form an image of a dog, but you say the word dog and it doesn't mean anything because the sound, "dog," doesn't look a bit like a little four-legged creature. It takes about 15 months to develop these skills and then break into language.

This happened to the entire species from about one million years ago down to about 50 thousand years ago with the evolution of Cro-Magnon man. We were able to manipulate images, but not yet symbols. We lived just like the advanced animals and our world was a place of chaos. I call this era, Before Story Time, because we couldn't tell stories yet. Life was a bewildering, unpredictable and totally uncontrollable series of sensory input that left us in amazement. Obviously, if we can't yet make up stories because we don't have language or we don't have intellectual skills, then we don't have God. There is no need for God. There is no need even for meaning. We can't impose meaning on our circumstances. We can't identify patterns, see rhythms, precedents and so every new situation catches us unawares. We respond as the animals, instinctually, to every new situation.

As a species, we left this stage perhaps 50 thousand years ago. As individuals, each one of us left that stage at 15 months, although periodically we regress back into that. Sometimes an event in my life is so traumatic that I temporarily regress into a Before Story stage. I have no way of making up a story to account for the event. I'm just totally bewildered by life, I can't impose any kind of meaning on it or pattern to it and so I'm floored by it. Most of us from age 15 months onward manage to break through that. Then we go into stage two of the process that I call During Story Time or the period in human history where we make up stories.

The first level of story is what I call the Event Story. A discrete event happens in my life and having participated in the experience, I then create a story to hold onto the memory of it. This memory or story I create can help me or hinder me. For instance, if I'm walking down the street and a pretty lady drops her glove in front of me, I can think, "Boy, is this a hint? Can I pick up the glove and maybe it will lead to something. Perhaps this person will turn out to be my soul mate?" I create a whole story in my head about a dropped glove. Maybe it will lead to love and this will be my hint from the universe. But I'm making up this story about the significance of a dropped glove.

I know a person who was mugged ten years ago. She was beaten up and her handbag was stolen and ten years later she is still suffering from this. She believes that she is a victim, totally vulnerable, that life sucks, you can't trust men and that you have to always watch out over your shoulder. Ten years after the event, the story she created around it is still crucifying her. These Event Stories have the potential to make life meaningful for us or they have the ability to crucify us, because it is always the story that causes the problem. The experience is over and done with, but ten years after the event the story around the event is still crucifying this woman.

The second level of stories I call Personal Myths. This is where I string a lot of Event Stories and make them my identity. For instance, if you're sitting on a plane for six hours with someone and they turn to you and say, "Chuck, is your name Chuck? Tell me about yourself." For the next six hours, you tell a whole bunch of Event Stories, string them together and act as if that is who you are. Very often, these events that you conjure up and the Personal Myth that you create from stringing events together is non-representative and doesn't adequately reflect who you really are.

My two brothers and I were raised in the same family, but I guarantee you that if you asked them or me to tell you who we are, we will give you totally different stories about our parents. Every one of us creates a Personal Myth. The Personal Myth is that group of Event Stories that I string together and is what gives me my sense of identity. Very often they are a non-representative group of stories, but this is my Personal Myth and I hold tenaciously onto it. To the extent that I'm buying into this Personal Myth, I'm totally identified with these specific events. As we move into spirituality, we have to let go of all of these things.

The third level is History. History is the Personal Myth of the group where we string together a lot of experiences we have had as a group and we make that our identity. There was an interesting experiment done where English and French High School students were asked to write a list of the 30 most important battles fought between England and France. The French and English students wrote their 30 battles and they were all correct. There was one problem however, there was almost no overlap between the two lists because the French students had been told a version of history of the wars that they had won and the English students had their version. History is also a non-representative sample of the experiences of an entire group. History allows us to form an identity as a nation or community and it allows us to be prejudiced, engage in genocide and kill people. This is what happens when history is taken as truth and the story we create around history becomes our identity as a people and as a nation.

The fourth level is what I call a Cosmology. A Cosmology is our attempt to create a story around the entire species, the trajectory and the meaning of the species throughout our evolution. This places humanity in one of several possible positions. If we subscribe to the Judeo/Christian model, it places man very firmly at the center of the universe as the most important thing the universe has ever created with the right to despoil and to dominate nature as mere resources for humans. If we were Saint Francis, we would see all sentient beings as our brothers and sisters. If we are practicing Buddhists with a Bodhisattva vow, we would see all sentient beings as our brothers and sisters. The story we tell ourselves at the highest level, the cosmological level, is also going to be the making of us or the breaking of us. These are the stories that we begin to tell each other and tell ourselves as a group.

It seems to me that for most of recorded history from the evolution of Cro-Magnon man, we have lived in the During Story Time phase of our evolution. Occasionally we slip back into a Before Story Time when we are totally bewildered by life, but mainly we are stuck in the During Story Time. Only a few intrepid souls have managed to break through from "During Story Time" into After Story Time.

What happens when an intrepid explorer of spirit breaks beyond During Story Time into After Story Time? What happens when the Buddha, Jesus and Gandhi figures break through that barrier? What happens is pure mysticism. They have precipitated themselves into the void that is the origin of all possibility. We can then say with Buddhism that form is emptiness and emptiness is form; in that void, lies all possibility. In any articulated manifestation of this void, any physical thing in the world whether it is a comet, planet, human being or a tulip, all contain within themselves the totality of the void because they are an expression of the pure consciousness at the heart of this void. That is what happens.

What happens again is that there is no need for God. There are no Gods necessary, no stories necessary and no need to impose meaning on anything because meaning is unnecessary when the memory comes back and we remember who we are. We are bite-size bits of God having an experience as human beings and we don't need to impose understanding anymore. We don't need to create patterns or identify precedents because we have now managed to come into contact once more with the entire gestalt. There is no need for religion at this stage. The gods diminish at this stage and so with Buddhism we will say if you meet the Buddha on the road, kill him. You can only kill the Buddha if you have reached After Story Time. If you attempt to kill the Buddha During Story Time, you are in big trouble. When Meister Eckhart said, "I pray daily to God to rid me of God," you can only afford to do that if you've broken through into After Story Time. If you try to kill God when you are still in During Story Time there is bedlam and chaos. Eventually it has to be done. Every one of us needs to go beyond this place, but we encounter three different problems when we get to that stage.

The first one is that if I manage to break through beyond the stories where I no longer have to tell myself stories, I no longer believe in the Event Stories I've made up to justify my anger or my feeling of victim-hood. I no longer need to create the Personal Mythology by a selective garnering of some things that happened to me as a child and create my identity around that. I'm no longer going to buy into the History of the tribe or the nation or even the species because I know that it is all made up. I no longer have to have a Cosmology showing my place in the universe because I've gone to the heart of that which created and birthed the universe. Initially, when I reach that state, the temptation will be to think that it is a blah experience. If I have no story, am I really alive? If I have no story, is it a dead blah experience? It only appears to be because it is so different. It is like what happened when the great prophets, the Buddha, Jesus and Muhammad figures broke through the prevailing understanding of religion and were all branded atheists. The model of God and spirituality that they were moving towards was so radically different that to the person stuck in the old tradition, they appeared to be atheistic. If we break through into After Story Time, the mystical origin of all possibility, it appears to the outside observer like going into blah-ness or blah-hood. How can there be vitality when there is no story? The truth is that there is the ultimate vitality because we are at the core of all possibility from which all creation and all stories spring.

The second problem when we break into After Story Time is that we confuse Before Story Time with After Story Time because neither of them have stories attached. It is a little like someone building a house. Initially he has an empty lot, puts up scaffolding, builds his house and then takes away the scaffolding. The first state and the last state are scaffolding-less. It is possible to confuse them except you have a house in one and only an empty lot in the other. Because neither has scaffolding, we think they are the same thing. We can confuse the Before Story Time with After Story Time because there is no story left, but they are totally different because one is enlightenment and the other is bewilderment.

When we have really moved into After Story Time then we begin to understand that the scriptures of all traditions are merely petrified stories that initially created a child-like awe and allowed us to evolve as a species but thereafter only results in childish fantasies and the stagnation of human possibility. Even the scriptures need to be let go of and all stories need to be let go of.

What happens to the story of December 25? What happens to the birth story of Jesus? This is a story that initially looks like a brutal intervention by a distant demanding deity into human history to foist the second person of the blessed trinity upon us. What happens when we let go of the story is a radical awakening of humanity to the Christ consciousness at the core of every one of us. Then we get it! We get it that the word has become flesh. The word did not become flesh two thousand years ago with the birth of a baby in Bethlehem whose parents were from Nazareth. It happens in the birth of every baby. Every baby is the word made flesh in our midst. Every time any one of us breaks through During Story Time into After Story Time and begins to savor Christ consciousness, then the word is made flesh again and again in our midst. Every baby is a reminder to us of the extraordinary miracle where not only does love become flesh, but the greater miracle that flesh can become love.

My prayer for you and for our world is that during the Christmas season, we will have the courage to make flesh become love.

To Be or Not to Be—Some Ideas on the Abortion Debate

"Great knowledge sees all in one. Small knowledge breaks down into the many."

Chuang Tzu

WHEN COUPLES COME to my office for counseling, one of the first things I do with them is a quick review of good communication. I give them a two-page handout with ten tips. Communication, of course, is more complicated than that but it helps to have a simplified summary that can easily be remembered, and which, if practiced, is very effective. Item number four on my summary involves detaching from a preconceived outcome when in discussion with another.

But there are two poles to the dance of detachment. No matter what the topic, if there are intelligent, moral and spiritual people on both sides of the debate, then there must be some value in both positions. That is the first pole of the dance. So, I am far better served by trying genuinely to understand the value in my "opponent's" viewpoint than in trying to cram my position down his throat. The wise one learns more from the fool than the fool learns from the wise one, for the wise one realizes that everyone can teach him something, while the fool thinks that nobody can teach him anything.

The second pole of the dance, however, is the truth that not all viewpoints are equally good or equally valid. For instance, the opinions of the Ku Klux Klan and of the NAACP are certainly not equally valid when it comes to Black rights. Moreover, it is a performative contradiction and a logical fallacy to hold that all positions are equal.

As we make moral choices, we have to negotiate the balance between these poles.

The mathematician in me tends to approach a topic by first considering its widest possible context, then progressively narrowing the examination through a series of concentric, nested contexts. In this article, I want to begin with a look at moral thinking, and then focus, in subsequent sections on increasingly pertinent sub-contexts until I get specifically to the question of abortion.

I believe that morality is to ethics as engineering is to pure mathematics. In other words, morality is applied ethics just as engineering is applied mathematics. I could also say that ethics is the science of living, while morality is the art of living. They are complementary pieces.

There is also a vitally important distinction to be made between moral values and moral laws. While there are absolute moral values, e.g., respect for life, truth, another's reputation, property, sexuality, etc., I do not believe that there are any absolute moral laws. Of course, the values must be enshrined in precepts, but these precepts are not God-given, unalterable laws to be blindly obeyed whatever the circumstance. For example, while respect for truth is important, there are occasions when the moral thing to do is tell a lie. If I could save innocent lives, in a time of ethnic cleansing by telling the marauding mob that "No, I am not hiding members of the 'accursed' group in my house," then, I believe, I am morally mandated to tell a lie.

In practice, the very governments and religions that legislate on these absolute values are the ones who most frequently contravene them and justify these contraventions as being both expedient and even good.

Then there is the consideration of the different ways males and females approach making moral decisions. It is, perhaps, a trifle simplistic and stereotypical, but there is value to the following distinction: for males, morality is the application of will power to revealed legislated ethical principles. "Here are the pertinent ethical laws, use your will power and that will ensure a moral decision." For females, morality is the exercise of choice in the widest possible human context. "There is a moral decision to be made and who will be affected by it? Where will the ripples end?"

Personally, I favor using a combination of these. It's not that one system is good and the other bad, or that one is antiquated and the other is modern. Rather, when making a moral decision, I need to consider the widest possible human context, then consider the pertinent ethical principles, and finally, exercise the necessary will power.

Some years ago, the archbishop of Chicago, Joseph Cardinal Bernadin, coined the phrase "the Seamless Garment approach." It means that any discussion of the sanctity of life needs to be evenly applied to the death penalty, killing in self-defense, warfare and abortion. We cannot hold one to different standards than another.

I find an interesting split in America. The Liberal Left is very much against capital punishment, warfare, and only reluctantly agrees to killing in self-defense. It is very vociferously, however, in favor of the Pro-choice lobby. The Conservative Right, on the other hand, is outraged at the Pro-choice thinking, while very enthusiastically promoting capital punishment, war and killing in self-defense. Both sides blissfully ignore the Seamless Garment criterion.

The Conservative Right often hides its very anti-life agenda of promoting capital punishment, war and killing in self-defense behind the self-righteous slogan "Pro Life." And the Liberal Left is disingenuous in using the "Pro Choice" slogan. The issue in not about freedom to choose across all issues and areas of moral decision making, but very specifically about freedom to choose to have or not have an abortion. It doesn't help serious discussion to cloud the issues with these "bumper sticker" types of claims.

Until I understand what life is, I can't grasp what personhood means and then the "abortion debate" is mired in emotional charges and counter-charges. So when does life begin? It depends on whom you are listening to. Currently, the Roman Catholic Church teaches that life begins at conception: "There is no pre-existence, rather, at the moment of conception God creates a brand new soul and infuses it into the zygote." However, the Roman Catholic Church did not always hold that view. Thomas Aquinas (1225-1274), the "angelic doctor," basing his work on contemporary medical "facts," taught that it took 40 days for an embryo to develop into a medically recognizable boy, but 80 days to develop into a medically recognizable girl. This was established via postmortems on pregnant women.

Another view is that life begins at the "quickening" or the time when a mother first feels movement in her womb. Quite another notion is that life only begins when the fetus has reached viability. Given the advances in postnatal medical care, this is fast becoming a non-viable position! Still another notion is that life only begins when the freshly delivered infant takes its first breath.

Establishing when life begins is a tricky business. Moreover, I want to make an important distinction between life and human life; between the native intelligence of an organism and the notion of en-soulment. I believe that everything on the planet is alive, whether it is a rose, an elephant or a concert pianist. In fact, I see three kinds of intelligence: the creative intelligence which brought that life form into existence for the first time by setting up a morphogenetic field and a proto-template through which cosmic energy flowed, resulting in the physicalization of the idea and secondly, a sustaining intelligence that enabled each created thing to thrive in its environment by harvesting what it needed via photosynthesis or mineral extraction, etc.; and thirdly, a re-gifting intelligence which, on the "death" of the organism, distributed its molecular components into the ecosystem, while releasing its energy back into the cosmos for other creative endeavors. Thus, everything on the planet has life. It is not a question of when life begins, but, rather, of when human life begins. At what stage is the embryo/fetus en-souled? This is a vital question and one that neither medical science nor the legal system can answer. It is a spiritual question, perhaps even a mystical question. When does human life, as distinct from the life of the spacesuit begin? When does the soul arrive?

At what stage, then, does abortion involve the taking of a human life? Let me use an analogy. Four people are each building a house. John clears his site, but then somebody dumps a whole pile of garbage there; Judy digs her foundations and footings but somebody comes with a backhoe and fills them all in; James gets as far as framing and roofing his abode but somebody burns it to the ground; and Jennifer has completed her house and is living in it when somebody sets off a bomb as she sleeps. At what stage of the building process can the owner claim: "Someone is trying to trash my lot or someone is destroying my house or someone is making an attempt on my life!"

In order to examine the notion of personhood we need to ask; who is a person and who or what confers personhood. Is it a legal issue and therefore, either the lawmakers or attorneys get to decide when an entity is a human person? Or is it a biological issue to be decided by the medical community? Or is it, perhaps, a theological issue and personhood can only be conferred by religious authorities? Or, maybe, it's a private issue and only the pregnant mother can decide when it has "become a person"?

In the transition from life to human life to personhood, who is the arbiter? The awarding of the title person has had a rather checkered career. Different cultures and different epochs have traversed that terrain at different speeds, but here, to simplify it greatly, is the basic chronology. The first beings to be awarded the title were adult, freeborn males. Then, after the Civil War in America, personhood was awarded to corporations. Next came freedorn to adult females. Before this time, they were the property of their husbands. Later, children were awarded personhood. And, finally, slaves were accorded this honor. A report from South Africa in the 1840's showed the number of big game shot by authorities and settlers. In one year, under the category mammals, the records showed: 400 Bushmen-females. And when the British discovered Tasmania, they did not believe that the natives were human. To immortalize that attitude, having exterminated the lot, they sent the last two, a male and a female, to a taxidermist and then shipped the exhibits back to the British Museum. Only recently were these remains returned to Tasmania.

Who confers personhood? Can it be withheld or withdrawn? Before females, children and slaves were accorded personhood, were they not people? And what happens when a regime rescinds personhood, as has occurred many times in human history? Typically, this process goes through four stages. Firstly, we de-humanize the person or group; then, we vilify them; thirdly, we ostracize them; and, finally, we exterminate them.

Are we in danger of doing that to the unborn; deny them personhood, in the first place, or rescind a previous legislative recognition? Can we say that a fetus is a person if the mother is happy to continue the pregnancy, but only a "clump of cells" if the mother decides to abort it? Is biology a gift or a curse, whether you are male or female? Is gender a part of each individual's carefully planned and enthusiastically embraced mission for any particular incarnation, or is it a cruel, sick joke perpetrated on us by a randomly evolving cosmos?

May society say to a female: "You are a woman; you've got a womb; bear children!" May society say to a male: "You are a man; you've got testosterone; bear arms!" Do both men and women have the right to say to society: "Take your laws off my body?"

Are we here as channels of life? And does that mean that women have to deal life through limitless birthing while men deal death through limitless killing? I believe that conceiving life and taking life are huge decisions with great moral, social and mystical repercussions.

I should like to propose the "moral equation" which might go as following: $ax_1 + bx_2 + cx_3 + dx_4$ Where,

x_1 represents the rights of the mother.

x_2 represents the rights of the unborn.

x_3 represents the rights of the father.

x_4 represents the rights of society.

These are four important sources of input in this decision, but not all four factors are equally weighted. I believe that (a) is greater than (b); (b) is greater than (c); and (c) is greater than (d). While the rights of the mother are the most important, in my opinion, they may not always outweigh the other three combined.

The rights of the unborn are complicated. While the mother, father and society can represent their viewpoints; the unborn cannot represent its viewpoint. So, in fact, society has two kinds of rights here: its own, since birth is how society propagates itself and those of the unborn. If a five-year-old child were being molested or seriously neglected within its family, society reserves the right to intervene and override the parents.

Societal concerns on this issue span the spectrum from nations in which abortion is enforced, i.e., China, or to communities in which the pregnant woman has no legal say at all about her reproductive rights and may not avail herself of contraception or termination of pregnancy.

What of the father's rights? If a woman decides to carry a child to birth, then the father is expected, indeed legally mandated, to support it for the next 18 years. What if he didn't want to be a father in the first place? Does he have the right to say "No"? And if he feels very strongly that his child go full term and be birthed, does he have no rights here? Are we in danger of just swinging from one pole to the other; a situation in which women had few procreation rights to a situation in which men have none?

And what of the special case when a teenager gets pregnant? Do her parents have no input into her decision? They are legally responsible for her other choices, but she can have an abortion without ever talking to them about it?

In the Pro-life versus Pro-choice debate there is a tug-of-war between extending rights and curtailing rights and how to represent both viewpoints? Let me employ two analogies to capture what might be the thinking of the Conservative Right and the Liberal Left.

In 18th Century Europe, the gentry had the right to duel. If one gentleman felt publicly insulted by another, he had the right to a challenge to defend his honor with pistols or swords. Frequently, these gentlemanly sorties ended with the death of one party. But it was not regarded as murder. However, if two working class men got into a barroom brawl where one of them then killed the other, that was regarded as murder. Imagine, then, a movement by working class men that the right to duel-to-the-death be extended to them. And, further, imagine society resolving the issue by deciding: Since taking life is intrinsically wrong, instead of extending this right to the working class, we need to abolish it for the gentry. I can imagine that kind of response from the Conservative Right: If abortion is morally wrong, rather than extend the availability to working class women, we need to ensure that upper class women cannot get access to it.

And the Liberal view might look like this, using an analogy from the drug culture. Since drug addicts are going to use needles anyway to shoot up and often use contaminated needles and dump their used needles where innocent others may be infected by them, let's give them clean needles so they don't compound their drug problem with toxic-needle-induced other illnesses, and risk the health of innocent bystanders into the bargain. So, in the abortion debate, it might look like this: Since women, from time immemorial, have availed of abortion, and since financially privileged women have always found a way around prohibitions against abortion, and since poorer women have always resorted to medically unsafe methods, why not, at least, ensure that all women have equal access to top quality medical care for this procedure?

And what of the responsibilities that go along with the rights? The mother, obviously, has the greatest responsibility. She will dedicate her own body to carrying, birthing and nursing her infant. There is responsibility for the father, who will be legally, emotionally and financially responsible for supporting the child to age 18. The parents of a pregnant teenager are responsible. Very often, they are the ones who wind up looking after their grandchild, if it is born, or dealing with their daughter should she choose an abortion. And society has its responsibilities. But, here, once again, I notice a split between the Liberal Left and the Conservative Right. The liberals support a woman's right to abortion, but, in fairness to them, if she carries the pregnancy to birth, they will help support her and her baby via a host of welfare programs. Moreover, they seem to be very concerned about creating the kind of global, national and local environment in which children can grow up in decent surroundings. On the other hand, I see the conservatives, who are vociferously against abortion, having either no interest in, or worse, actively creating economic and environmental conditions, which militate against the welfare of the mother and child, once they have forced her to carry her pregnancy to term. That is a very hypocritical stance.

I think it is very probable that after the first trimester, we are dealing with an en-souled human person. At that stage, abortion means killing an unborn baby, which is not to say that, in special circumstances, this may not only be acceptable, but may even be the morally responsible decision. But don't let's hide behind the "clump of cells" line anymore.

In the case of late term abortions, I have two strong concerns for the fetus because I believe it is, at that stage, an en-souled human being and late term abortion is a euphemism for a very barbaric medical procedure.

I believe that teenagers need more parental input before choosing an abortion because they need, at the very least, to be exposed to considering, in depth, the full range of the consequences and issues involved with it. As a psychologist, I well understand that there are teenagers within highly dysfunctional or even abusive families who are fearful of revealing their condition to parents. In such a case, some other responsible adult needs to be consulted before the teenager makes such a momentous decision.

The Conservative Right chafes at the Liberal Left's efforts to legislate a moratorium on the sale of certain kinds of guns. They are upset even at the suggestion of a "waiting period" of a few days, while a background check is being made on a prospective gun buyer. Why, then, are the liberals so incensed that a woman who wants an abortion may have to wait a few days and seek counsel before going ahead with the procedure? Handguns kill about 10,000 Americans each year; abortions account for about 1.6 million killings a year in the United States.

However, if a mother's physical life were in danger by carrying a pregnancy to term, or if her psychological state would be seriously affected by the pregnancy, or if familial or financial circumstances were such that it would be a crushing weight on the family to have another member, then, I believe the mother would be morally justified in terminating the pregnancy, as early in the first trimester as possible.

In cases of rape or incest, I believe it is the pregnant woman's moral right not to have the trauma and indignity of the crime compounded by the added insult of carrying, birthing and raising a child of the perpetrator. Again, I would hope this could happen as early as possible after conception.

On all moral questions, conscience is the ultimate arbiter, but it must be a well-informed conscience. For mature people seeking to make spiritual choices, especially in life-and-death situations, it is incumbent upon them that they put real effort, time and consultation into forming their viewpoints. This is as true of abortion as it is of warfare.

Experiment "homo sapiens" needs to evolve beyond the primitive position that taking human life is an adequate response to solving human problems.